10/15

MADGINFORD

MAD

Books should be returned or renewed by the last
date above. Renew by phone **03000 41 31 31** or
online *www.kent.gov.uk/libs*

AFTERSHOCK

Also by Matthew Green

The Wizard of the Nile: The Hunt for Joseph Kony

Matthew Green

Aftershock

The Untold Story of Surviving Peace

Portobello
BOOKS

Published by Portobello Books 2015

Portobello Books
12 Addison Avenue
London
W11 4QR

Copyright © Matthew Green 2015

The right of Matthew Green to be identified as the author of this work has
been asserted by him in accordance with the Copyright, Designs and
Patents Act 1988

A CIP catalogue record is available from the British Library

9 8 7 6 5 4 3 2 1

ISBN 978 1 84627 329 2 (hardback)
ISBN 978 1 84627 330 8 (trade paperback)
ISBN 978 1 84627 448 0 (ebook)

Typeset by Avon DataSet Ltd, Bidford on Avon, Warwickshire

Printed and bound by CPI Group (UK) Ltd, Croydon, CR0 4YY

This book is dedicated to the men and women who appear in these pages. They told their stories with one aim: to help others fighting their own silent battles.

One of the marvels of the world
Is the sight of a soul sitting in prison
With the key in its hand
Covered with dust
With a cleansing waterfall an inch away

Jalaluddin Rumi,
thirteenth-century Persian poet

Contents

Prologue

The highway cut through open country. From the cab of his truck, Hugh Forsyth could make out the ridge lines of faraway mountains, flanked by dark patches of forest. With any luck, they'd reach camp before sundown.

Hugh saw the private take another look in the wing mirror. The road was no longer empty: there was a car behind and it was gaining on them. Fast.

Hugh watched as the car overtook then swerved in front of their truck. More irritated than alarmed, he guessed it was teenagers, hoping to goad the soldiers into a duel.

As they rounded a bend, the driver of the speeding car misjudged the turn, veered off the highway and ploughed down a grassy bank. The private stopped the truck and Hugh stepped onto the tarmac. As the occupants began clambering out of the car, Hugh jogged towards them, thinking someone might be hurt. It was then he realised all the men were armed.

One of the gunmen levelled a pistol and pointed it in his face. For a moment they locked eyes. Hugh automatically reached for his rifle but found himself clutching only air: he had left his weapon in the cab.

The barrel did not touch Hugh's skin, but he felt the press of its snout all the same. It was as if somebody had taken a pair of tongs, picked up a ten-pence piece, dipped it in liquid nitrogen then pressed it flat against his forehead. In that instant, he felt he had been branded.

The sensation triggered a volley of thoughts. First: the certainty he was about to be killed. Second: the certainty that the private would die next. The third certainty was, paradoxically, harder to bear: both their deaths would be his fault because he had broken the one unbreakable commandment drummed into him since his sergeant-major father packed him off to military boarding school aged thirteen: never go anywhere without your weapon.

Hugh froze and it seemed like a very long time before the man with the pistol began to speak.

'Fuck off back to England!' he shouted. 'We don't need your help.'

Hugh edged backwards, then turned and stumbled towards the truck. As he ran, his mind began rehearsing what it would feel like if a bullet slammed into the back of his skull.

'I had tears streaming down by then. I was waiting for my face to explode,' Hugh recalled. 'I couldn't even breathe.'

He clambered into the cab and saw his humiliation reflected in the face of the private. Hugh's rifle was where he had left it – wedged beside his seat.

'When I got up close and he could see I actually had tears down my face, I was like: "Fuck off. Let's go."'

Hugh told the driver never to tell anyone what he had seen.

And then a loop began to play, a loop that would only get louder as the years went by: *You're not all that, when it comes down to it. You're not all that, at all.*

Introduction

The Spiral

For Dean Upson, a fly-fishing enthusiast who lives in Maidstone, the trigger is the smell of petrol. The fumes take him back to a desperate day rescuing casualties in a Chinook helicopter. Sounds are drowned out by the roar of the engines, his uniform is stained with blood and he is cradling an Afghan girl in his arms – a girl who will not survive.

For Stewart Mackay, a young man who lives in the Scottish borders, the trigger is the smell of fresh bread. The aroma yanked him out of the aisles at the supermarket where he used to work as a cleaner. Once again, he was first man on patrol, passing glass-fronted shops where Pashtun bakers flipped round, unleavened loaves. He felt the sun beat down and a prickly sensation he came to know well in Afghanistan – the sensation of being watched. His supervisor would tap him on the shoulder and he would start awake, clutching his mop like a rifle.

For Cheryl's husband Carl, the trigger is raised voices – reminding him of the screams of women in Bosnia. One day she will return to their home in Liverpool to find 'Don't Shout' scrawled across the living-room walls in marker pen. When Carl is anxious she sometimes catches him performing an involuntary mime: cocking a weapon with empty hands.

In Somerset, I went for a drink with an Army major who had served in the Gulf War. She flinched at the thunk-thunk sound of a fruit machine spitting coins. In south-west London, I met Roland Riggs, who had served in Northern Ireland in 1971 and 1972. He cannot help glancing up as he walks down the high street, scanning for a slightly open sash window or missing roof tiles. He is on the lookout for snipers, more than forty years after leaving Belfast and Londonderry.

For many, the trigger is an anniversary – particularly of a comrade's death. As the day approaches, a corrosive sense of guilt begins to creep in – the kind of guilt that can only be felt by those who have forged a bond under fire, then felt that bond break. Fireworks are a universal bane – the bangs and smoke reminiscent of gunfire and the smell of cordite. But for some the trigger can be as innocent as the twinkle of fairy lights on a Christmas tree – evoking the red or green diodes blinking on military equipment.

Sometimes the trigger is a word. For one soldier the mere mention of 'Afghanistan' sent him into a paroxysm of uncontrollable shakes.

On Remembrance Sunday, we drop a coin in a tin and pin a poppy on a lapel to honour the fallen. The ritual, begun by the Royal British Legion in 1921, ensures that the sacrifices made by generations of soldiers are not forgotten. Yet there are those among us for whom remembering is not a choice, for whom the boundaries between past and present blur, and for whom every day brings a fresh reminder. This book is about the British ex-servicemen and women still fighting wars in their minds.

The story is both very new and as old as war itself. From Homer's *Iliad* and the plays of Shakespeare to Tim O'Brien's stories of Vietnam in *The Things They Carried*, and *The Yellow Birds*, the novel by Iraq War veteran Kevin Powers, writers have explored the rage, alienation and melancholy that have followed soldiers home from battle. The centenary of the First World War has prompted a new wave of public fascination with the plight of the men who fought in the trenches, where the term 'shell shock' was coined to describe the strange symptoms of those who broke down: vacant eyes, trembling limbs and shuffling gaits. The struggles of a contemporary generation of service personnel and their families, by contrast, are taking place largely behind closed doors, with symptoms that cannot be seen. 'I can roll my sleeve up, I can pull my pants down, and I can show you seven feet of scars,' said one former special forces soldier. 'But I can't show you the seven hundred feet of scars in my head.'

Today, stories of homecoming hold a special significance. Since 2001, more than 220,000 members of the Armed Forces have been deployed to Iraq and Afghanistan – where 632 service personnel have died and many more been wounded. In addition, growing numbers are leaving the military as the Army shrinks to its smallest size since the Napoleonic Wars. Some 20,000 personnel leave the forces each year – many returning to a civilian world they last knew as teenagers.

The number seeking help is growing fast. In the spring of 2015, Combat Stress, the biggest veterans' mental health charity, reported that the number of ex-forces seeking help in the past year had risen by 26 per cent year on year – an increase driven mainly by individuals who fought in Afghanistan and Iraq. Nobody knows how many more will come forward in years to come. With memories fresh of Britain's campaign in Afghanistan, there is a great deal of goodwill towards those who serve – as the phenomenal fund-raising success of Help for Heroes and other charities has shown. Nevertheless, there is widespread concern in the military that public generosity may dwindle as recent campaigns fade into the past, even as demand for support continues to rise.

Against this backdrop, I set out to answer a simple question: how does war break people, and how best might they be healed? I wanted to understand how ex-forces navigate the transition home from the battle-zone and who is there to help them. Above all, I wanted to hear what lessons soldiers might have to teach anybody – military or civilian – who may be burdened by those species of grief, anger, despair or remorse that time alone appears powerless to heal.

It seemed like a fitting moment to begin the journey. At the start of the First World War, Dr Charles Samuel Myers, the Cambridge don turned military physician, had treated 'Case One' of the 'shell shock' epidemic that rippled through the trenches. A century later, I spent almost two years travelling around Britain, speaking to people who were still grappling with the after-effects of conflicts fought in my lifetime: Afghanistan, Iraq, Northern Ireland, the Falklands, Bosnia and other, smaller campaigns. My aim was to track down members of a scattered community of veterans who had returned physically whole but emotionally shattered.

Let me be clear: this book does not intend to imply that all former combatants are psychologically damaged. Large numbers go on to make a smooth transition to civilian life and some see their time in the military as the highlight of their lives, an experience that made them more resilient to life's vicissitudes, not less. Yet it is equally true that there are tens of thousands who have suffered serious psychological injuries over the years, and who continue to live with the consequences every day. My goal was to document some of their stories, and the struggles of their loved ones – a hidden army of wives, partners, children and parents who are Britain's true conscripts.

The journey was a homecoming of sorts of my own. For fourteen years I had worked as a correspondent for Reuters and the *Financial Times*, most recently in Pakistan and Afghanistan, and before that in countries across Africa. In 2003, I accompanied a convoy of US Marines spearheading the invasion of Iraq, arriving in Baghdad on the day statues of Saddam Hussein began to topple. Seven years later, I spent time embedded with American soldiers and Marines in Afghanistan. Throughout my career,

I had devoted myself to trying to understand conflicts, politics and personalities in faraway places. This enquiry presented a chance to traverse an invisible – but equally real – inner landscape, a little-explored region of our collective national consciousness. I hoped my time among soldiers on the ground would serve as a passport into what at first seemed like a forbidding, closed-off military subculture, curiously divorced from mainstream British life.

Entering this world was not always easy. Journalists are not permitted to speak to serving military personnel without permission from the Ministry of Defence and though such restrictions do not apply to ex-forces, an age-old code of silence endures. Many families will remember an ancestor comparable to my own grandfather Charles Green who fought in the First World War at the age of nineteen, serving in the third battalion of the Grenadier Guards. His unit faced heavy fighting, shelling and gas attacks in 1918 but he barely acknowledged his ordeal when he returned home. A younger generation of soldiers has begun to break this silence, yet most of those who suffer are reluctant to seek help, fearing what others may think, or afraid to admit the scope of their pain, even to themselves.

Finding people willing to talk was largely a question of serendipity. I contacted service charities, large and small, tapped journalist colleagues for military contacts, approached friends of friends who had served, and messaged individuals active on social media. I visited over fifty villages, towns and cities across England, Scotland and Wales and spoke to more than a hundred serving or former military personnel, some over the course of many months. I also interviewed dozens of people involved in their care, including parents and partners as well as therapists and psychiatrists. The individuals you will meet in these pages include a former sniper in the Royal Marines; an NHS nurse who ran a medical outpost in Iraq; young men who fought in Afghanistan; and a fifteen-year veteran of the SAS – who was given permission by the elite regiment to speak in depth about his personal battles. All of them agreed to meet me because they believed that others might draw some comfort, perhaps even wisdom, from what they had to say.

The book divides into two halves. The first charts the descent that awaits those soldiers who face the greatest difficulties when they leave the military. The second explores the paths some have found to healing. One Falklands veteran called the downward journey the 'The Shit Chute'. I came to know it as the Spiral. The descent can take years to unfold and may feature alcohol abuse, relationship breakdown, angry outbursts and, in the worst cases, prison, homelessness or suicide.

For some, this journey is linked to a condition known as post-traumatic stress disorder, or PTSD. According to Ministry of Defence-funded studies by the King's Centre for Military Health Research, PTSD probably affects 7 per cent of those who served in combat roles in Afghanistan and Iraq – twice the rate of the condition found among the civilian population. The King's Centre data, based largely on questionnaires, has become a standard reference for the government and media. However, some question how far its statistical analysis can truly be said to capture the intensely subjective world of the psychic burden carried by the military.

The symptoms of PTSD can include nightmares, crippling anxiety, intrusive thoughts and flashbacks, in which the sufferer repeatedly relives a life-threatening or horrific experience as if it were happening all over again. For others, there is a cold numbness – as if their loves ones are sealed behind a pane of glass. It is not merely a disorder of the psyche, but an intensely physical condition – manifesting in gut-twisting terror, the hot flash of rage or chest-crushing despair. For those who suffer the worst cases, it can dominate every waking moment.

Though much of the public discussion around military mental health centres on PTSD, I was to discover that for many leaving the services can be a far more disconcerting experience than anything they have seen on tour. Almost overnight the psychological scaffolding that may have sustained them since they left school is dismantled, their sense of purpose and camaraderie dissolved. There is a kind of reverse culture shock as they enter a world where the rules and certainties that have shaped their lives no longer apply.

While the fast-growing numbers of soldiers seeking help for PTSD have made headlines, other problems loom even larger, in particular alcohol abuse, which is a far more prevalent issue in the military. Research published by the King's Centre in early 2015 has also suggested that service personnel may be twice as likely to suffer from depression and anxiety as the general working population, and a previous study from the University of Manchester found young men leaving the Army are at three times greater risk of suicide. Many are extremely reluctant to seek help. It is perhaps not surprising, then, that when they do finally open up, they are often barely able to contain their feelings.

'The presentation of these men when you first see them in the clinic is surprisingly similar,' said Dr Keron Fletcher, a consultant psychiatrist who has more than seventeen years of experience working with ex-forces.

'It's usual to find men who find it difficult to express themselves. However, once you start exploring and asking more direct questions, surprisingly high numbers of these men weep. That is so unusual for men in a clinic to weep, but that is one of the characteristic features of the way these people present. They weep.'

History teaches that the psychological wounds of war have proved stubbornly difficult to treat. On my travels, I sought to evaluate the current system of care. Through the Military Covenant, the government has promised that those who serve should face no disadvantage in the provision of services in comparison with the civilian population, and in certain cases – such as for the wounded and bereaved – should be given special consideration. The pledge was enshrined in the Armed Forces Act 2011, which obliges the government to report each year on progress towards its implementation. I found that the gap between rhetoric and reality looms large.

Millions of pounds of public and private money have been spent on expanding services in recent years, and attitudes towards psychiatric casualties have evolved dramatically since Myers's day, when a number of soldiers with 'shell shock' were shot at dawn. Despite the progress, many of those in need of help are not receiving adequate support. The MoD is responsible for caring for personnel as long as they are in uniform, but as soon as they leave the job passes to the NHS and a growing military charity sector. While some are lucky and do eventually find the right care, many more are frustrated by a labyrinth of disjointed services that frequently fail to provide the help they need to make a lasting recovery. Despite the government's pledges to ex-forces, I met military families across Britain who feel abandoned and betrayed.

The second part of the book asks how recovery might be possible. After hitting the lowest point of the Spiral, some have managed to escape the grip of the past and have discovered a new and more profound relationship to life. After years of being trained to focus on external threats, the men and women I met showed that the path to healing lies in unearthing a trove of resources buried within. The many people who told me their stories did so because they wanted to share their discoveries and sketch a map to guide those still groping for a way out.

As I embarked on my journey, many ex-forces warned me to be wary of the stories I heard – mindful that the first casualty of war is often the truth. With this advice in mind, I did my utmost to verify the events recounted in these pages – cross-referencing what I was told with accounts in books and newspapers, speaking to colleagues and superiors, or viewing correspondence, photographs and other documents. The people in this book are real – some requested I identify them only by their first name or initials, and in several cases I have made explicit use of pseudonyms. Nevertheless, history is never final, and events described are collections of memories, prone to warp with time, not works of military history.

Threaded throughout these accounts is an exploration of how our understanding of war's impact on the mind has evolved, from the 'shell shock' seen in the trenches to the PTSD diagnosed today. I learned that military psychiatry is a field which seems to go round in circles: knowledge is gained in war, lost in peace, then rediscovered during the next bout of hostilities. Many of the debates that raged over 'shell shock' in Myers's day have returned in new guises, and there is still no consensus on the best approach to tackling the emotional hangover of combat. For this discussion, I have drawn on the work and insights of writers including John Hopkins, Edgar Jones, Peter Leese, Aly Renwick, Ben Shephard, Nafsika Thalassis and Simon Wessely, who have marshalled an astonishing wealth of primary material.

Though there has been no breakthrough in treating PTSD comparable to the discovery of penicillin to fight infection, significant new theories of how trauma affects the brain and body have emerged in recent years, offering promising new avenues for research. Such ideas might have been slow to percolate into the British military-medical establishment, but the stories of recovery I heard convinced me that they might be harnessed to spare future generations of service people some of the suffering endured by their predecessors. I do not pretend to have found all the answers, but I hope the stories in this book will help fuel a broader debate – already taking place quietly in many parts of the country – on how mental health services might be reimagined to address a fundamental dilemma: how to reach those people suffering from conditions that, by their nature, make them reluctant to seek help.

As my journey drew to a close, I came to believe that the gulf separating service personnel and civilians is not as wide as I had assumed. Aspects of the anguish the people in this book have endured will be familiar to anybody who has confronted their own darkness – you do not have to go to war for your mind to become uninhabitable; to feel like you can't change, but nor can you stay as you are. For the men and women I met, war forged a crucible for the same fundamental struggle that life will at some point force virtually all of us to confront: the quest to find meaning in despair.

Britain's soldiers are often portrayed as heroes, villains or victims – they are more accurately described as professionals. I hope they will find in these pages a reality that they recognise. For the rest of us, my intent is to offer an insight into a variety of heroism that is open to all: learning to endure suffering, and be transformed by it.

PART I

1

'Welcome Home, Soldier Boy'

The hard return from war

Blairgowrie is a small town in northern Perthshire, flanking the clear, fast-flowing waters of the river Ericht. The nucleus of Blair, as the locals call it, is comprised of stolid slate-roofed cottages and elegant Victorian homes clustered around a triangular green named the Wellmeadow. On the town's outskirts, rows of pebbled-dashed council houses form a buffer zone against the surrounding countryside, dominated by the scarps of the Sidlaw Hills. The views from these homes are by turns beautiful and bleak: the slopes erupt with golden-yellow gorse in spring; winter brings a light dusting of snow. The town was once famous for its watermills, but these days jobs are scarce and many teenagers leave the estates for Perth, an hour away on a number 57 bus, or the much bigger cities of Edinburgh, Glasgow and Dundee. Some see an escape route in the Army. Among them was a seventeen-year-old named Aaron Black.

The British Army has long prided itself on taking boys from tough backgrounds and turning them into men, and in many respects Aaron was an ideal candidate. His mother, June Black, had separated from his father soon after he was born and a subsequent relationship had imploded after years of quarrels marked by hard words, broken doors at their council house and visits from the police. As Aaron entered his teenage years he began to clash with June, misbehave at school and drink. Aged fourteen, he came to the attention of the social services. Teachers described a bright, energetic boy who would do well if he avoided the pull of what one termed 'the disruptive route'. When Aaron decided to join the Army, June felt a wash of relief.

After completing his training as a combat infantryman, Aaron joined his fellow recruits for a passing-out parade in the summer of 2008 at Catterick Garrison in North Yorkshire. All wore polished boots, a khaki dress uniform and a glengarry hat adorned with a black cockfeather with a white tip – the emblem of the Royal Regiment of Scotland. Mothers and fathers looked on as their sons, most not long out of school, began their new lives as soldiers. In Blairgowrie, Aaron's friends had nicknamed him 'Black Swan' for his long neck. In his new battalion, the Black Watch, he was known simply as 'Blackie'.

June knew the war in Afghanistan was a serious business. For more than a year, hearses had been ferrying Union Jack-draped coffins down the high street of Royal Wootton Bassett, a village in Wiltshire near the airbase used to repatriate the dead. As the caskets arrived with greater frequency, local people had begun to organise vigils emblematic of Britain's growing sacrifice. But still, when June spotted Aaron, marching shoulder-to-shoulder with the other immaculate young men, the possibility he might not come home was far from her mind. She felt nothing but pride, certain that the Army would be the making of her son.

Soon afterwards, Aaron's unit – Two Platoon, Alpha Company – was sent to Kenya for live-fire exercises ahead of the mission to Afghanistan the following spring. The sparse conditions at the arid Archer's Post range – nicknamed 'Archer's Roast' – helped the young men to bond. Aaron's quick wit and frank style of talking went down well in the macho culture of the Black Watch, renowned as one of the most aggressive units in the British Army. Aaron got on well with almost everyone, but he forged a particularly close friendship with another young soldier named James Forrester. James was a little older, and as a lance corporal, was a rank up from Aaron, still a fresh-faced private. But the pair had both joined the Army as a ticket out of small-town Scotland, and shared a no-holds-barred sense of humour.

After their training in Kenya, Two Platoon returned to the austere confines of Fort George, an eighteenth-century castle on the north-east coast of Scotland, to begin the countdown to their deployment. The windswept fort was not a popular posting – soldiers nicknamed it 'Alcatraz' – and Aaron and James took every chance they could to scrape together the £30 taxi fare to their favourite haunts in the nearest town of Inverness: a rowdy pub named Johnny Foxes and a nightclub called Love2Love. Aaron drank vodka, while James sipped rosé – an unusual choice in the Black Watch, where recruits were more likely to reach for a bottle of Buckfast, a sugary, caffeine-laced and highly alcoholic beverage colloquially known as 'wreck the hoose juice'.

Aaron would entertain the other soldiers at Fort George by striding into the corridor and shouting quotes from the comedy film *Anchorman*, or he'd barge into James's room without knocking and help himself to cigarettes or toast. Once he took a new pair of James's trainers and posted a picture of himself wearing them on Facebook. When James confronted him, Aaron replied: 'What's mine is mine and what's yours is mine.' James could only shoot him a quizzical glance.

A few nights before they were due to fly out, Aaron revealed a more sensitive streak as he and James shared a drink with another soldier at Fort George. As the conversation deepened, Aaron spoke in increasingly emotional tones about the risks ahead. Turning to the pair he asked: 'You realise we might actually die in Afghanistan?' James was reluctant to pursue Aaron's train of thought, irritated at his morbid line of questioning. When their friend dozed off at the end of the night's drinking, James and Aaron lightened the mood by drawing on his face with boot polish.

In March 2009, James and Aaron found themselves seated in

the back of an RAF TriStar transport plane, headed for Kandahar Airfield, a hub of the coalition war effort. It was dark and word came down for the men to don their body armour for the final approach – a stomach-jolting dive designed to minimise the risk of being shot down. As they stepped onto the tarmac, both young men knew they were crossing another threshold: they were going to war, and they could hardly wait.

I first met James Forrester one Saturday morning in the bar of the Beveridge Park Hotel in Kirkcaldy, an industrial town on the east coast of Scotland, once renowned for its linoleum factories, and a traditional recruiting ground for the Black Watch. Framed photographs of soul singers crowded the wallpaper and we found ourselves subject to the laconic gazes of Barry White and Luther Vandross.

James had left the Army a few years earlier and found work on the production line at an American pigment manufacturer, which operated a plant outside his nearby home town of Methil in old coal-mining country. He was twenty-six years old and had close-cropped black hair, a pale complexion and a rangy build. A tattoo on his forearm said: 'Live Fast and Die Young', but I soon discovered there was no trace of arrogance about him. As he talked me through the tour, he took pains to explain points a civilian might not immediately grasp – such as the tendency of the rocket-propelled grenades, or RPGs, fired by the Taliban to veer wildly off target, or the importance of carefully calibrating the metal detectors they used to sweep paths for buried bombs. He would take my pen and sketch out the disposition of troops and terrain in the 'contacts' – Army speak for firefights – he and Aaron had faced. He spoke of his friend with a mixture of deep affection and exasperated amusement.

'Everything I did in Afghan, he was the one that was behind me,' James told me. 'My go-to guy.'

There was always a glint of humour in James's eyes. Yet as he relived the most difficult operations, or 'ops', he would absently pick at his fingertips and his face acquired the cast of a much older man.

When Aaron and James arrived in Afghanistan, the pair soon discovered that in some respects Kandahar Airfield was a softer billet than Fort George. The Black Watch camp was perched at the end of the runway, where fast jets took off for dawn and dusk patrols. Bar the occasional rocket fired into the base by the Taliban, the sprawling tent-town felt remote from the fighting. Life between ops revolved around a dusty quadrangle where soldiers from the United States, Britain, Canada and a host of other nations frequented Tim Hortons coffee shop, Pizza Hut, Subway and a T.G.I. Friday's franchise decorated with kitsch Americana. The one drawback was the lack of alcohol: the closest thing on offer to beer was bottles of non-alcoholic Beck's. Membership of the Black Watch conferred a certain cachet, however. American troops, aware of the battalion's fearsome reputation, would ask: 'Are you guys some kind of Scottish Special Forces or something?' Aaron and James would narrow their eyes, nod darkly and mutter: 'Aye.'

The two friends did not have to wait long for their first test. Chinooks flew Alpha Company to the headquarters at Camp Bastion in Helmand Province, the region where the vast majority of British forces were located. From Camp Bastion, they drove in a column of armoured vehicles to a village where they set up a new base for the Afghan police, who had been overrun a few weeks earlier.

With the outpost established, their commander decided to use their final day on the ground to try to gather more intelligence on the location of the nearest Taliban positions. Two Platoon would advance until they encountered the 'FLET' – the Forward Line of Enemy Troops. The soldiers divided into two 'multiples' of about a dozen men and began to push forward. James was in the first wave, while Aaron followed, backed by two six-wheeled

Mastiff armoured vehicles. They advanced through a maze of mud walls and into a patch of dense foliage and drainage ditches ideal for close-quarter guerrilla warfare.

'One of the guys in our team spotted three gunmen on a roof,' James told me. 'We got round to try and get as close as we could.'

James ducked behind some undergrowth and found himself crouched alongside Dennis Boila, a courageous and respected Fijian corporal – James admiringly referred to him as a 'total machine'. The gunmen were twenty metres away.

'It was my first real contact,' James said. 'All these leaves started falling. It never really registered: three guys shooting at us.'

James began moving into the open to start firing but Dennis pulled him into cover behind a wall, saying: 'It's too hot, Jimmy.'

The two men moved into a ditch and James fired his first rounds in combat. His rifle jammed almost immediately and he began popping off grenades from a launcher slung under the barrel. Then he grabbed one of the rocket tubes the soldiers carried in their packs, and pointed it towards the undergrowth. In his excitement, James did not bother to insert the earplugs provided with the tube and was deafened by the blast. Behind them, one of the Mastiffs advanced through a gap in a wall and triggered a buried bomb. Aaron was close enough to see the shockwave flip the vehicle.

'A boy lost his leg,' James said. 'Foot got caught under the brake pedal.'

When Aaron caught up his face showed his dismay at missing out.

'When he jumped in the ditch he was chomping at the bit to get involved,' James said. 'Everyone wants the best story.'

Aaron volunteered to run to a compound where they suspected some Taliban might be hiding and fling a grenade but his superior vetoed the idea as too risky. In the ditch, meanwhile, James fired more rounds at the Taliban and was joined by several other young privates – including Robert McLaren, who hailed from a tiny hamlet on the island of Mull, off the west coast of Scotland.

Robert was new to their unit, having only recently completed infantry training, and had only arrived in Afghanistan a month earlier. He had fitted in quickly with Two Platoon, however – helped by his status as a Rangers fan, his winning smile and his eagerness to get involved in the action. As the Taliban fled, the three young men savoured their first taste of the euphoria of being shot at and surviving.

'The guys were laughing and joking, chain-smoking,' James said. 'Think I smoked about nine fags in ten minutes.'

Lieutenant Rob Colquhoun, commander of Two Platoon, called for air support to provide a show of force to discourage the Taliban from attacking again – and an American A10 tank-buster swooped low. The platoon advanced into an orchard and one of the soldiers found a flip-flop next to a pile of empty brass casings, marking a Taliban firing point. They asked a farmer which way the gunmen had gone. The man looked at them, stone-faced, but said nothing. Colquhoun handed him the flip-flop and said: 'When he comes back, give him his shoe.'

As they conducted a succession of similar operations, Aaron and James began to relish the adventure, confident that the Black Watch had the upper hand in their skirmishes with the Taliban. It was only when they were flown to Zhari, a Taliban stronghold west of Kandahar Airfield, that the mood changed. For several days, Two Platoon took the lead as the company pursued a group of hardened Taliban fighters through a punishing landscape of irrigation ditches, vineyards and mysterious mud-walled compounds until the gunmen abruptly switched tactics and chose to stand and fight.

The Taliban took up positions in a tree-line, pinning down part of Two Platoon in an open field. Dennis Boila's section, which included Robert McLaren, the young private from Mull, was forced to shelter behind fist-sized clods of earth as rounds zipped overhead. It was only a matter of time before somebody would be hit. The Black Watch troops decided to try to regain the initiative by seeing if they could fire back at the Taliban fighters from the vantage point of a mud-brick outhouse – the soldiers called them grape huts.

Some way back from the fighting, a sergeant told James to run over to the grape hut with one of the platoon's collapsible ladders so Boila's men could use it to scramble up the side.

'Aye,' said James. 'Blackie can come.'

James glanced across at Aaron, who nodded.

The pair ran to the grape hut as rounds cracked through the air like electricity, their figures lumbering, laden down with kit. They reached the entrance and found a private named Mark Connolly sheltering near the door. Aaron peered inside and called to Robert.

'You good?'

Robert gave him one of his big grins.

'Yeah. I'm good.'

James and Aaron felt safe enough in the lee of the grape hut's fortress-like walls to smoke a couple of hasty cigarettes before once more braving Taliban fire to dash back to their unit. From there, they were ordered to follow another group of soldiers who were advancing into a ditch to try to outflank the enemy. The two friends had just begun to push through the undergrowth when a boom rolled through the fields and vineyards and compounds and time seemed to freeze. Their eyes darted to the epicentre of the blast – the grape hut, where Aaron had last seen Robert.

The concrete-hard walls acted as a funnel, forcing the shock-wave upwards and hurling a column of dust and debris high into the air. After what seemed like a very long time, a mangled rifle crashed to earth. A few moments later, Aaron and James heard the news on their radios: Robert had been killed in action. James watched Aaron's jaw go slack and his eyes widen.

'I can still mind Blackie's face when that happened, when it came over he was a KIA,' James told me. 'It was like: "Fuck, eh?" – disbelief.'

James said he and Corporal Alisdair Welshman, his section commander, knew the only choice was to press on with the operation: 'Me and him were like, though it seems harsh to say, "Suck it up and get on with it, think about it later."'

James and Aaron's section pushed forward a hundred metres or so then held their ground, as other soldiers tended to the casualties. Mark Connolly had suffered serious burns and shrapnel injuries when the blast wave rolled through the grape hut entrance, and was loaded onto a helicopter. Others scoured the area for Robert's remains – the first man Alpha Company had lost. Smoke poured from a crater in the floor of the grape hut where he had taken his last step, triggering a buried bomb.

Their trap sprung, the Taliban began to hammer Two Platoon with mortar fire and Chinese-made rockets. James recalled that they were pinned down for the good part of an hour. As the impacts crept closer, both young men began to feel that there was a good chance they might also be killed. Despite many previous close-calls, it was their first time to know real fear.

'I would genuinely say I was actually proper scared,' James said. 'I think the main emotion for a couple of days after that was anger. The only positive thing that came out of that op was we killed a lot of them the next day.'

Soon afterwards, Chinooks ferried Alpha Company back to their camp near the runway at Kandahar Airfield. One night they formed up to watch Robert's Union Jack-draped coffin being unloaded from a Mastiff and carried up the ramp of a Hercules transport plane. Hundreds of troops from the United States and other coalition countries turned out for the ceremony. James held his salute so long his arm began to ache. Robert had died two weeks before his twenty-first birthday. His parents, Alasdair and Linda McLaren, later told me they had been surprised when he had announced his intention to join the infantry – they had hoped he would go to university. Robert had been keen on sport and they had imagined him as a physiotherapist.

'You think it hit Aaron hard?' I asked James.

'It did, yeah,' he said. 'I still mind his face – it's his face that stands out. His face dropped. We'd just been there, we'd just seen him. We'd been in that building . . . When we found out that it happened, we came to the realisation it wasn't just dust that came out of the top of the grape hut . . .'

James paused.

He and Aaron barely had time to absorb the shock of Robert's death before they were deployed on Operation Panther's Claw – the Army's biggest operation of the war. Just after midnight on 19 June 2009, a fleet of ten Chinook helicopters began to take off in two groups, laden with 350 soldiers of the Black Watch. Their mission was to push back the Taliban from a segment of territory on the west bank of the Helmand River as part of Britain's biggest airborne military operation since the Second World War.

Aaron and James were by now well used to the drill of air assaults, waiting for the eerie green interior light of the Chinook to dim as a crewman made a 'V-for-victory' sign denoting two minutes to landing. Their section disembarked safely and trekked through the night until they reached their designated target: a Taliban-controlled bazaar. The gunmen had fled, but had sown the area liberally with improvised explosive devices, or IEDs. Shortly after sunrise, one of the privates discovered that their patrol had walked over a pressure plate linked to three mortar bombs – it only failed to explode because the battery attached to the detonator had died. As the sun rose, an Afghan soldier stepped beyond the spray paint used to mark the paths that had been swept with a metal detector. He triggered a mine and lost everything up to his abdomen and died before he could be airlifted. A patrol base established nearby was named 'Wahid' in his memory.

James and Aaron's unit took up position in a shop, found a fridge filled with soft drinks, left a few dollars and began sunbathing. Their sister unit, Bravo Company, was involved in heavy fighting on the other side of the village, but their area seemed quieter – although a stray round once ricocheted off a doorway next to Aaron with a puff of dust. They had been there for several days when Aaron approached James to collect his water ration. James handed him his six bottles and Aaron stepped outside. Moments later, James was deafened by a huge blast and dust turned everything black.

'I thought Blackie had walked on an IED,' James said. 'I felt the walls, couldn't see that far in front, worked my way round, put my helmet on, grabbed a med kit, metal detector. Then there was shouting: "He's still alive!"'

A British army truck had triggered a deeply buried IED and the pressure wave had blown Aaron through a doorway and on top of another private. The back of the truck was shredded but the driver was saved by armour shielding the cab. Aaron never talked much about the incident, though James said he would sometimes ask him if he remembered the time he had nearly been blown up. 'Aye, Blackie,' James would reply, and roll his eyes.

'I don't know how he felt about that,' James told me. 'He never spoke about it in a deep way.'

Shortly after Panther's Claw, the pair went on their two-week mid-tour R & R. They arrived in Edinburgh, still wearing their desert combat gear, and headed to a sportswear shop to buy armfuls of T-shirts and jeans, flush with money saved. They asked the young woman behind the counter for an Army discount. She looked at them warily and said: 'I thought you guys were cadets.'

James produced his Army ID and they received 30 per cent off. Afterwards, James, Aaron and Stuart Nicholson, another Black Watch soldier from Blairgowrie, sat drinking together at Edinburgh Waverley station, watching as one by one their trains pulled away. Nobody said as much, but none of them seemed ready to go their separate ways. Eventually, James made his way back to Methil and Aaron returned to Blairgowrie, where he took up residence on June's sofa.

Before her son went to war, June had made talismans to keep him safe. She had Googled images of ethereal-looking angels, printed them out on her computer, then Sellotaped them to pieces of cardboard – she called them 'Angel Protection Cards'. Aaron told her he wore the home-made charms under his body armour, though June suspected this was a white lie. While Aaron was in Afghanistan, June had focused on her job working for HM Revenue and Customs, telling herself her son was simply 'at work'. She had gained only the briefest of glimpses into his trials through his sparse 'e-blueys' – blue aerogrammes sent via the military. Though his tone was mostly cheerful, even flippant, the last letter he sent before going on mid-tour leave finished on a brooding note: '*Worst day of my life in the last op. Tell you about it when I get back. Love Aaron xxx.*'

When Aaron had arrived at her doorstep, June was relieved to see he looked fitter than ever and had a handsome tan. He wanted to make the most of his R & R and was planning to go to T in the Park, a music festival outside Perth, with his big sister Jenna. Aaron said nothing about his experiences in Afghanistan until one day, sitting on the sofa, he turned to June and declared: 'I'll speak about this only once . . .'

Aaron's voice was clotted in a way that June had never heard before, and she felt the energy drain from the room. He recounted how Robert McLaren had flashed him one of his big grins from the darkened interior of the grape hut, minutes before he was killed. Then he fell silent for a moment.

'What do you think they send back?' he finally asked.

June looked at her son, uncertain what he meant.

'It's just sandbags in the coffins, Mum,' Aaron said. 'There's nothing left.'

On his return to Afghanistan, Aaron was confronted with

more casualties. On the morning of 31 August the Taliban fired an RPG at a group of Black Watch soldiers on a rooftop. Sergeant Stuart Millar and Private Kevin Elliott were killed and several others wounded. Aaron watched from another rooftop as soldiers struggled over rough ground to remove their remains on stretchers. James was given the grim task of helping to pack away their blood-stained gear. Two months later, Aaron and James were on their way home. A total of 110 British troops would be killed in 2009, and many more wounded – the two friends had survived Britain's bloodiest summer of the war.

Alpha Company flew back via Cyprus, where the Army had introduced a mandatory break known as 'decompression': thirty-six hours of briefings, beers and barbecues on the beach before they were reunited with their families. Back at Fort George, James and Aaron made straight for Love2Love. They ordered bottles of champagne and sprayed them across the bar like racing drivers. Girls crowded around with outstretched glasses.

'We thought we were playboys,' James told me, with a rueful grin. 'We were just drunks.'

The next day the returning troops were given a stress debriefing, and warned about the mood swings they might face as the adrenalin from the thrill-ride in Afghanistan began to subside. James paid scant attention, and Aaron was too hungover to attend. Certainly, the pair might have been forgiven for feeling a certain sense of swagger. Aaron, whose school reports had been mixed, was described in his post-tour appraisal as one of the best soldiers in his platoon: 'cheerful, well-motivated and keen to learn'. Calm under fire, he displayed a good level of 'well-controlled aggression' in combat. James was assessed in similarly glowing terms.

For the first time in their lives, the pair had money to burn and a month's leave to kill. They treated themselves to a visit to the Inver Ink tattoo parlour. Aaron had 'Black' inscribed across the back of his neck in Tibetan characters and James emblazoned his forearm with: 'Live Fast and Die Young'. One evening, the two friends joined Mark Connolly, recovered by then from the blast at the grape hut, for a drink in a corner of Johnny Foxes. Aaron spoke for all of them when he said: 'This novelty's never going to wear off. I'm going to feel like this forever.'

Inevitably, sparks began to fly. One night, a girl yelled: 'Baby killers!' Another remonstrated with James: 'Are you in the Army too? Why don't you just fuck off back to Afghan and get yourself blown up?'

'Are you for real?' James shot back.

Meanwhile, Aaron was embroiled in a heated discussion with bouncers who were refusing to let him back inside Johnny Foxes.

'I was fighting the Taliban last week,' Aaron said. 'Do you mind letting me in for a drink?'

Even through the fog of alcohol, James cringed at his friend's sense of entitlement and gently warned him he would regret his words in the morning.

In December, the Black Watch staged welcome-home parades in the cities of its heartlands – Inverness, Perth, Aberfeldy, Kircaldy, Dunfermline and Dundee. June watched the procession through the centre of Perth, where a Shetland pony named Cruachan III, the mascot of the Royal Regiment of Scotland, led the Black Watch soldiers past Argos and Caffè Nero to the skirl of bagpipes. Passers-by clapped and shouted: 'Well done, lads.' June wondered what it must be like to be one of the relatives of the five men who had not returned. She spotted her son and waved.

June's colleagues at the tax office had helped her to improvise a welcome-home banner using a piece of the kind of black material used to line a rockery and some red plastic letters. June had considered spelling out 'Welcome Home Aaron – Hero', but one of her younger workmates suggested that sounded a little sugary. She settled instead on 'Welcome Home Aaron – Soldier Boy'. The women did not have enough 'O's and so replaced them with hearts. June draped the banner from an upstairs window.

When Aaron reached home, he looked at his mother askance. 'Soldier boy?' he said. 'What's that all about?'

They went into the kitchen and June put on the kettle.

When their month-long post-tour leave was over, and normal duties resumed at Fort George, Aaron asked James Forrester to lend him £300. The more than £10,000 in savings he accrued after serving in Afghanistan had been spent, much of it on alcohol. One day he went missing at Fort George and was later found sleeping off a hangover in a bathtub. Aaron confided something of his distress in a text to his older sister.

'I feel like I'm losing it Jenna, I need someone to help me,' he wrote. 'My head's a mess. Yeah, I'm always down, don't know why. I'm never happy. Ever since I got back from Afghan, I was happy for a month or two, then I just dropped.'

Jenna asked what the matter was and Aaron responded: 'I don't know, everything really, I don't even know it's happening, but it must be. I need help with my aggression, I don't know what else to do.'

The trouble deepened when Aaron failed to return to Fort George after a period of leave. June suggested he seek help.

'I tried mum, but they wouldn't help me,' Aaron texted. 'I feel like I'm going mental. My head's fucked. I don't know what else I can do.'

June exchanged several messages with one of Aaron's colleagues who sent her a text when Aaron finally reappeared to reassure her he would receive the appropriate care.

'I've got him back safe and sound. He's in with the doctor at 09.00 tomorrow. We can start to help him now.'

Aaron's superiors began to keep a closer eye on him, but his drinking continued on nights out from Fort George and during visits home. In November, he got into a fight at a pub in Blairgowrie. Police arrived and handcuffed him. Aaron asked one of the officers if he could have a cigarette then ran off down the street – still in handcuffs. When the case later came to court, a regimental police sergeant wrote a letter saying the action was 'out of character' and he was given a £135 fine.

Six months after returning from Afghanistan, Aaron handed in his year's notice to leave the Army. His welfare officer and an Army careers adviser tried to dissuade him, but Aaron dreamed of following the path of other ex-forces who had landed lucrative expatriate jobs protecting ships from pirates off the coast of Africa. In May 2011, Aaron returned to Blairgowrie, where he once again took up residence on June's sofa.

'*Finish with the army today, new job tomorrow,*' he posted on Facebook. '*Anyone know what you're meant to take with you, lol?*'

A friend helped Aaron find a temporary job at a roofing company but he sometimes failed to turn up on a Monday. By July, he had been let go and was claiming Jobseeker's Allowance. Aaron received another blow when his friend Mark Connolly was killed. After surviving the blast in the grape hut, Connolly had died after being punched in a brawl outside a bar at a British base in Germany.

In Afghanistan, Aaron's commander had praised his 'well-controlled aggression'. In Blairgowrie, his control began to slip. A few days after Connolly's death Aaron headbutted a friend in a pub fight, knocking out his front tooth. He was once more arrested and charged.

June posted on Facebook: '*Welcome to the real world, son.*'

Aaron 'Liked' the comment and wrote: '*Yep, lol.*'

'*Trying to work out how to function as a civvie, harder than I thought,*' Aaron later posted. '*You have to cook your own meals and that!*'

In June, Aaron posted on his mother's Facebook wall: '*Happy fathers day . . . mother xxxx*'.

The comment reflected Aaron's sometimes acerbic sense of humour regarding the turmoil of his upbringing.

'*Thank you,*' June replied. '*Hard doing two jobs . . . Bumpy ride sometimes along the way x*'.

Aaron clicked 'Like'.

As Aaron struggled to adjust, June's relief at her son's safe return gradually gave way to frustration. She was tired of coming home from work and finding him sitting on the sofa staring into space, or being woken by the ping of the microwave as he barged in after a night's drinking. Aaron's plan to make a living chasing pirates sounded to June like a pipe dream. She worried that an assault conviction would close doors on him.

As a younger woman, June had lived in a series of bedsits in London. One evening she had fallen into conversation with a hard-bitten Irishwoman in an East End pub. June had asked her for advice on her latest bout of man trouble, and the woman had shot back: 'There's no room on my raft.' The words cut June, and she had cauterised the wound by adopting the mantra as her own. When she read a story in the *Scottish Sun* saying the government was planning to order local authorities to give ex-forces priority on waiting lists for council homes, she saw a catalyst to lift Aaron from his malaise.

One afternoon, a housing officer showed mother and son around a one-bedroom bungalow in Blairgowrie, on the other side of the river Ericht from their estate. The flat had been occupied by an elderly wheelchair-bound man – a cement ramp led to the front door and handrails adorned the bathroom. Cigarette smoke stained the walls and there was a smell in the bedroom hinting at the recent use of a commode. Aaron delivered his verdict with characteristic bluntness: 'I hate it, Mum.'

June thought of her own bedsit years in London and told Aaron the flat would serve as a stepping stone. She loaned him some paint rollers from her shed and the council gave Aaron some vouchers, which he used to buy some white gloss, cream emulsion and wallpaper. He wanted to replace the doorknobs, but June gave him some silver paint to brighten up the ones he had.

As June watched her son's attempts to set up home, she could not help thinking that a young man who had been fighting the

Taliban before his twenty-first birthday seemed curiously ill-equipped to look after himself. When his second-hand washing machine broke down the first time he used it, he did not seem capable of bailing out the dirty water. Aaron brought her his laundry instead.

One night in early December, Aaron passed by June's kitchen and asked to borrow twenty pounds. He needed money to travel to Perth the next day to face his assault charge. June had hesitated: she was planning to gather the family for a Christmas Day lunch at the Angus Hotel on the Wellmeadow, where she had once worked as a cleaner. Tickets cost forty pounds and she did not want Aaron skipping it because of another hangover. She pushed her doubts aside and gave him the money.

'What about Christmas, Aaron?' June had asked. 'I'll pay your forty, but if you go drinking with your mates on Christmas Eve and don't turn up, I'll lose my forty quid.'

'"Have you done this? Done that?"' Aaron said, mimicking her. 'Mum, you're always nip-nip-nipping at me.'

Aaron told her that he would soon get a job earning £70,000 a year tax free working in maritime security.

'Well, I hope you give me that twenty pound back, Aaron – and the twenty pound before that,' June replied. 'You'll be the bairn with a great life earning 70K – the bairn that never speaks to me again.'

June looked at her son.

'You're getting awfully thin – are you eating well?'

Aaron shrugged.

'What about forces' charities? Have you sought help?'

'No one ever got back to me.'

'Let me know what happens in court tomorrow, Aaron.'

'Do you care?'

'Of course I care, Aaron.'

Their conversation ended and Aaron bolted out the back door. In his next Facebook post, he joked about his 'Black Swan' nickname, writing:'*Wish I was actually a swan, I'd be well away south for the winter.*' He appeared in court in Perth and the case was adjourned. That evening, he struck a rueful tone on Facebook:

'*Aww well, I'll learn one day I'm sure.*'

A girl had posted:'*What's up with you?*'

'*Nothing honey,*' Aaron replied.'*Just learning new things every day. How are you?*'

Aaron changed his Facebook status from 'in a relationship' to 'single', having broken up with his latest girlfriend.

'*Lucky escape,*' he posted, '*aye, for her.*'

Aaron's spirits seemed to lift at the prospect of catching up with Stuart Nicholson, who was visiting Blairgowrie on leave, but he later posted lyrics from a Rihanna song lamenting a lost love. The next day he updated his status:'*shit, benders starting again*'.

A friend later told June that during the subsequent bout of drinking, Aaron had revealed that there was an image from Afghanistan that he could not get out of his mind. 'Is it bad enough the stuff I've seen?' Aaron had asked. 'Haven't others seen worse than me?'

On Friday 16 December, a group of Aaron's friends went out drinking. Aaron, who had been banned from most of the pubs in Blairgowrie, stayed in his flat. Shortly after midnight, June was woken by the sound of knocking. Her teenage son John called from the landing: 'Mum, there's police outside.' Blizzards had swept Perthshire in the run-up to Christmas, turning the Sidlaws white, and the officers' breath misted as they waited on the step.

June pulled her dressing gown over her pyjamas and ushered the police into the kitchen. The memory of her son dropping off his washing flashed through her mind as they announced the reason for their visit. Aaron had been found hanged from the loft hatch of his bungalow. He was twenty-two.

Police had been called to his address and seen his silhouette from the street. Aaron had been wearing his combat boots from Afghanistan and had carefully laid out his medals on the kitchen counter, crowded with empty bottles of Stella Artois and an overflowing ashtray. He had placed his Afghanistan ribbon beside a medallion cut with the shape of a crucifix. A photo of an ex-girlfriend stood nearby along with a CD of songs compiled as a memorial tribute for the funeral of Darren Lackie, a soldier in the Black Watch who had fought alongside Aaron, but who later died during a holiday in Portugal, aged twenty-one. The CD bore the motto: 'The Brave Don't Live Long, But the Cautious Don't Live at All'. The washing machine was still pooled with dirty water. Aaron had placed his remaining pre-Christmas money on the worktop: thirty-two pence, in coppers.

The police asked June to check her mobile. Aaron had sent her a text at ten to midnight. June was afraid to open it, but the officers insisted.

It said: '*Goodbye XXX*'.

June's first thought: *I never did his washing.*

In the weeks after his death, Aaron appeared to June in dreams. She would spot him in a crowd and try in vain to catch his eye. Or she would be driving home across the bridge over the river Ericht when shapeless grey forms would crowd the road. As June cursed at them to move, a bright image of Aaron dressed in uniform illuminated her windscreen. 'Mum,' he called, and June jolted awake.

Soon the shock gave way to remorse. June had thought that finding Aaron a home of his own would help him stand on his own feet. Instead, she felt she had found him his 'death house'. She tormented herself with the thought that had she heard Aaron's final text, she might have called her son, asked him what he had meant by '*Goodbye XXX*'.

In the 1980s, June had worked alongside investigators at HM Customs and Excise in London. In grief, what June called her 'professional head' took charge and she began to pose questions. She could not understand how her son could have performed so courageously in Afghanistan, only to die by his own hand, seven months after leaving the Army.

Much as June yearned for a chance to speak to Aaron, she also had questions for the MoD. The Crown Office and Procurator Fiscal Service, the Scottish prosecution service, has the power to investigate a sudden death if it deems an inquiry would be in the public interest. June, who had once toyed with hopes of studying law, began to lobby judicial officials in Perth to examine the case of her son. At one meeting, she noticed several entries on Aaron's medical records were marked 'confidential'. She asked the procurator fiscal what they might contain. Though such files might often hold little more than dental records, the fiscal requested them anyway. June waited for the documents to arrive, desperate for any clues into the mystery that consumed her: what had been going on in the mind of her son when he came home from war?

2

'Case One'

'Shell shock' and the origins of military psychiatry

At the outbreak of the First World War, another twenty-year-old private was experiencing his first taste of life on the front line. Like many of the thousands of young British soldiers who crossed the Channel, he had at first relished the chance to join a great battle for civilisation, even if the whole adventure was expected to be over by Christmas. His feelings changed abruptly at 1.30 p.m. on 31 October 1914 when, crawling under some barbed wire, he was caught in a barrage of German shells.

One shell landed so close that the blast tore away his haversack. The shockwave from another struck him with the force of a punch in the head – though curiously left no pain. Dazed but alive, he wriggled free of the wire and stumbled back into a trench, where his comrades were stunned to discover that he had survived the inferno with only a burn on his little finger. They soon realised that he was not quite unscathed. Bathed in a cold sweat, he began to tremble and cry out that he was going blind.

Two soldiers, one on either side, led him to a dressing station. From there he was transported to a hospital where he was seen by Dr Charles Myers, the brilliant, contentious Cambridge psychologist seconded to the Royal Army Medical Corps. The soldier told Myers he had 'rather been enjoying' the war until the shelling. He had since lost his sense of taste and smell, his vision had blurred, a burning sensation hurt his eyes and he was unable to get up. His mind raced with thoughts of the explosions and he would wake in tears. A donnish figure with next to no clinical experience, Myers tried hypnosis, a common treatment at the time, but achieved little. Two weeks after his ordeal, the soldier was sent to London to convalesce.

History does not record the name of the soldier, but Myers dubbed him 'Case One' in an article he published in the *Lancet* in February 1915 entitled 'A Contribution to the Study of Shell Shock'. It was the first time that the phrase, popular slang among soldiers, had appeared in a medical journal. In writing his article, Myers had fired the starting gun for a century of controversy over the question of how war might damage a soldier's mind, and how best it might be repaired.

Contemporary discourse around the psychological cost of combat revolves around a clunkier, more technical-sounding label: post-traumatic stress disorder, a diagnosis that was first codified in America in 1980, and then adopted in Britain some years later. The journey from 'shell shock' to PTSD represents more than the inevitable evolution of medical terminology, however. Both phrases are products of different eras in our beliefs about the after-effects of war. These beliefs have exerted a profound influence on the lives of troubled soldiers – whether they are empty-faced veterans of the Western Front, or present-day ex-forces grappling with personal legacies from Afghanistan. In each case, unspoken assumptions about trauma, memory and the mind have shaped the way we respond. Equally importantly, these assumptions have also shaped the way these men and women have seen themselves.

While medical science has made giant strides in the past century, military psychiatry has described no parallel arc from ignorance to enlightenment. Since 'Case One' lurched into the dressing station, the field has been notable as much for the way knowledge has been periodically forgotten or ignored as it has been for its breakthroughs. Questions posed by First World War physicians have returned to puzzle modern-day researchers equipped with a battery of brain-imaging devices that would have been unimaginable in early 1915, when the British Army in France hastily appointed Myers as chief 'Specialist in Nervous Shock'.

Myers and his contemporaries argued over whether 'shell shock' was the result of microscopic damage to the brain and nervous system caused by the concussive impact of explosions, or the consequence of an emotional collapse born of horror and fear. This mind–body dichotomy remains at the core of modern debates over trauma: are mental scars primarily psychological in nature? Or are they best understood in terms of physiological changes in the body and brain? The answers are not merely of academic interest. For the men and women I would meet, they are a matter of life and death.

When Myers sat down to pen his article for the *Lancet*, he was not the first writer to grapple with the interplay of mind and body in time of war. Poets and historians have tackled the theme since antiquity. The earliest recorded instances date from the Assyrian dynasty, which existed in ancient Mesopotamia, now modern-day Iraq, from 1300 to 609 BC. Scribes recounted how battle-weary soldiers were plagued by despair, forgetfulness and nightmarish apparitions – visitations from the spirits of the men they had slain. Centuries later, the Ancient Greeks explored the emotional landscape of combat in more depth, notably through the *Iliad*, Homer's epic of the Trojan Wars. American psychiatrist Jonathan Shay has argued that the predations of the warrior Achilles described in the text – the oldest in western literature – foreshadow the undoing of character suffered by many of his patients who fought in Vietnam.

Several hundred years after the appearance of the *Iliad*, the Greek historian Herodotus described how curious symptoms could linger after war. Epizelus, an Athenian warrior who fought bravely at the Battle of Marathon in 490 BC, went blind from fright when the fighter standing next to him was killed. At the subsequent Battle of Thermopylae Pass – the 'Hot Gates' – the Spartan commander Leonidas dismissed his men because he could see they were spent from previous encounters: 'they had no heart for the fight and were unwilling to take their share of the danger'. Among them was a warrior named Aristodemus, so shaken he was nicknamed 'the Trembler'.

More than a thousand years later, the Norse saga known as *Heimskringla* vividly described warriors' altered states. Frenzied berserkers 'went about without armour and were mad like hounds or wolves, and bit their shields and were strong as bears or bulls'. But it was left to William Shakespeare, writing in the late sixteenth century, to embark on a subtler exploration of the relationship between war, memory and malaise. In the play *Henry IV, Part I*, Lady Percy frets over the 'thick-eyed musing' that has settled upon her husband Hotspur since his return from battle.

> Tell me, sweet lord, what is't that takes from thee
> Thy stomach, pleasure and thy golden sleep?
> Why dost thou bend thine eyes upon the earth,
> And start so often when thou sit'st alone?

Hotspur's insomnia, exaggerated startle-response and loss of libido have become an oft-quoted reference for researchers combing historical records for early evidence of PTSD-like symptoms.

As conflict erupted in continental Europe in the seventeenth century, physicians encountered growing numbers of soldiers gripped by the morbid introspection familiar from ages past. In 1678, a Swiss doctor coined the diagnosis 'nostalgia' – characterised by low mood, loss of appetite and stupor. The Germans noted similar complaints and Spanish counterparts described the condition as '*estar roto*' – 'being broken'. The doctors tended to attribute these doldrums to homesickness, rather than the less convenient possibility that the men were scared of being killed.

Technology evolved, and so did psychosomatic illness. In the Napoleonic Wars at the start of the nineteenth century, doctors described cases of 'wind contusions' – twitching, tingling and partial paralysis seen among soldiers who had narrowly escaped a passing projectile. But it was the American Civil War (1861– 1865) that heralded a new age of industrialised conflict. Soldiers subjected to the more accurate fire from weapons with rifled barrels and the murderous impact of the Gatling gun suffered from mysterious chest pains, shortness of breath and palpitations – lumped under the diagnosis 'soldier's heart'. British troops later reported similar cardiovascular troubles in the Boer War. Medical officers, unaccustomed to thinking in psychological terms, assumed that the twinges were caused by the tightness of their cartridge belts.

In the Russo-Japanese War of 1904–5, the massive firepower and intricate trench systems provided a foretaste of the 'shell shock' epidemic that struck the British Army a decade later. Russia repatriated more than 2,000 psychiatric casualties and became the first modern army to acknowledge the legitimacy of war neuroses. But it was in the mudscapes of the Western Front that military psychiatry can truly be said to have begun. The sheer scale of the mobilisation – with more than a million British troops deployed in France and Flanders at any given moment – redefined what it meant to go to war. Dr William H. R. Rivers, an anthropologist and medical psychologist who treated the war poet Siegfried Sassoon at Craiglockhart Hospital outside Edinburgh, captured the mood of the times when he wrote that men had been faced with 'strains such as have never previously been known in the history of mankind'.

From a modern perspective, the baffling panoply of symptoms that confronted Myers, Rivers and their fellow 'shell shock' doctors have a macabre, other-worldly ring: palsied hands, strange walks, stammers, tremors and tics. Some spoke of nightmares or the kind of waking visions of the dead recorded in the Ancient

World; others could only offer mute, glassy-eyed stares. While such symptoms were not new, the trickle of shuffling, disconsolate men would eventually grow into a horde.

According to conventional medical lore, the 'shell shock' epidemic should never have happened. Nervous reactions had traditionally been the domain of upper-middle-class women prone to spells of what was then known as 'hysteria' – emotional outbursts and fainting fits presumed to be caused by some hereditary taint. The Royal Army Medical Corps Training Manual for 1911 contained only two categories of mental disorder: brain damage and insanity. As the historian Ben Shephard has noted, the Edwardians saw war as a test of manhood. Men were either sick, well, wounded or mad. Anyone else who was unwilling or unable to fight was necessarily a coward, and might deserve to be shot. As the war intensified, such simplistic distinctions began to dissolve.

In his book *Shell Shock*, Peter Leese describes how, at the start of the war, a rumour began to spread of a new kind of casualty. In September 1914, a group of men had been discovered standing on duty – alert and ready for action, but no longer alive. 'Every normal attitude of life was imitated by these men,' reported *The Times History of The War*. 'Their bodies were found posing in all manner of positions, and the illusion was so complete that often the living would speak to the dead before realising their true state of affairs.' This chilling image seemed to capture the aura of mystery and fear surrounding the strange new malady. Some believed the colossal firepower of the new artillery systems could cause virtually undetectable brain damage. Others dismissed the condition as a figment of the imagination or an excuse for malingering.

In some cases, soldiers could trace their collapse to a single horrifying event. In *Enduring the Great War*, Alexander Watson cites the example of an officer who suffered a terrible 'turn' after touching what he thought was a living man, only for the back of the corpse's head to roll off. Charles Wilson, later Lord Moran, who served as a medical officer, described how a stretcher-bearer temporarily lost his senses after a shell killed three of his comrades, spattering him with their gore. Yet the enduring theme was the accumulated strain of living with the ever-present threat of being maimed or buried alive. 'Artillery was the great leveller,' wrote a front-line soldier. 'The first to be affected were the young ones who'd just come out. They would go to one of the older ones – older in service that is – and maybe even cuddle up to him and start crying.' By December 1914, only four months into the war, an estimated 7 to 10 per cent of officers and 3 to 4 per cent of ordinary soldiers admitted to hospitals in Boulogne had been sent home after suffering some form of breakdown.

The Army's gut reaction was to treat collapse as a disciplinary matter – evidence of a weak character rather than a medical condition. But as the cases multiplied, a heated argument erupted in the medical press over the causes. As the historian John Hopkins has noted, psychiatric casualties were given a wide variety of labels – many were diagnosed with 'neurasthenia', an all-encompassing Victorian term for nervous exhaustion. But it was the terse phrase 'shell shock' that resonated most strongly with the public, distilling the collective sense of fear and fascination at the scale of the devastation unleashed by the modern tools of war.

The medical debate was framed by Victorian-era assumptions about the supposed physical origins of mental illness. While some British doctors had begun to embrace more complex theories of the mind, many assumed that the roots of lasting psychological disorders lay in damage to the nervous system or genetic defects in the brain. This orthodoxy was apparent in a controversy over the origins of the memory loss, anxiety and lassitude observed among survivors of train disasters. Their condition was dubbed 'railway spine' – reflecting a belief that their symptoms stemmed from inflammation of the spinal cord caused by the impact of the crash. One doctor explained their lack of visible symptoms with the analogy of a watch that stopped after being dropped on the ground, even though its glass face remained intact.

On the continent, physicians had begun to develop more sophisticated theories of trauma that pre-empted the modern concept of PTSD. At the vast Salpêtrière mental hospital in Paris, pioneering French neurologists Jean-Martin Charcot and Pierre Janet drew links between the symptoms of 'hysterical' patients and their traumatic memories – which they dubbed 'parasites of the mind'. In subsequent years, Sigmund Freud, the Viennese psychiatrist, also a pupil of Charcot, began to elaborate his famous theories of the unconscious that would eventually transform psychotherapy. Such ideas had yet to gain widespread acceptance in Britain, however. It was thus only natural that Dr Frederick Mott, a respected neuropathologist working at the newly opened Maudsley Hospital in London, would begin his investigation into 'shell shock' by conducting physiological studies of affected soldiers and dissecting the brains of servicemen killed in blasts.

As Mott peered into his microscope, the Army groped for a response. Command was loath to recognise psychological injury as a legitimate condition in case it provided soldiers with a pretext for malingering that could spark a mass exodus from the trenches. Generals placed great faith in the cohesive power of the traditional Army structures of platoon, battalion and regiment.

For those deemed to have deserted their posts, the penalty was clear – a blindfolded appointment with a firing squad. One such soldier was twenty-three-year-old Albert Troughton, who described his predicament in a final letter to his family on 21 April 1915: 'All my comrades have been slaughtered which I think everyone should know,' he wrote. 'I have been silly to go away [desert] but if you knew how worried I was, and almost off my head . . . Goodbye to all at home. Goodbye, Goodbye.' When dawn broke, Troughton became one of more than 300 British soldiers who were executed during the First World War.

There can be no greater symbol of military callousness than

the practice of shooting those who gave way under intolerable strain, but the reality was not so clear-cut. Officers and medics often argued for clemency for the accused and so only about 10 per cent of some 3,000 death sentences were carried out. As professors Edgar Jones and Simon Wessely have noted, some of the men were executed for non-military capital offences and far from all had been diagnosed with 'shell shock'. In any case, it was stigma that proved the biggest deterrent to breakdown, not 'therapy by firing squad', as one contemporary doctor bleakly described the executions.

As concern over 'shell shock' mounted in Britain, the military was forced to evolve a more nuanced response. Late in 1915, the Army warily acknowledged what Ben Shephard describes as 'a grey area between cowardice and madness'. Command decreed that psychiatric casualties would be divided into two groups – those that had been caused by direct exposure to enemy fire, and those who had gradually succumbed to the gnawing fear of being killed. The Army looked far more favourably on members of the former category, whose casualty reports were marked with the letter 'W' for 'Wounded'. They were awarded the same coveted gold stripe worn by men who had been shot or hit by shrapnel.

If, however, a man's breakdown was not obviously due to enemy fire, his file would be labelled 'S' – for 'Sickness' – and he was not entitled to a stripe or sometimes even a pension. The message was clear: being concussed by a shell was acceptable, but there should be no glamour attached to mental defeat. When doctors amassed more data, it became increasingly obvious that the new classification system was based on wishful thinking. As Myers had argued from the outset, psychological strain – not brain damage caused by shellfire – was by far the biggest cause of 'shell shock'.

A portly, inquisitive academic who chafed at the Army's rule-bound culture, Myers believed the military's policy of automatically sending psychiatric casualties back to Britain had consigned many good men to needless psychological ruin. He believed most would quickly recover if they were treated with a few days of rest and decent food near the front – preferably within earshot of the guns. Crucially, such men must be constantly reminded that they were expected to return to battle. Myers's strategy was not entirely original. The Russians had observed that panic-stricken soldiers rallied much faster if they stayed near their units, and the French had adopted a similar approach in the trenches. Despite these precedents, the Army remained deaf to Myers's pleas, fearing his proposed front-line treatment centres would degenerate into burdensome camps populated by 'lunatics'.

It would take the catastrophic offensive at the Somme for command to reconsider. At 7.30 a.m. on 1 July 1916, officers began blowing their whistles to send men over the top. Advancing at a slow walk, they were mown down in droves – what one historian termed a form of 'mass suicide'. By the end of the day, the Army had suffered almost 57,000 casualties, including more than 19,000 dead – its worst single-day loss. Sixty per cent of officers who took part on the first day were killed and many 'Pals Battalions', units of men who had enlisted from the same town, were wiped out. In the following months, 'shell shock' cases multiplied fivefold. British generals began to fear the mounting toll of psychiatric casualties could cost them the war. Reluctantly, they followed Myers's advice and set up four tented treatment centres in the field.

It was by then widely recognised that the vast majority of 'shell shock' cases were psychological in origin, and the term had begun to lose credibility among doctors. Even Myers, who introduced the phrase into the medical literature, argued that it had become unhelpful, noting that some men had even begun to boast about receiving the diagnosis. In June 1917, the General Staff issued an order sharply limiting the use of the label 'shell shock' to avoid any implication that psychiatric casualties had collapsed due to physical injury. Leonard Gameson, a temporary captain in the Royal Army Medical Corps, summed up the military's view: 'Discourage the diagnosis. The fewer there were of such cases, the better, the easier, the cheaper.'

With 'shell shock' all but abolished, men sent to Myers's forward treatment centres would henceforth be labelled NYDN – 'Not Yet Diagnosed (Nervous)' – to emphasise that they may simply be suffering from a temporary collapse rather than incurable brain damage. Medical staff left all but the most severe cases in no doubt they would soon be expected to resume fighting. Myers's principles of forward psychiatry would later become known by the acronym PIE, for proximity, immediacy and expectancy (of return to duty) and have remained a cornerstone of British military psychiatry to this day.

Myers's moment of triumph was, however, short-lived. The Army leaned on him not to publish a new paper on 'shell shock' and reduced his responsibilities, while elevating his rival, the ambitious neurologist Gordon Holmes, renowned for his toughness. Exhausted by his many trips to the front and feeling sidelined, Myers requested a transfer to Britain. He thought the Army's 'wasteful procrastination' had denied many thousands of men a chance to recover. The Army saw him as a meddler whose compassion had made it harder to win.

Before the war, the infant disciplines of psychology and psychiatry had yet to gain much traction in mainstream British medicine. The influx of 'shell shock' cases from France electrified the field, raising hopes among a small vanguard of practitioners that lessons learned in war would fertilise a new era of peacetime treatments for hitherto incurable disorders. Practitioners divided loosely into two schools, identified by Eric Leed as 'analytic' and 'disciplinary'. The former sought to painstakingly unearth hidden conflicts and release bottled-up emotions. The latter clamped a lid on fear and sent men back to the front, sometimes with treatments that sounded worse than German shells.

The archetypal 'analyst' was Rivers, the Craiglockhart psychologist, who had accompanied Myers on an anthropological expedition to the islands off New Guinea in 1898. Rivers drew on Freud's theories to argue that 'shell shock' was an involuntary reaction produced when the patient faced an irreconcilable conflict between his sense of duty to his comrades and his innate will to live. His encounter with Sassoon, the war poet, was dramatised to great acclaim by the novelist Pat Barker in her book *Regeneration*, but their therapist–client relationship was not typical. Although there was considerable medical interest in psychoanalysis in Britain at the time, there was also plenty of margin for those inclined to a harsher approach.

The best-known – and most extreme – 'disciplinarian' was Lewis Yealland, a young, driven Canadian physician at Queen Square Hospital in Bloomsbury. He believed that very few of even the most ingrained cases of 'shell shock' could not be cured through a combination of shouted commands and the application of a strong electric current. Patients were strapped into chairs and told they could not leave the room until they were well. 'The current can be made extremely painful if it is necessary to supply the disciplinary element which must be invoked if the patient is one of those who prefer not to recover,' Yealland wrote. Although Yealland only treated a very small number of soldiers in this way and mainly used gentler therapies, the cruelty involved would cloud his legacy.

By the end of the war, more than a dozen 'shell shock' hospitals had sprung up across Britain, mostly offering treatments not much more sophisticated than gymnastics, woodwork and vegetable gardening, or the more passive methods of massages, rest in hushed wards, milk diets and baths. While officers had a better chance of meaningful care, conscripts could expect more cursory help and the least fortunate were incarcerated in prison-like asylums under the label 'Service Lunatic'. The historian Edgar Jones estimates that the total number of British psychiatric casualties was at least 240,000. Three years after the war, there were still 15,000 veterans in hospital with 'shell shock' and 65,000 were receiving payments for mental problems.

The scale of the problem prompted the government to set up a committee under Lord Southborough, a retired civil servant, to investigate how to prevent such an epidemic in future wars. A roster of notable medical officers and 'shell shock' doctors made submissions, but one was conspicuous by his absence: Myers. He later wrote that it would have been too painful for him to recall his wartime work so soon, and it would take him years to write his book *Shell Shock in France 1914–18*, which was only published after the Second World War had begun.

The creation of the committee was nonetheless a significant step, marking the first official recognition in Britain that the mental stability of a fighting force was as important as physical fitness, even if there was much talk of 'feeble-mindedness' and 'cowardice'. Perhaps predictably, the committee's report placed the interests of the military above the welfare of the individual soldier, concluding that fighting men should not be allowed to think that loss of control provided an 'honourable avenue of escape' from the battlefield. Though the committee recognised that there were limits to what even the most gallant officers could endure, the Army was still reluctant to acknowledge the inevitability of psychiatric casualties. The official view remained that well-led professional troops were virtually immune to breakdown.

What relevance do attitudes towards 'shell shock' have for today's soldiers? As I would discover, though Army thinking has evolved considerably in the past century, echoes of the officially sanctioned stigma of Myers's day remain a potent obstacle to help-seeking. The tension faced by officers in the trenches between their desire to treat individuals humanely and the imperative of discouraging mass breakdown has reappeared in various forms throughout Britain's subsequent conflicts, and it is only very recently that the issue has been treated with a greater degree of openness.

The larger impact of the First World War on Britain's national psyche is impossible to quantify. At its peak, 5.7 million people served in the forces. The fact that many more did not succumb to the strain is a testament to human endurance, but returning soldiers said little. I am told my grandfather Charles Green only spoke once to my father, John Green, about his experiences – pointing to a mark on his thigh caused by a bullet. Where the round was fired and how he survived, he did not say. The burden my grandfather carried must have shaped my father's childhood, and I have sometimes wondered whether it has also coloured my own life in unknowable ways, part of an intangible web of war experiences transmitted invisibly between generations in so many British families.

It fell to Harry Patch, the oldest surviving veteran of the trenches, to speak for a taciturn generation. Patch had fought through the swamp-like cataclysm of the battle of Passchendaele in 1917, but never spoke of it with his wife. He only began to talk about his ordeals after his hundredth birthday. Patch told a BBC interviewer how he had shot a German in the shoulder, ankle and above the knee to avoid killing him. He would still see the flash of a bomb when staff at his nursing home turned on the light in an adjacent room when he was dozing. When Patch died on 25 July 2009, he was 111 years, one month, one week and one day old.

'It wasn't worth it,' he said. 'No war is worth it. No war is worth the loss of a couple of lives, let alone thousands. T'isn't worth it . . . the First World War, if you boil it down, what was it? Nothing but a family row.'

3

'The Trigger'

Outwardly untouched, wounded within

No obvious signs marked the man waiting at the wheel of a white four-wheel drive as anybody out of the ordinary. Though he retained the fighter's physique of his days as a recruit boxing champion in the Royal Marines, the regulation haircut and shaggy moustache he had sported on tour were long gone. His blond thatch touched his collar, and with his laconic demeanour he could have passed for a surfer moved to the coast for the swell. The only hint of his past was a discreet logo stitched on his navy blue sweater in gold thread depicting a pair of crossed rifles.

We drove out of the station car park and past the promenade, where a January wind slapped waves against the sea wall, still festooned with Christmas lights. The man, who requested I call him A.J., lived with his wife Karen and two teenage sons a little further out of town. A Gibson Les Paul guitar hung on the living-room wall and Jen, his pointer, was curled asleep in a basket in front of an electric fire. A.J. settled back on his sofa and swung his legs up onto a footrest as we ate cheese sandwiches. He had an almost palpable aura of calm. It was a quality that had kept him alive.

In Afghanistan, A.J. had served as a sniper. As such, his role had been to kill enemy soldiers in a cool and methodical fashion. Unlike infantrymen such as Aaron Black and James Forrester, who often found themselves firing through dense undergrowth in the adrenalin-fuelled heat of close-quarter battles, A.J.'s role had been to observe Taliban fighters from a distance, set up a shot and pull the trigger. They died without even knowing they were being watched. The scope on his rifle was so powerful he could clearly see their faces.

He had rehearsed the drill a thousand times in training: check the distance with a laser rangefinder, line up the cross hairs, and count down from three to ensure a steady shot. As a seventeen-year-old recruit he had often wondered whether he would be able to perform the procedure with his sights resting on another human being. In Helmand he had discovered that it was simpler than he thought – there was no remorse attached to shooting somebody who was intent on killing him or his comrades.

'Shooting somebody seemed easy – it wasn't the biggest decision, or the biggest fear,' he explained. 'The biggest fear was us getting hurt and all that came from that. I would quite happily fire to prevent any of ours getting hurt.'

We spoke at length that afternoon – revisiting several of what A.J. called his 'Big Five' – the incidents that had caused his PTSD. Though his voice never wavered, our conversation was marked by long moments of silent reflection as he seemed to almost listen for the right words. Several times, when speaking of the 'Big Five', I noticed that while his face betrayed no hint of emotion he would slowly clench his toes.

As was the case with several of the ex-forces I met, I was put in touch with A.J. by a retired officer who connected us via email. A.J. wrote back some weeks later to say he was happy to tell his story, believing that other people battling PTSD might draw comfort from realising they were not alone.

'The stress from combat is something I did not expect to suffer with,' he wrote. 'However, when I was told at discharge that there is no cure and it will last for life, I refused to accept this as a married man and father of two. There is a way.' We had met for lunch in a pub in Exeter and some weeks later he invited me to visit him at his home further down the coast.

It was perhaps inevitable that after spending eighteen years in the Marines, A.J. had remained close to the sea. The son of a Yorkshire trawlerman, he had fond memories of accompanying his father on fishing trips on their boat. The family had run a high-class fishmongers, but tighter regulations in the late 1980s made the trawler business untenable and his father encouraged him to join the military. He had visited the Army Careers Office in Hull, where recruiters had been impressed that he could manage more than six pull-ups. They suggested he try for the Marines, the elite commando unit famous for its gruelling training course and coveted green beret. A.J. turned out to be a natural soldier, earning the King's Badge, awarded to the best Marine in each intake, and flooring fully fledged commandos in a corp boxing championship. Before long he was selected for the arduous training in marksmanship, concealment and stalking to qualify as a sniper.

He first went to Afghanistan in late 2001 after the Taliban government was toppled by a combination of US airstrikes, Special Forces operations and Northern Alliance militias. The Marines were deployed to mountainous terrain in eastern Afghanistan to try to prevent Osama bin Laden and his followers fleeing into Pakistan. They arrived long after the al-Qaeda leader had fled, and barely a shot was fired. But by the time A.J.'s unit, 45 Commando, returned to Afghanistan in September 2006, it was clear that lack of action would no longer be a problem.

At the start of the tour, he participated in Operation Slate – a mission to secure a hydroelectric dam near Gereshk, a town on the Helmand River. The plan was to use two companies of Marines – several hundred men – to form a perimeter to allow Royal Engineers to construct an outpost for a unit of Afghan police. The Marines left a compound known as Forward Operating Base, or FOB Price, before dawn and drove south towards Gereshk. As the convoy of British armoured vehicles entered the settlement, black-clad men lining the main street stared in silence.

'Everything was just Taliban – wasn't a single smile or a wave from any of the blokes,' A.J. said.

His sniper rifle was too unwieldy to use at close quarters so he gripped a handgun as he rode in a turret. The convoy paused and he saw an old man with flowing grey beard and turban watching him from an alleyway. Their eyes met and the elder drew a finger across his throat.

'He knew what was coming when we got to the dam.'

The Marines reached the dam and formed a perimeter so the engineers could start to deploy their earth-moving equipment. Moments later the first Taliban mortar bomb whistled overhead. For the next thirty-six hours the Marines were thrust into a non-stop fight for their lives.

The Taliban were well-practised at hitting the dam and their shells rained down with appalling ferocity, forcing the Marines to dig shallow holes they called 'shell scrapes' or deeper trenches to shield themselves from the devastating blasts and shrapnel. At one point A.J. was briefing a troop sergeant when they both heard the loudest explosion yet and dived into a shell scrape, wrapped together like animals cornered in a burrow. A.J. pointed across from the couch to his television to show how far away the round had struck then somehow failed to explode.

'We looked at each other – that was the mortar to kill us,' A.J. said. 'It's probably still there now.'

The Marines hit back with mortars of their own, while jets roared overhead and bombed Taliban positions. As a sniper, A.J. acted as eyes and ears for the rest of the Marines, carefully spotting targets and either calling in mortar fire or counting down from three and squeezing his trigger. He had soon made his first kill and before long the tally was mounting. Throughout, the engineers calmly marshalled their earth-moving equipment, a surreal spectacle amid the mayhem. A.J. noticed one of the soldiers driving a digger was wearing ear defenders – and wondered for a moment if he was trying to muffle the sound of the equipment, or the bullets zipping past his wagon. A woman officer, rifle slung across her back, directed the work as calmly as if she was supervising a building site.

At one point A.J. and a fellow sniper joined a group of Afghan police officers locked in a gun battle with the Taliban. The Marines gestured to the Afghans to stay down but one of the young men dashed forward to fire an RPG. The rocket slammed into a Taliban position and A.J. exchanged an approving glance with another Marine as if to say: 'Fair one.'

Then there was a burst of gunfire and the policeman fell a few paces in front of him. Another Afghan policeman ran forward to try to help his wounded friend and was also shot down. Hoping they might be saved, the Marines mobilised a quad bike to ferry them back to a helicopter landing area. A.J. rode with the pair in the back of a trailer, once more drawing his handgun in case he needed to stage a close-quarter defence. He worked with a Marine medic to try to staunch the arterial flow but the trailer floor was soon slick with blood and he watched as their life forces started to fade. The pair could not have been much more than sixteen or seventeen years old. It would be years before A.J. would learn how deeply the image of the teenagers' faces had been engraved onto his memory.

Large numbers of Taliban were killed, but they proved a determined enemy – the fire had been so intense at times that A.J. marvelled he had not been hit. Nevertheless, the strain of combat left a physical imprint. He had suffered a concussion after banging his head while taking cover and each time he pulled the trigger on his sniper rifle, the shockwave from the recoil of the high-calibre .338 round rippled through his body. His head soon began to feel numb and his ears rang with a maddening high-pitched sound that lasted for days after the shooting had ceased.

As the tour progressed, A.J. was deployed to Sangin, a small town on the Helmand River. A notorious Taliban stronghold, Sangin was used as a hub for smuggling the opium used to make heroin, and the insurgents were intent on winning it back after soldiers from the Parachute Regiment had narrowly managed to hold their position in the town centre in intense close-quarter fighting a few months before. A.J.'s unit was based four kilometres away from the centre in an outpost known as FOB Robinson, resupplied infrequently by Chinook helicopters that ran a constant risk of being shot down. An outer ring of wire cages filled with earth formed the first line of defence. The Marines bedded down in buildings in an inner circle nicknamed the 'Dust Bowl'. A tower made of mud bricks stood in the centre and A.J. took turns with the other snipers to man a makeshift bunker on the top, cradling their rifles and scanning the dun-coloured landscape for any sign of the Taliban.

Nowhere in Sangin was safe, but the tower was particularly exposed. FOB Robinson had been set up by a previous rotation of Canadian troops on a slope, giving Taliban fighters concealed in the town a clear arc of fire. They exploited this weakness to lay down barrages of terrifying intensity – hammering the base with heavy 120mm mortars that made the ground shake. Sometimes as many as thirty rounds would slam into the ground in a single attack. Prone soldiers watched as grains of sand leapt in front of their faces with each shuddering impact.

While other Marines took cover, A.J. and his sniper team would remain on the tower – scanning the surrounding patchwork of landscape for any sign of the enemy. The Paras had lost two soldiers and a linguist six months earlier when a shell had hit a similar tower in the centre of Sangin. Each time the crump of a mortar being fired echoed across the landscape, A.J. flinched, suspended for thirty seconds in a zone between life and death. It was only when he heard an ear-splitting blast as the shell struck home that he knew he was still alive.

'Anything happened, any "bang" – you had to be involved,' A.J. said. 'People were relying on your optics, especially at night – you could see more.'

As the mortar rounds fell about him, he was keenly aware that if he lost the deadly game of hide-and-seek with the Taliban, Marines would pay with their lives. He did his best to push aside the fear, concentrating on making rapid calculations based on the pattern of the incoming fire to try to plot where the mortar team might be concealed. There was no shortage of potential hiding places: the scrappy sprawl of dwellings in Sangin, the thick foliage of the river-hugging 'green zone' and a sinister-looking ruin – the North Fort – located almost a kilometre away.

If working on the tower was dangerous, then the snipers' other duties put them even further in harm's way. A.J. and his sniper partner often ventured out of Robinson, concealing themselves on outcrops to watch the Taliban fighters as they attempted to blend in with the locals. They knew from monitoring enemy radios that the Taliban were intent on scoring a propaganda coup by shooting down one of the Chinooks that periodically landed at the base. Sometimes A.J. and his team would approach the insurgent positions in the darkness, carefully set up a rifle, wait for first light, then count down from three.

'You'd hear them on the radio saying: "Get the weapon, the helicopter's coming, we're going to take out the helicopter today,"' A.J. said. 'We used to lie there, finger on the trigger, round up the chamber – ready to engage a head or a body.'

Sometimes, the Taliban turned the tables – luring A.J. and his partner into a spot where one of their snipers had a clear aim. Once a bullet sliced through the air between them. Another time they found themselves in a sniper-on-sniper duel – resolving the contest by locating their adversary and directing fire from two .50 calibre machine guns. In an account A.J. later sent me by email, he emphasised how intimate the war felt – snipers on both sides trying very hard to kill one another.

'This was personal,' he wrote. 'The Taliban wanted us dead. We had a big impact on them and they would target us directly.'

At dusk, A.J. would once again take up position on the tower – often spotting more Taliban to shoot. When darkness fell, he switched on a thermal imaging device, sensitive enough to pick up the body heat of deer, foxes or dogs. Sometimes he detected groups of two or three Taliban trying to plant roadside bombs about a kilometre from Robinson. A.J. would cut their activity short with his rifle – or call in a Javelin anti-tank missile that lit up the night with a searing flash.

One freezing January night, just before 11.00 p.m., he was about to climb down from the rooftop to hand over the watch when he felt an unusual pang. He did not hear a spoken command, exactly, nor was the sensation that of being tapped on the shoulder. Yet he felt as if a silent voice was urging him to take one last look. Like an old computer, his thermal scope took a while to reboot. When it flickered back to life, something stirred on the North Fort. He watched a heat spot bob up and down, as if something was beckoning him from the battlements.

'It was spooky; I think I've got a guardian angel,' he told me with a wry smile. 'It went down, then came back up. Then another one came up – then there were two.'

Whatever it was, it was no fox, deer or dog. He picked up a field telephone and called Robinson's duty room.

'Stand the men to,' he said. 'We're about to get attacked.'

He had shot at targets on the North Fort before and knew the precise range – 728 metres. As yawning Marines stumbled out of their quarters, pulling on combat helmets and quickly taking up their positions, A.J. saw two men pop up on the ruin. Squinting through his scope, he tracked his rifle to the point where the cross hairs were hovering just beneath a black turban.

A flash of light flooded his eyepiece. The man in his sights had lit the propellant on a rocket. Viewed through his optics the glow of the fuse illuminated his target like a halo. He fired. The man fell, and his rocket arced into the night's sky with a fizzing *wushhhh*. True to A.J.'s intuition, the blast signalled the start of a carefully planned attack. Orange muzzle flashes flickered around the base as Taliban fighters began to open fire from positions less than a hundred metres from the earth-filled cages marking Robinson's perimeter.

A.J.'s warning had meant the Marines were ready and the night lit up with the laser-like streaks of glow-in-the-dark tracers. He remained on the tower, counting down from three, over and over. The next day the Afghan linguist who monitored the Taliban radios grabbed his hand.

'You killed him!' he said.

A.J. was puzzled. Then he learned that his 728-metre shot had martyred the Taliban commander in Sangin.

The kill was testament to his skill, yet it did nothing to soothe his nerves. He had always been self-reliant, content with his own company and often happier sharing a quiet drink than in a rowdy barroom. But he watched the Marines preparing for patrols with a stab of envy – their camaraderie left him feeling even more isolated in his nest. When the others were resting, he would be hard at work reinforcing the makeshift fortifications on the tower. Somebody nicknamed him Rommel after the German general known for his preoccupation with defence.

A.J. said: 'Let's say five or six mortars come in an hour. Goes quiet. They say: "Stand down. It's over." I couldn't switch off. You're just left feeling on edge – look around, see some people making drinks, taking body armour off, getting a shower. How do you know a bomb's not going to land any minute? If we got ten minutes spare, I'd be filling sandbags.'

One night, he took a short break in one of the sturdier bunkers in Robinson – a reinforced shipping container. With mild amusement, he realised he had wet himself. Another sniper bumbled inside and confessed that the same thing happened to him every night. They both laughed. These fleeting moments of respite were their only antidote to the tension.

One day, mortar rounds were once more falling on Robinson, creeping ever closer to the tower. A shell exploded just outside the base walls, then one hit inside the perimeter. The next struck close to their building. A.J. agreed with his partner that the next time they heard a mortar being fired they would scramble down from the tower during the thirty-second lull before impact. There was another dull thud and, his survival instincts kicking in, he threw himself off the tower.

Laden with body armour and ammunition, he slammed into the ground on his backside, pain lancing up his spine. He struggled on for another week, but he was reduced to a crawl at the end of patrols and could not lie flat to fire. His commander had no choice but to send him back to Camp Bastion for medical attention.

On the day he was due to leave, the Marines were skirmishing with the Taliban just outside Robinson. A.J. provided cover from a rooftop while another sniper was sharp-eyed enough to spot a patch of disturbed earth 200 metres away. It was a classic 'combat indicator' – a tell-tale sign of a buried bomb. A.J.'s colleague was given permission to fire at the soil with a carefully aimed shot. There was a huge blast and a mushroom-shaped plume of white phosphorous smoke billowed high into the air. Had a vehicle rolled over the bomb, Marines would no doubt have been wounded or killed. A.J. would later regret not recommending his friend for a decoration.

With the gunfire still crackling outside Robinson, A.J. ex-changed a hurried handshake with the man next to him. He unloaded his rifle, then staggered with his kit onto the rear ramp of a Chinook. He was devastated to be leaving but he knew he had no choice: the aircraft only landed every two weeks and would be on the ground for no more than ten seconds. As the helicopter raced across the hard-packed desert, he could not know that his hardest battle lay ahead.

*

The Royal Marines' spiritual centre of gravity is situated on the Devon coast at the Commando Training Centre at Lympstone, a collection of four-storey barrack blocks and offices overlooking the mudflats of the river Exe. As a young Marine, A.J. had jogged across the estuary in formation with his fellow recruits, tracing out the number of their unit in figures so big they were visible to passengers on passing trains. Six months after coming home from Afghanistan, he returned – this time to attend a promotion course for the rank of sergeant, a big step in his career.

Ever since he had arrived back in Britain, A.J. had known that something was wrong. Four days after leaving Robinson, he had found himself at Dreghorn Barracks in Edinburgh, where he was sent for three weeks of intensive rehabilitation for his back. While the rest of 45 Commando would be returning home as a team, stopping off in Cyprus for thirty-six hours of 'decompression', A.J. felt disconnected and alone. Once he was walking across the parade square to the dining hall when a cannon was fired as part of the preparations for a ceremony. He dived to the ground and rolled under a car. Other soldiers shot him bemused glances and he felt shaken and embarrassed. Unable to sleep, he was constantly on edge. Though the Royal Marines had pioneered efforts to raise awareness of 'operational stress', he kept his problems to himself.

By the time he returned to Lympstone, A.J. felt worse. At one point he lost his memory for several days. On another occasion, he struggled during a map-reading exercise and his classmates burst out laughing – wondering how a sniper who had served two tours in Afghanistan could not perform one of the basic skills of his craft. One of the training exercises precisely replicated an incident he had been part of in Afghanistan and made his head spin.

'It was horrible. I felt totally sick,' he had written to me. Though he seemed to perform well, he vomited as soon as he was alone. He began to skip lessons and wander aimlessly around the base or spend long periods staring across the river Exe.

Despite his growing anxiety, A.J. managed to earn his promotion. He was assigned a role as an instructor at Lympstone and hoped he would feel better as he settled into his new routine, but his distress soon became impossible to hide. Once he organised a realistic casualty exercise – so realistic that one of the Marines broke down, threw aside his weapon and left the course. As he lectured classes on the painstaking task of preparing orders for battle, he would suddenly find himself back on the tower in Robinson, braced for a fresh barrage of mortar rounds. He only realised he had trailed off in mid-sentence when his audience began to murmur.

He said: 'I'd suddenly snap out of it – I'd say: "Mate, tell me what I was saying." It became a laughing point – people were going: "Is he losing it?"'

One day, A.J. had been due to give a lecture when another sergeant found him sitting in the canteen, gazing into space. He felt as if he was encased in a glass dome – the world beyond seemed remote and unreal.

'It was all about me, it was all about Afghan, all about my world – you live in a bubble,' he said, illustrating his point by touching his fingertips together to form a globe.

'The only things that matter are actually right here and within arm's reach – anything else, you can't take it in. Can't think about yesterday – gone. Can't think about tomorrow – just in a bubble.

'It would be just as easy to make a cup of tea as it was to walk out the door and never come back,' he said. 'You're emotionally numb. You don't really care about anyone else's emotions – they don't matter.'

A.J.'s superiors took his plight seriously and he was assigned sessions of a therapy known as EMDR – eye movement desensitisation and reprocessing, one of the standard treatments for PTSD used by the military and NHS. In an EMDR session, the therapist asks the client to recall a visual image of a traumatic memory, the accompanying emotion and where that is felt in the body. The goal is then to release the trapped feelings using bilateral stimulation of the brain – either by the therapist moving their fingers back and forth in front of the client's eyes or by using flashing lights. A similar effect can be achieved using special sound tracks played through headphones or through hand taps or buzzers held in the patient's hands. The therapy can sometimes achieve remarkable results. In A.J.'s case, it made him feel worse – the seemingly endless sessions brought the terror and horror of the 'Big Five' flooding back.

I'm a soldier, A.J. had felt like telling his therapist. *Why am I pouring my heart out? Why am I crying in front of you?* He began to question whether it would have been better to have kept silent and followed the traditional soldierly mantras of 'man up' and 'crack on'.

'They actually said to me: "You've persisted to a point where it won't work,"' A.J. told me. '"You've topped out with EMDR – don't do any more."'

With the therapy showing no signs of a breakthrough, A.J. was medically discharged from the Marines. As his last day approached, he spent much of his time alone at home. Looking back, he could see that his chain of command, while sympathetic, had been uncertain how best to handle him.

'It's a funny one: you want help and don't want help, so they didn't know what to do,' he said. 'I'd be angry at them. They'd be worried that they're causing you stress. They didn't know where the fine line was, whether to intervene too much or step back. I knew I needed to be away from the military. Because I'm a sergeant they assumed I've got the level-headedness to organise it and sort it out myself.'

In reality, A.J.'s despair was deepening. On his last day as a Marine, Karen went to work. He got up from the kitchen and walked towards the garage door. A silent voice was calling. This was not the benign whisper he had heard on the tower. At our first meeting in Exeter, he told me he could only think of one word to describe the voice. He had hesitated to share it because he realised how outlandish it sounded; he had felt like the Devil had been summoning him from the garage. His message: *'Everything will be easy if you come with me.'*

A.J. preferred not to speak in detail about the following moments; suffice to say that the thought of his two sons finding him prompted him to step back from the brink. He charged out of the house, ran through the streets leading towards the seafront, and reached the beach.

As he ran, parallel to the breaking waves, something shifted. A.J., always articulate in his descriptions of his inner world, found it hard to convey the change. In the depths of his darkness he made momentary contact with a profound sense of peace. He had never been particularly religious, but it was only the sphere of the spiritual that seemed to offer something approaching an appropriate vocabulary to describe the clarity he felt. Later he would call it 'meeting God', though he was aware that this shorthand could easily be misinterpreted, and did not even begin to capture what he had experienced. As he walked home, he was filled with a conviction that he owed it to himself and his family to get well again.

Despite the epiphany on the sand, A.J.'s hopes of a rapid recovery proved elusive. He was tormented by feelings of guilt over the death of a member of his company who had been killed by an IED in ground he had kept safe for months from his nest on the tower. Part of his mind insisted that his friend might have lived had he not been sent home injured. He ruminated over a conversation they had shared several days before the Chinook lifted him out of Sangin. A.J. explained in an email:

> During a mortar attack, he had asked me where best to take cover up at my end of the camp. I froze, didn't

answer him and made my way to the roof in a daze. Once there I was able to engage the firers. I had let him down – not told him where to take cover. I was focused on retaliation.

The next day we spoke and I said sorry for not helping him. It was fine, he was cool and to soothe my concerns he said I could make it up to him with a beer once we were back in the UK. I never got a chance to buy him that beer. He was killed by an IED in ground I had been in control of.

Because A.J. had been repatriated with his injury, he was able to attend the funeral. 'The hardest thing I have ever done: laid a friend in the ground having felt responsible for the device being laid in my territory whilst I was "off watch". This funeral felt like it was my creation. Guilt – even innocent guilt – is an evil thing.'

As time passed, his underlying sense of anxiety constantly took on new forms, a shape-shifter immune to the power of logic. When a car he did not recognise parked outside his house, he rang the police, convinced it belonged to a hit man come to kill him. He became fixated on helmet-camera footage shot in Afghanistan and uploaded onto YouTube. 'It was a first sign I think of depression and a macabre interest in death,' he explained.

The obsession morphed into a fascination with YouTube clips about a conspiracy theory that predicted a massive object known as 'Planet X' would sweep through the solar system, triggering a reversal in the polarity of the earth's magnetic field that would destroy civilisation. To A.J. the theory seemed plausible – even urgent. He later realised that the prospect of calamity striking from the heavens served as a proxy for the fear of falling mortar rounds that had infected him in Sangin.

One day, he was out driving with Karen and his children in Exeter when another driver barged past him as he was reversing out of a parking space. He threw his car into gear and pursued the man until they were both forced to stop at a roundabout. A.J. jumped out and began running towards the driver, who managed to accelerate and swerve around the circle. A.J. caught a glimpse of his panic-stricken face as he sped past and began to sprint after him, then realised the chase was futile, and stood in the road bellowing obscenities. As he calmed down, he gradually became aware that a queue of people were staring at him from a bus stop.

'I would have just kept beating him until he was dead, I know I would,' A.J. said quietly. 'I had no control. And that's when I knew I needed some help.'

4

'Delayed Massive Trauma'

Soldiers, therapists and the 'invention' of PTSD

In 1944, a psychiatrist named Major Dugmore Hunter was serving in the Eighth Army as it advanced into Italy from North Africa. In a memorandum, he set out his views on treating soldiers who broke down. '"Hysterical" screaming and jibbering can often be stopped at once by means of a sharp command, a gallon or two of cold water, or the abrupt application of the flat of the hand to the side of the face,' he wrote. 'These are to be regarded as common-sense forms of first aid.' There was, however, no cure for 'poor moral fibre'.

In today's Army, Hunter's successors are broadcasting a somewhat gentler message. In 2011, with British troops still fighting in Afghanistan, the MoD launched a publicity campaign called 'Don't Bottle It Up' to challenge an ingrained culture of stigma around mental health. Posters appeared at bases across Britain encouraging soldiers to come forward if they were having problems. The British Forces Broadcasting Service began running a clip of a soldier trapped in a giant bottle, screaming a silent cry as he pummelled the glass. There was a poetry competition and a stand-up comedian sought to break down barriers in a segment dubbed 'Nervous Laughter'.

The Army had never attempted anything like it. Not only did the campaign acknowledge the existence of mental health problems among service personnel, it granted them a degree of legitimacy that would have been unthinkable even a few years earlier. The exhortation was no longer 'suck it up, buttercup', as one Army wife assessed the prevailing attitude in her husband's regiment in the 1990s. The new message: it is not weak to put up your hand, it is sensibly strong.

The question of whether the campaign was a sign of real progress or merely a cosmetic change would be critical in determining whether contemporary forces could expect proper support. Across Britain I heard contradictory reports. Jake Wood, a reservist who fought in Sangin and wrote a book about his experiences of PTSD called *Among You*, said he had been treated impeccably by his commander and there had been no whisper of prejudice against men in his company who suffered stress reactions in the aftermath of intense fighting. The only time he came up against unhelpful attitudes was from a handful of senior individuals based in Camp Bastion who had little experience of combat.

'Among the troops actually fighting on the ground, I neither heard of nor encountered any stigma – ever,' Jake said. 'I only ever saw empathy, forged from shared experience.'

Others described a less enlightened attitude. 'The boys would have ripped the piss out of you for years if they even found out you'd been to see a therapist,' said Ian, a young former soldier from York, who served a tour in Afghanistan and later found work as a window cleaner. 'It's just the Army banter – they'd make you feel a lot worse about the situation even though they think they're cheering you up.'

Some of those who did seek help ended up feeling broken and discarded. One serving Army captain reported that he and several other soldiers he knew had been treated with an attitude bordering on contempt by their superiors when they were diagnosed with mental health problems and their careers had suffered. 'In a nutshell, it's a shambles,' he told me.

To understand more about this current system of care, I started

by taking a deeper look at the way it had evolved since the end
of the First World War, when the Army was still reeling from the
debacle of 'shell shock'.

In the interwar years, military psychiatry receded to the outer rim
of medicine. There was no systematic clinical effort to distil the
wealth of experience acquired by Myers and other British 'shell
shock' doctors. In the 1920s, the pioneering American psychiatrist
Abram Kardiner worked extensively with US veterans of the
First World War to develop sophisticated theories of trauma, but
his work had scant influence on military policy. Generals had
absorbed some lessons – the Field Service Regulations of 1929
acknowledged the conditions of modern war could quickly wear
men down and warned that the individual soldier should not be
pushed beyond the point of exhaustion. But the official view
was summed up by Lieutenant Colonel Lord Gort VC, who
argued that 'shell shock' was 'practically non-existent' in 'first-
class divisions' and should be thought of as a form of 'disgrace'
to the soldier. In other words, psychiatric casualties represented a
regrettable breach, rather than an inevitable consequence of war.

At the outbreak of the Second World War, there were only
half a dozen regular Army officers with varying degrees of psychiatric training and the British Expeditionary Force in France
made no plans to adopt the forward psychiatry model developed
by Myers. His principles were only rediscovered more or less
by accident in May 1941 when Germans surrounded the Allied
garrison at Tobruk on the Libyan coast. Australian medics were
forced to open a 'war neurosis clinic' in an underground shelter
within earshot of the guns – precisely the kind of front-line care
Myers had advocated.

Public attitudes were changing, however. The experience of
'shell shock' had left an indelible impression on society and the
death penalty for desertion had been abolished in 1930. Victorian
notions of duty and self-sacrifice had begun to erode and

generals risked a backlash if they were seen to treat men callously. The hard-driving American commander Lieutenant General George S. Patton Jr sparked outrage when, during a visit to a hospital in Sicily, he slapped a young psychiatric casualty with his glove. He told another: 'You're just a goddamned coward.' The incidents forced Patton to make a public apology and cost him his command.

As the Second World War intensified, the Army, eager to exploit scientific progress in all areas of combat, turned to the fast-developing discipline of psychiatry to try to minimise the incidence of breakdown. In April 1942, the War Office established its first dedicated Directorate of Army Psychiatry and by 1945 there were over 300 psychiatrists working for the Army, many serving overseas. As the war progressed, rudimentary intelligence and aptitude tests were introduced for recruits in the belief that 'dullards', 'lifelong neurotics' and 'misfits' were more likely to have difficulties. Psychologists also played a role in officer selection, devising 'Leaderless Group' tasks still used in the British Army today.

Treatments varied according to the temperament of psychiatrists. In Tripoli, a rugged, powerfully built disciplinarian named Major Harold Palmer believed the key ingredient in recovery was to restore a sense of duty. He would begin by reducing patients to tears in their initial interview before subsequently offering them a chance at redemption by returning to the front. Palmer likened his technique to that of a Salvation Army evangelist, first 'knocking a sinner sideways', then exalting them to repentance. He triumphantly reported that his methods had returned 98 per cent of patients to 'full duty', though, as the historian Ben Shephard has pointed out, only about a third returned to their original units and the rest found jobs elsewhere in the Army.

In Italy, Major Dugmore Hunter concentrated on prevention. Acutely conscious of the need to minimise 'wastage' as the war entered its final stage, he focused on distinguishing men who would be 'curable' if treated quickly from inherently weak-willed soldiers who would forever be a burden. Hunter believed this latter group – the 'poorest sort of human material' – should be deliberately pushed to breaking point. 'The manpower problem remains acute,' he wrote. 'It is therefore essential that we get the last ounce every man is capable of giving before we discard him as a fighting soldier.' Inferior men should be treated like a 'cheap car': run to the limit, then discarded.

Despite the increasingly prominent role of psychiatrists, command still regarded stigma as an essential counterweight to 'exhaustion' among troops, and there was widespread suspicion, even hostility, towards 'nut-pickers' and 'trick cyclists'. Winston Churchill voiced a widely held view when he warned in a memorandum that letting psychiatrists loose among soldiers might propagate the very neuroses they aimed to prevent. 'I am sure it would be possible to restrict as much as possible the work of these gentlemen, who are capable of doing an immense amount of harm with what may very easily degenerate into charlatanry,' Churchill wrote. 'There are quite enough hangers-on and camp-followers already.'

There was no clearer evidence of the official use of stigma than in Britain's Bomber Command. Unexpectedly high rates of breakdown among aircrews at the start of the war sparked fears that a systemic collapse in morale would leave Britain dangerously exposed to invasion. In the spring of 1940 the RAF took drastic action: hundreds of those who were too shaken to continue flying would henceforth be stripped of their wings and have 'Lack of Moral Fibre' marked on their files. Some were sent to labour in coal mines. Group Captain Leonard Cheshire VC, an iconic bomber ace, dealt briskly with 'LMF' for fear it might be contagious. 'I was ruthless with moral fibre cases, I had to be,' he wrote. 'We were airmen, not psychiatrists.' All the more poignant, then, that Cheshire himself would suffer devastating bouts of depression after the war.

Outside the military, civilian doctors began to look beyond the baths, massages and electricity used as treatments in the last war. Among them was an ambitious psychiatrist named William Sargant who was confronted with an influx of dazed survivors from the disaster at Dunkirk in the summer of 1940, some 'raging mutinously', some in a state of 'abject neurotic collapse'. Sargant gave one mute and trembling soldier a shot of sodium amytal – a fast-acting barbiturate used to induce a catharsis of pent-up emotions – and the man rapidly brightened. Encouraged, Sargant began to give similar injections to other patients, including a quaking man with a paralysed hand. The man's hand functioned again and he relived how he had come across his own severely wounded brother lying by the roadside, who had begged him to shoot him. The paralysed hand had fired the shot. Sargant became an evangelical advocate of drug-based therapies which he used on thousands of patients, dismissing psychotherapy as just 'talk, talk, talk'. Known as a risk-taker and self-publicist, Sargant was adored by some patients – others saw him as the 'Devil Incarnate'.

Meanwhile, at the Northfield Military Hospital near Birmingham, psychiatrists were taking radical steps in the opposite direction. Drugs were still used, notably to plunge the severest patients into a deep sleep: staff watched them crawl on the floor or grapple with imaginary adversaries while still unconscious. But Northfield would be best remembered for a bold but short-lived attempt by the psychiatrists Wilfred Bion and John Rickman to weld the 800 patients into a new form of self-governing therapeutic community. Wards elected representatives and men gathered for group sessions: the collective was seen as both the patient and the method of treatment. Blurring the roles of psychiatrist and commanding officer, the pair sought to galvanise the men into a communal 'war' against their neuroses. Their martial values appealed to the Army, but the initiative came to an ignominious end only six weeks after it began. Rickman and Bion were sacked when chaotic scenes in the hospital cinema hall left an unedifying trail of discarded newspapers and used condoms – a breakdown in discipline that was the precise opposite of their goal.

Group therapy was revived on a smaller scale by their successors, however, and clerks, matron's staff, cooks and even senior Army officers joined in with the patients. One supervisor cleared a ward, named it 'The Hospital Club' and left it empty. When the patients began to protest, he told them to organise the club themselves. Inmates frequently wrecked their new project, but were left in charge of repairs. Other patients vented their frustrations by brutally satirising their doctors in a newsletter called the *Psyche*. Although the concept of the therapeutic community fell out of fashion as a new pharmaceutical age dawned in the 1950s, the 'Northfield experiments' became psychotherapy folklore.

The other significant legacy of the war was the growing amount of research challenging the Army's reluctance to accept that psychiatric casualties were inevitable. A study by American psychiatrist John Appel concluded that the idea of 'getting used to combat' was a myth and that the average soldier could endure between 200 and 240 days of fighting before becoming ineffective. Lord Moran, who served as Churchill's personal physician, expressed the point succinctly in *Anatomy of Courage*, his study of wartime psychology, published in 1945: 'Men wear out in war like clothes.'

In some respects, the Army's embrace of psychiatry can be read as a success story. Selection prevented many young men who might have clogged the 'shell shock' hospitals of the First World War from ever reaching the front, and there were advances in talk- and drug-based treatments. Yet the war produced no new consensus on how men broke down, or on the best way to help those that did. By the outbreak of the Korean War in 1950, the forward model pioneered by Myers had once again been forgotten. It would be thirty years before the advent of a new, more enduring era in the psychology of war – heralded by the return of hundreds of thousands of American soldiers from the jungles of Vietnam.

In the 1982 film *First Blood*, Sylvester Stallone plays a fictional former Green Beret named John Rambo who declares war on a brutal small-town police chief. After using his prowess in guerrilla warfare to best massed ranks of police and National Guard, Rambo – a man of few words – finally breaks his silence in a confrontation with Colonel Sam Trautman, his former commanding officer. Breaking down, the bare-chested, machine-gun-toting commando reveals his vulnerability through the most childlike of gestures: pressing his head against Trautman's chest.

The archetypal disturbed Vietnam veteran has become such a familiar on-screen trope that it is easy to forget that the war was initially seen as a success story for military psychiatry. Pentagon doctors congratulated themselves on having applied the lessons of the past to record lower rates of psychological casualties than in any previous war. By the mid-1970s, this optimistic assessment had capsized. Large numbers of veterans were plagued by drug and alcohol problems, alienated from society and unable to maintain jobs or relationships. Though not quite Rambos-in-waiting, their suffering was acute.

While the American government was reluctant to acknowledge the veterans' plight, a group of psychoanalysts closely aligned with the anti-war movement took up their cause. Among them were Chaim Shatan, a New York psychoanalyst, and Robert Jay Lifton, one of the most influential American psychiatrists of his generation, who had spent years working with survivors of the atomic bombing of Hiroshima. The two men attended a series of 'rap groups' – mass meetings organised by Vietnam Veterans Against the War, a pressure group founded by disillusioned former soldiers. The constellation of hyper-vigilance, insomnia, paranoia and explosive rage reported by many convinced Shatan and Lifton that they were dealing with a new type of disorder, one that did not appear in any existing manuals.

Shatan and Lifton read literature on the survivors of the Nazi Holocaust, reports on burn and acid victims and the writings of Kardiner, the American psychiatrist who had worked with First World War veterans. They compiled a list of the most common symptoms of traumatic neuroses and cross-referenced them with the clinical records of 700 Vietnam veterans. Lifton initially described their condition as 'post-Vietnam syndrome'. According to Shatan, this was caused by a 'delayed massive trauma'. A coalition of like-minded psychiatrists who had worked with diverse groups of veterans and survivors of rape, child abuse and the Nazi Holocaust began to lobby the medical establishment to recognise the potentially devastating long-term impact of life-threatening events. In 1980, after much painstaking deliberation by committees, the American Psychiatric Association adopted the new and unwieldy diagnostic category of PTSD in the third edition of the American Psychiatric Association's *Diagnostic and Statistical Manual of Mental Disorders*, the profession's bible.

Since Myers's time, the assumption had been that an otherwise healthy soldier should never suffer more than a transient collapse. A stressful event could only produce a prolonged reaction if it activated some pre-existing, hidden vulnerability – a hereditary defect or damage dating back to early childhood. PTSD turned this thinking on its head. The cause was – by definition – trauma, not faulty genes or parental neglect. The symptoms were no longer seen as evidence of an underlying flaw, rather they were a natural reaction to an abnormal event. Some went as far as to argue that those who pushed themselves the hardest were the most liable to break down. From this perspective, PTSD was far from a sign of weakness – it was a badge of strength.

The new diagnosis ran into fierce opposition from the outset. Critics pointed out that the 'invention' of PTSD did not follow any scientific breakthrough or carefully controlled research – rather it was the result of well-organised lobbying by psychiatrists passionately opposed to the Vietnam War. Some saw the diagnosis as a spurious mishmash of conditions already well described in the literature. The fact that PTSD had evolved from such a wide range of proposed conditions – 'the rape trauma syndrome', 'the battered woman syndrome', 'the Vietnam veterans' syndrome' and 'the abused child syndrome' – seemed to muddy the concept further.

Other psychiatrists recognised the importance of trauma, but were concerned that the emphasis on 'disorder' in PTSD carried unhelpful connotations of permanent damage and disease that would privilege drug-based treatments over therapies designed to help people find meaning in their experiences. Among them was Professor Charles Figley, one of America's leading trauma specialists. Figley began his career as a psychologist after serving a combat tour as a US Marine in Vietnam in 1965 and he participated in the deliberations that led to the creation of PTSD. He told me he would have preferred the formulation to categorise long-term stress reactions as 'injuries' – implying they could be managed and ultimately healed.

'If you're running every day carrying eight-pound weights in each hand, it's inevitable that eventually you'll trip over and hurt yourself. If somebody labels that as a "disorder" you'll think: "I'm sick, I have a disease, I need medication,"' Figley told me. 'In actual fact, you are suffering from an injury and what you need is rehabilitation to recover.'

There was a dispute, too, over the broader utility of a diagnosis forged at a unique, highly polarised juncture in American history. Some believed that PTSD was caused by a universal trauma reaction hardwired during the course of human evolution. Others were convinced that the concept of a 'traumatic memory' was a social and political construct that did not exist in other cultures and historical epochs. Such sceptics pointed out that there is scant evidence to suggest that those who suffered from 'shell shock' in the First World War reported anything akin to the flashbacks described by Vietnam veterans – the phenomenon seems to have emerged in parallel with the diffusion of cinema and television. For some doctors in Europe, the proliferation of the catch-all American diagnosis of PTSD was to psychiatry what the creation of the 'Big Mac' had been to food.

The controversies linger, yet for many people – soldier or civilian – the elaboration of PTSD was a profound source of comfort. Danny White, a former Royal Marine who served two tours in Northern Ireland between 1989 and 1992, spoke for many when he told me of the despair and frustration he had felt until he was diagnosed.

'I just wanted to smash my head open, almost peel my head open – let it all fly out,' Danny told me at his home in a quiet village in East Sussex. 'Then it was almost like a relief that all of a sudden you had the diagnosis – it was tangible, you weren't going mad, you had something that someone else had had. This ray of hope: "You're going to be all right."'

Given the ambivalence Britain's military has often shown to psychiatry, it was perhaps unsurprising that the Army harboured scant enthusiasm for the new diagnosis of PTSD. The prevailing view was that the condition might affect American conscripts in Vietnam, renowned for taking drugs and murdering their own officers – a practice known as 'fragging' – but certainly not well-trained British regulars. It would take the shock of a new conflict for that view to shift. In 1982 – two years after the official adoption of PTSD in America – Argentine forces occupied a small archipelago in the South Atlantic known as the Falkland Islands. The fallout from the subsequent conflict would trigger a tectonic shift in attitudes towards mental health that is still unfolding today.

The pivotal figure in military psychiatry at the time was an Irish physician named Dr Morgan O'Connell. Having joined the Royal Navy as a medical student, he set sail as a psychiatrist aboard the SS *Canberra*, a P&O cruise liner serving as a medical facility for Britain's 26,000-strong Task Force. He turned to the work of Robert H. Ahrenfeldt, an Army psychiatrist who served in the Second World War, to see what he might glean.

'It was almost as if in the aftermath of that horrible war, people just wanted to get back to civilian life and put behind them everything to do with war, including military psychiatry,' O'Connell told me, when we met at the Royal Maritime Club in Portsmouth. 'The whole of Europe dismissed PTSD.'

In common with many in the early days of the Falklands War, O'Connell assumed the Argentines were bluffing and the fleet would not steam much further than the Isle of Wight. As hostilities commenced after an 8,000-mile voyage he treated dozens of psychiatric casualties, including shocked survivors of a Sea King helicopter crash and HMS *Ardent*, a frigate sunk by Argentine aircraft. As a uniformed psychiatrist, he believed he was in a unique position to help men minimise the risk of long-term problems by helping them confront their feelings of terror and bereavement collectively in the immediate aftermath of a disaster.

Buoyed by a swift victory in the seventy-four-day conflict, the military anticipated few problems as the men returned to a heroes' welcome. But O'Connell soon sensed that trouble was brewing behind the smiles. One Royal Marine described how he had been looking forward to taking his wife for a Big Mac. When they reached McDonald's in Plymouth he suddenly found himself cowering under a table – then turned to find another Marine in exactly the same position. They both laughed at their predicament – realising they had instinctively dived after hearing low-flying jets rehearsing for a display.

O'Connell began to conduct surveys of sailors and Marines who had joined the Task Force and a control sample who had stayed in Britain. At first he saw no difference between the two groups, but within a few years growing numbers of veterans were reporting symptoms.

'We'd lost ships before – we're familiar with grief and bereavement reactions and anxiety disorders. But they weren't getting better,' O'Connell said. One of his registrars began to wonder whether the men might be suffering from the new American diagnosis of PTSD.

'Sure enough,' O'Connell said, 'that's what it was.'

Concerned that the problem, known by the catch-all title of 'stress', was not being taken seriously enough, O'Connell approached the Army and RAF to suggest they join a Royal Navy project to make an awareness-raising video.

'The Army said there is a problem, but we'd rather not talk about it because it's bad for regimental morale,' O'Connell said. 'The RAF said: "Stress? We call that LMF (Lack of Moral Fibre) and we kick them out." Finally, the Army and RAF accepted that there must be something in this for the Navy to take it so seriously.'

O'Connell set up Britain's first treatment programme for PTSD in 1987 at Royal Naval Hospital Haslar, the Navy hospital located across the water from Portsmouth docks. About a third of the men who attended his four-week outpatient regime returned to duty – but many relapsed when they were deployed in the Gulf War in 1990. O'Connell would continue to lobby for greater attention to psychological well-being in a later role as the MoD's chief psychiatrist. A wise and compassionate man with a gentle sense of humour, he helped veterans even after he retired in 1996 through his work at Combat Stress and other charities.

O'Connell was by no means alone in his concern for ex-forces, however. Another psychiatrist would emerge as a talismanic figure among hundreds of veterans who served in conflicts from the First World War to the Gulf, and he was about as far from a military man as it was possible to imagine. His name was Dr

Dafydd Alun Jones – otherwise known as 'D.A.' – and at the age of eighty-three he was still ministering to former soldiers. One autumn day, I went to visit his home on the island of Anglesey off the coast of North Wales.

One of Jones's sons came to collect me from the station at Caernarfon, a town dominated by the fairy-tale battlements of its thirteenth-century castle, and we drove over the suspension bridge across the Menai Strait leading to the island. Late in the year, the countryside had a desolate aspect and the sky was smoke-grey. Jones lived in a rambling farmhouse and greeted me warmly at the door clad in a three-piece suit and tie in the style of a country doctor. He led me into a spacious kitchen where he served me a home-made pie and glasses of crisp apple juice, the product of an orchard he had planted in the garden in 1959. As we talked, a pheasant strutted across the lawn.

Jones had become intrigued by the problems facing ex-forces in the early 1980s when he treated an airman who had been shot down over Europe during the Second World War. The Gestapo had run him down with dogs in the foothills of the Pyrenees and he had spent years as a prisoner of war. On his return home, the former flier had plunged into alcoholism and depression. Jones took up his cause and he was awarded a long-overdue war pension. It was the beginning of Jones's one-man crusade to rescue men from the Spiral, waged through a roving psychiatric clinic he ran for ex-forces in towns and cities across Britain, and a war of attrition with pension tribunals. Reluctant to turn anybody away, Jones would routinely receive calls from clients held by police. 'Yes, I know him,' he would tell a sceptical custody sergeant. 'What's he done this time?'

A fierce advocate of Welsh independence, Jones relished his role as a bane of the British establishment. His maverick style and the perennial glint in his eye appealed to ex-forces angered by the lack of support from the military. No doubt some saw in him a father figure. Jones summed up his own self-image in a comment he made to a medical conference in the 1980s: 'I am a white-robed druid bearing no arms. I salve the fallen warrior.' By his own estimate, he had treated more than 2,500 veterans – among them an old soldier who had served near the Khyber Pass on the frontier of Imperial India, the modern border of Afghanistan and Pakistan, and a sailor who crewed a midget submarine in the Second World War.

When I met Jones, he was still grieving for the loss of Ty Gwyn – Welsh for the White House – a twenty-bed private psychiatric clinic set up in 1994 in a country house on the edge of Llandudno further along the coast. Former patients remember a hallowed sanctuary where a restored sense of camaraderie served as a potent healer. Veterans were referred to Ty Gwyn from across the country by NHS doctors, and sometimes judges. Some referred themselves, turning up before dawn and waiting in their cars as they summoned the courage to knock on the door.

Ty Gwyn's graceful architecture and seclusion were reminiscent of Craiglockhart, the hospital outside Edinburgh that treated 'shell-shocked' officers during the First World War. A turret commanded panoramic sea views and the men went for day-long hikes in the nearby peaks of Snowdonia, fishing trips off the coast or bike rides and go-karting. Staff turned a blind eye to a degree of eccentricity and rule-bending. An ex-Royal Marine scooped out a mini-golf course in the grounds and one man brought a budgerigar that flitted around his room. A Falklands veteran once caused consternation among staff when he presented an Argentine soldier who had fought on the other side for a psychiatric assessment. Though Ty Gwyn was in principle a dry house, the men would visit local pubs and there were sometimes fights. Occupants called Ty Gwyn 'Last Chance Saloon' – Jones compared it to the sweat lodges Native American warriors used to purify themselves after a battle.

'Ty Gwyn was some kind of white magic,' he said with a grin at once mischievous and triumphant. 'It worked! There was nothing quite like it.'

By the time Ty Gwyn closed for commercial reasons in 2004, some 550 patients had passed through its doors, representing every conflict involving British forces since the First World War. With the house destined to be turned into deluxe apartments, many of its patients were left bereft. Some kept in touch with Jones for years afterwards. One of them was Roland Riggs, who served tours in Northern Ireland in 1971 and 1972 and lived near me in south-west London. Roland, who arrived in Belfast at the age of eighteen, was forever grateful that staff at Ty Gwyn had helped him to finally confront the mental scars inflicted by the riots, shootings and bombs.

'The hardest thing with Ty Gwyn was to go through the front door. Many guys have walked up to it and turned around,' Roland told me. 'If I hadn't had gone there I would have been in prison or dead – that's a guarantee. Ty Gwyn saved a lot of us.'

A decade after Ty Gwyn was shut down, and more than forty years after serving in Northern Ireland, Roland was still making the two-day round trip to see the psychiatrist he knew as 'D.A.' every month.

While Jones was working at Ty Gwyn, there were broader rumblings of discontent among servicemen who felt the military had ignored their psychological wounds. In 2001, some 2,000 British military personnel launched a class action lawsuit accusing the government of failing to take steps to prevent or adequately treat PTSD they had suffered in conflicts prior to 1996, primarily the Falklands, Northern Ireland, the Gulf War and Bosnia. The case brought together sixteen expert witnesses – eight on each side – and led to what was perhaps the most extensive review of the literature on war trauma to date. The judge ultimately dismissed the case, partly on the grounds that the military had provided care consistent with the level of medical knowledge in Britain at the time. The government had been spared damages that could have run into many millions of pounds, but the hearings had exposed the dearth of recent data on the scale of psychological problems within the British military.

While the MoD had traditionally been reluctant to fund research into PTSD, the class action prompted it to start financing large-scale studies of serving personnel by the King's Centre for Military Health Research in London, which had previously investigated mysterious symptoms among veterans of the 1991 campaign to liberate Kuwait collectively known as Gulf War syndrome. As the campaigns in Iraq and Afghanistan intensified, the military also sought to encourage soldiers to come forward with their problems by expanding a system known as Trauma Risk Management, or TRiM, pioneered by the Royal Marines in the mid-1990s.

The system works like this: a number of personnel in each unit are trained as 'TRiM practitioners' – the psychological equivalent of medics who treat physical wounds caused by bullets or bombs. Their role is to watch out for signs of stress among their colleagues and perhaps take a soldier aside for a chat, particularly if they have witnessed a potentially traumatic event, such as the death of a colleague. TRiM practitioners are not therapists, but are trained to assess whether to refer somebody for specialist help.

The scheme has been hailed as a huge step forward for military mental health, though it has its limits – particularly because some personnel may be reluctant to admit their feelings to TRiM-trained superiors for fear of harming their chances of promotion. Nevertheless, the military believes the system has contributed to a gradual erosion of stigma around mental health problems, with service personnel typically seeking help much earlier than in the past. The 'Don't Bottle It Up' campaign launched in 2011 was another sign of its greater willingness to acknowledge the issue.

At Army headquarters near the Hampshire town of Andover,

I met Captain Theresa Jackson, one of the coordinators of the publicity drive. She showed me a selection of stories published in forces' magazines based on accounts by personnel who had successfully sought treatment for depression or PTSD. Among them was a tough Glaswegian colour sergeant named Terry Lowe. A thirty-three-year-old veteran of tours in Iraq and Afghanistan, Lowe had spoken candidly about his experience of wartime trauma at a series of 'roadshows' for younger soldiers. Nobody could accuse Lowe of being weak: he had shrugged off a suicide bombing in Iraq that killed two British soldiers and wounded more than a dozen. In an interview with *Sixth Sense*, the forces' newspaper in Germany, he described the events in Afghanistan that caused his PTSD.

'I knew something was a wee bit wrong when we were caught in a horseshoe ambush, and after I called in fire support to smash the compound I found two dead civilians and five wounded that were being used as a shield by the Taliban,' Lowe said. 'Something about those civilians was totally different.'

Shortly afterwards Lowe trod on a pressure plate that detonated a bomb buried behind him, killing two of his colleagues. The blast left him so dazed he was momentarily convinced that he too was dead. He began to remove his helmet and body armour while bullets were still flying and only came to his senses when others rushed to his aid. On his return home, Lowe started a classic path down the Spiral: he drank to extremes, suffered road rage and started fights. After receiving therapy from the Army, he volunteered to return to Afghanistan. Lowe proved his PTSD would not hold him back when he led his men into cover to return fire at Taliban fighters, *Sixth Sense* reported.

'You have got to ask yourself if you have three of us on the ground with PTSD, and the other two aren't admitting it ... who is the bigger liability?' Lowe said.

Perhaps the most poignant 'roadshow' presentation was delivered by Michael Iddon, a forty-eight-year-old Falklands veteran known as Iddy. Aged eighteen, Iddy had served as a combat medic on the *Sir Galahad* landing ship. On the afternoon of 8 June 1982, Argentine Skyhawk warplanes attacked the *Sir Galahad* and the *Sir Tristram*, a similar vessel, as they prepared to disembark troops at Bluff Cove. Explosions and fires aboard the *Sir Galahad* turned the vessel into a floating inferno, claiming the lives of forty-eight soldiers and crew, including thirty-two members of the Welsh Guards. Another 150 men were wounded, many suffering horrific burns in one of the worst military disasters Britain had suffered since the Second World War. Iddy was one of the last to abandon ship and almost drowned when he did eventually reach a life raft. He spent the rest of the war treating grievously wounded soldiers.

Sixth Sense pulled no punches with Iddy's story, informing readers that he had not dared to have children and was divorcing his wife because his PTSD symptoms had crushed his libido and left him scared of giving her a black eye during the night. Iddy had tried to kill himself in the toilet of a fast-food restaurant and had only been saved by chance when somebody needing to use the cubicle had started banging on the door.

'There are blank voices in my head, things it's maybe best not to remember, and then those memories are here as if it was last night, this morning, today, five minutes ago, right now,' Iddy told *Sixth Sense*.

'Go it alone and if you are lucky you will survive it. If you're not, you'll end up on a park bench drunk and dead. I don't want that for you lads, and I don't want you to go through what I'm going through now. My advice is to get treated, because if you don't you're screwed.'

5

'Lager Therapy'

Pouring petrol on the fire

When British soldiers go to war, their commanders encourage
them to write a letter to their next of kin to be opened in the
event they are killed. James Forrester, the young lance corporal
in the Black Watch, deferred the task until Alpha Company were
told they would be heading to Sangin, which by the summer of
2009 had acquired a well-deserved reputation as a death trap. It
was dark and James donned a pair of night-vision goggles that
turned the world into pale shades of green and grey. He scrawled
out his 'death letter' and tucked it under the breastplate of his
body armour, where it would remain for the rest of the tour.

Two Platoon made their customary helicopter landing and
James and Aaron watched tracer fire light up the night as a
nearby unit of the Black Watch opened up on the Taliban.
Deployed to a quieter area, Two Platoon bedded down in a
compound to try to snatch a few hours' sleep – but the Taliban
had other ideas. Every twenty minutes or so, a gunman would
take a pot shot, making it impossible for anyone to drift off.
One of the soldiers decided to risk dashing across the roof
to try to provoke the shooter into giving away his position.
Before long, James, Aaron and the rest of their section were
taking turns doing star jumps. There was a tenuous sort of
military logic: if anyone could spot a muzzle flash then they
could shoot back or call in a missile strike. The real reason for

the display was bravado – the inevitable consequence of days spent dodging bullets.

The thrill of close combat is rarely spoken about much outside the military, but there is no doubt that there are intense highs to be had in a war zone. Like all highs, they come at a price, and the inevitable comedown can leave a soldier much more vulnerable to the Spiral. Adding alcohol to the mix can turn the descent into a free-fall.

One October afternoon, I returned to the east coast of Scotland to pay James another visit. As before, he stopped short of inviting me to his home town of Methil, saying he could not think of anywhere suitable for us to meet, and directed me to the bus station at the adjacent centre of Leven, overlooking the brooding waters of the Firth of Forth. It was only later that James told me he was worried that had I stopped in Methil I might have risked being mugged.

James led me up a parade of discount stores and shabby shops, then steered me into a pub called the Windsor. It was a Thursday lunchtime and there was a noisy crowd at the bar. We found a corner table under a screen showing horse racing and I bought James a pint of Tennent's.

On the surface, James appeared to be a model for the successful transition between the military and civilian worlds. He had left the Army after his second tour of Afghanistan and found work producing the silver sheen used in car paints and scratch cards. He had recently been taken on full time, elevating him above the crowd in Methil, where many worked on 'zero hours' contracts – spending their days waiting for a text message to summon them to a shift.

And yet, as I got to know James better, I learned that he had faced his own struggles after returning from Afghanistan with Aaron. The first sign of trouble had occurred before the deployment was over – during his mid-tour leave. After arriving in Edinburgh, James, Aaron and Stuart Nicholson had spent the afternoon drinking before James made the ninety-minute trip back to Methil. James had drunk a bottle of rosé on the train, then finished another two bottles he had asked his mother to leave in the fridge.

'I was absolutely belted,' James told me as he nursed his drink. 'I phone up my pals: "I've come back from Afghan." They were like: "Come to the Brig, we'll have a few pints."'

On the way to the Brig, a pub in Methil, James bought another bottle of rosé and drank half before playing a few rounds of pool with his friends.

'It was only ten o'clock at night. I was like: "Right lads, let's go and do something. Let's go to Kirkcaldy or something."'

One of the group, an acquaintance James barely knew, seemed to take offence.

'He was like: "What, is this not as exciting as Afghanistan?"'

'I was like "eh?"'

'He was like: "Are we not exciting enough for you? Do you want to just fuck off back to Afghan?"'

'I was like: "Aye." I snapped the pool cue on the table and hit him.'

James grinned.

'It was over before it started. Never tried to hurt him, just wanted to give him a scare – but it obviously scared them all.'

When the tour ended, James did not feel any different, but his friends sensed a shift. It was as if his many near-misses in combat had skewed his perception of risk. One night, walking home from a pub, James had felt inspired to recreate a scene from the film *First Blood* by leaping onto the side of a cliff from the Bawbee Bridge over the river Leven. He ended up plunging a good twenty feet but, like Rambo in the film, his fall was broken by branches. Another time, he was riding in a car driven by a fellow Black Watch soldier when it careered off an icy motorway. James felt curiously removed from the danger, as if the question of his survival was of merely academic interest.

'When you're out there, everything matters,' he said as we talked about Afghanistan. 'You get told to do something – you do it. If something needs to be done by a certain time, you get it done. Everything is ten times as speedy as what it is in the civilian world. When you get home, even waiting at a bar to get served winds you up – because you're used to everything being organised.'

The change in James would manifest in unexpected ways. One morning, a girlfriend told him how he had leapt up in his sleep and begun patrolling the bedroom, convinced he was being hunted by the Taliban. James had been drinking the previous night and could remember nothing. At an Army training range in Wales, the sound of a machine gun firing momentarily transported him back to a real-life firefight.

Though James's superiors grew concerned and kept a close eye on him, he did not feel that his experiences in Afghanistan had fazed him. Army friends did not treat him any differently, perhaps because they had changed too. Aaron had spoken for all of them when he had declared in Johnny Foxes that the buzz of homecoming would never end. But during brief interludes of sobriety, life seemed flatter than before their tour.

James said, 'Every now and again, me and him would joke: "By the way, the novelty's worn off." He really, really meant it.'

When James reached a stage where he could not eat or sleep without the aid of a drink, he went to see an Army medical officer, who ordered a blood test. The results suggested he'd better sober up fast. He believed he had managed to bring his drinking under control in large part because he had had to prepare for his second tour in 2011, a much quieter deployment than the six months he had served alongside Aaron. His hard edge began to soften, and before long his friends from Methil recognised him as the James they had once known.

James went outside for a cigarette, and as we surveyed the near-deserted high street, I asked what sort of jobs were available nearby. There was the pigment factory, where he worked, and a Diageo bottling plant, but he estimated that as many as twenty of his peer group had joined the Army.

'If you were to come here at ten o'clock in the morning, walk up the high street and across the road, it will take you about a mile to get past the dole queue,' he said. 'Aye, it's bad like.'

I asked him what his parents did for a living. His mother worked locally and his father had not had a job since the coal mines closed in the mid-1970s. He walked me back to the terminus so I could find a bus.

Alcohol has been central to military life since armies began – the term 'Dutch courage' derives from the gin that fortified seventeenth-century English troops fighting in the Low Countries during the Thirty Years' War. British regiments gave out spirits to soldiers during the Battle of Waterloo in 1815 and the Army reintroduced the rum ration to stiffen the resolve of troops in the harsh winter at the start of the First World War. One shaken officer expressed a common sentiment when he wrote: 'I drank three quarters of a glass of neat whiskey and carried on.' Lieutenant Colonel J. S. Y. Rogers, who served as a medical officer to the Black Watch, extolled the benefits of hard liquor at the 1922 'shell shock' inquiry: 'Had it not been for the rum ration, I do not think we should have won the war.'

In the century since then, the drinking culture has endured. The men I spoke to about their service in the 1970s, 1980s and 1990s uniformly described the central role of alcohol in military life. Superiors took a nod-and-a-wink attitude to heroic levels of consumption of subsidised lager at British bases in Germany, seeing it as a semi-official form of stress relief. There was even a term for it: 'lager therapy'. Drinking also played an important bonding role. In the Royal Engineers, for example, there was an initiation ritual called 'engineering' in which a new soldier had to down a pint glass filled across the optics – with nuts, pretzels and crisps thrown in. A common question for a new lad would be: 'Have you been "engineered" yet?' Frank Stowell, who served in Bosnia and Iraq during his 1999–2006 Army career, recalled the entry requirement for his unit: downing a litre bottle of Bell's whisky. 'I had to have my stomach pumped. I ended up waking up in hospital,' he said. 'The sergeant major gave me a little bit of a bollocking. Everyone else said: "Welcome to the regiment."' The bonding function of alcohol was not confined to the rank and file: in smart cavalry regiments, junior officers might be expected to buy rounds of champagne for the mess at lunchtime as a punishment for a misdemeanour.

Attitudes have started to change. In today's Army, troops are no longer allowed to consume alcohol when on front-line duty and lunchtime drinking in barracks is largely a thing of the past. The MoD says the number of unit bars has shrunk, opening hours are restricted, and a harder line is now taken on drunken behaviour. The Army is also piloting a scheme similar to the TRiM system used to spot soldiers who might be suffering from PTSD to encourage peer-to-peer monitoring of alcohol intake. Nevertheless, the scope of the alcohol problem suggests it may take time to erode.

In a paper published in 2007, the King's Centre for Military Health Research found that the rate of hazardous drinking in the military was 67 per cent among men, compared with 38 per cent for their civilian peers. The difference was even starker among servicewomen – 49 per cent of whom drank at hazardous levels, compared with 16 per cent of female civilians. When it came to severe drinking problems, proportions in the military were almost three times higher for men and nine times higher for women. Those at greatest risk included unmarried soldiers who had fought in combat roles – young men like James Forrester and Aaron Black.

The death of Mark Connolly, the private who had fought alongside James and Aaron in Afghanistan, was a particularly poignant example of the damage alcohol could inflict. After surviving the blast in the grape hut that had killed Robert McLaren, Connolly had died after a drunken brawl at a base in Germany. Private Paul McKay, a physical training instructor who had also fought in Afghanistan, had punched Connolly so hard he caused a fatal brain bleed. McKay, who claimed he was defending himself during the incident, was later cleared of manslaughter by a court-martial and has since left the Army. He told Army investigators: 'You don't know what it's like to kill your best mate.' The court heard that several soldiers had drunk large amounts that night – one was alleged to have downed eighteen bottles of beer.

In theory, a soldier who is drinking so much they are not able to perform their duties should be referred for medical help by the chain of command. In practice, many soldiers are unable to see the damage alcohol is doing, as I heard from Paula Berry, a former NHS alcohol specialist who had seen a rising number of soldiers at the fortnightly clinics she ran at two barracks in north-west England.

'Half the time you think you're superhuman – you can't see what's going on inside,' she said. 'When I see them they say: "I haven't got a problem with alcohol, but my missus has thrown me out twice this week. I've got a problem gambling, and I'm anxious and I'm depressed." They don't see alcohol has a lot to do with that.'

When problem drinkers leave the Army and are no longer subjected to military discipline and routine, their consumption can rapidly spin out of control. In my conversations with ex-forces, alcohol emerged as by far the most common fuel for journeys down the Spiral – the shared ingredient in bar-room fights; trouble with the police; arguments with partners; lost work opportunities; mounting debts; and, in the worst cases, suicide attempts. Although there were limited data on the scope of drinking problems among ex-forces, there was no shortage of examples of those who struggled.

In Runcorn, near Liverpool, I visited Daz, a middle-aged man
with a sallow complexion and a distracted air, who had served
in Northern Ireland and the Gulf War during a ten-year Army
career. When I met him through Blue Apple Heroes, a local
military charity, he was mourning the loss of his brother, a fellow
veteran who had committed suicide the previous year. Daz spent
much of his time confined to his flat in a parade overlooking
the turbid sweep of the river Mersey. 'Seen a lot of bad shit out
there,' he muttered, speaking of his time in the desert. 'Dead
Iraqi bodies everywhere. Just stank of rotten flesh. I can smell it
sometimes, now and again.'

Daz said he had turned to drink to dull the flashbacks and
paranoia that had begun to plague him with increasing intensity
in the years after he left the military. He would venture out to
buy three-litre bottles of cider first thing in the morning when
the streets were mostly empty.

'Sometimes I think I'm being followed. I've thought I've seen
people in the trees opposite,' he said. 'I think it's because you feel
safe when you're in the Army. When you're out, mixing with
civilians, it's different.'

Daz disappeared into his bedroom then returned carrying a
vintage bayonet he kept under his pillow – a comforting presence
in the night hours. When I spoke to him more than a year later,
he said he had begun receiving fortnightly visits from an NHS
mental health nurse and had tried to cut down his drinking by
switching from cider to export-strength lager.

In Dumfries, a market town in the Scottish borders, I met
Mark Frankland, a novelist from Lancashire who founded the
First Base Agency in 2003 to help people misusing drugs and
alcohol. In the past year, more and more ex-forces had begun
knocking on his door, some old-timers who served in the
Falklands or Northern Ireland, others young men who had done
a tour in Afghanistan or Iraq.

'There was a slowly growing number of guys coming in a

really bad state, usually drunk out of their heads, more or less reaching the point where people would describe them as being a tramp,' Mark said. 'When you get chatting, they would be ex-military. It would soon become apparent that the root of their problems had been mental health-type issues.'

One of the most memorable was a Falklands veteran named Derek Styles, known as Tinker. As a super-fit young man, Tinker had enjoyed a promising start to his Army career, competing in gymnastics tournaments around the world before he became one of the youngest members of the Parachute Regiment to fight at the Battle of Goose Green. After leaving the forces, he fell into a cycle of addiction and homelessness and developed a revolving-door relationship with Scottish prisons. In later life Tinker had survived by selling the *Big Issue*.

In a blog post, Mark had described him as 'wiry as a half-starved kangaroo' and said he carried a sadness about him 'like a tired old overcoat'. Little by little, he wrote, Tinker had told him more of what had happened at Goose Green, but never all of it.

'He could never quite manage to relive the final few minutes when the issue was resolved with bayonets,' Mark wrote. 'He might not have talked about those desperate moments of murderous violence, but he certainly never forgot them. How could he? They came back to him every night without fail. In Technicolor. His mind became his enemy – a hated, unmanageable VCR that replayed images of Goose Green day and night and night and day.'

It was obvious that Tinker's problems ran deeper than alcohol. Mark made enquiries with the NHS on Tinker's behalf and was told that ex-forces might wait nine months or more to see a psychotherapist. Mark raised £5,000 so the charity could pay for individual therapy sessions for ex-forces one morning a week. I met several young men who had served in Afghanistan who had benefited from the service, but Tinker did not manage more than a few sessions. He was fifty-one when he died.

★

For many ex-forces, reaching for a drink to deal with unwanted feelings is not so much a choice as a reflex instilled by military life. From the day they joined, they had imbibed the tacit message that the remedy for stress lay in the nearest bar. The results of long-term alcohol abuse could be bad enough. But when soldiers turned to alcohol to try to blot out the flashbacks, nightmares and anxiety caused by PTSD, their problems became exponentially worse.

One day I went to the town of Royal Leamington Spa to visit Dave Salt, who served multiple tours during his Army career, including in Afghanistan and Iraq. Dave lived in a bedsit on the ground floor of an imposing white house on a leafy avenue. A large Apple Mac computer set on a desk dominated his living space; next to it lay *The Post-Traumatic Stress Disorder Sourcebook: A Guide to Healing and Growth.*

The night before, Dave had attempted an experiment. He usually slept with a bedside light on, but he had decided to see what would happen if he left the light off when he took his usual dose of zopiclone sleeping tablets. Within minutes, he started sweating and felt panic rising. As he turned the light back on, a thought had formed: *It's still alive inside me.*

Despite its tranquil appearance, Leamington Spa was choked with hazards. In Tesco, the sound of the tannoy swept Dave back to dusty days in Basra or the rain-spattered streets of Belfast. Four weeks before I visited, he had suffered one of the worst flashbacks he could remember. Feeling palpitations, a sure sign he was about to lose control, Dave began to scream call signs that meant he had lost his rifle. The next thing he could recall was waking up in hospital.

As a teenager growing up in Stoke-on-Trent in the 1980s, then still the heart of Britain's pottery industry, Dave nursed big ambitions. After obtaining four A levels, he had been on track to become the first member of his family to go to university, but had decided to join the Army for a couple of years to gain some life experience first. He ended up serving pretty much everywhere it was possible to go in the Army in the past twenty years – Northern Ireland, the Balkans, Sierra Leone and Afghanistan. It was after his second tour of Iraq that things fell apart. Dave said he had never had a problem with drink, but when he began experiencing flashbacks and nightmares he drank a few more beers than usual to calm his nerves and settle his surging heart rate. Soon, he was drinking a bottle of vodka a day.

'The first half bottle of vodka is medicine, because it calms you down. You'd never know I had a drink,' Dave said. 'And it was better than any diazepam – whatever-pam – it was the best. And so it went on, until I was on about two and a half litres of vodka for breakfast. And you're in trouble then.'

As a corporal, Dave had his own room at the barracks in Germany. His night terrors were so severe that he packed up his clothes in suitcases and began to sleep in the wardrobe. When he did not turn up for parade one morning, his sergeant major burst in and discovered his hiding place.

'That's when they actually started to take me seriously. Because they weren't before – they were just saying: "Buck your ideas up. What's up with you? You're a professional soldier. You're a leader." I was always the commander of patrols and they just thought I was going through a bad patch. Eventually you crack. And that's exactly what I did – I cracked.'

Dave wandered out of the barracks towards a nearby railway line, intent on lying on the tracks, but two friends who had volunteered to keep a round-the-clock watch led him back to camp. Then the same thing happened again.

'I can blame myself for not getting help earlier, but soldiers don't reach out for help, they're independent – no surrender,' Dave said with a sad smile. 'That's the way it's drilled into us.'

In February 2008 the Army sent Dave to the Priory Group, a network of private clinics which then had a contract to provide in-patient psychiatry to the MoD. Dave was admitted for a three-week assessment and ended up staying for nine months, during which time he was also undergoing divorce proceedings.

'I was in such a state I could've probably killed somebody on the streets and not even known it,' Dave said. 'For the first months, I didn't open my mouth.'

Dave was medically discharged from the Army and, supported by a war pension, felt well enough to start a new life. But his civilian friends only seemed to care about money and status, and he began to miss the adventure of his Army days. He spent three years travelling the world teaching diving or skiing, before returning to Britain with a plan to train as a psychotherapist. Landing at Birmingham Airport, he told the taxi driver to take him somewhere quiet.

After settling in Leamington Spa, Dave began to realise he was not as well as he had thought. Intense flashbacks would transform the placid streets into scenes from Sarajevo, Baghdad or Belfast. He would yell 'gun' or 'bomb' – and once caused pandemonium in Tesco. By his own count, Dave had been admitted to hospital thirty-four times in the past three years, and had spent six months in a private clinic, but he still found it hard to resist the urge to blot out his PTSD symptoms with drink.

'One will always go with the other,' he said. 'Say I've been suffering three, four, five days on the trot – no sleep, flashbacks, nightmares. I'm going crazy, out of my mind. I'll start drinking because it will persuade me: "Just have half a litre of vodka." And it calms me down.'

Dave paused.

'I can't just have one, I can't just have two, three, four – it carries on and on. And we're not talking all day. I'm talking weeks. You don't suffer the PTSD but you suffer from pouring this poison down your neck which is killing you. You're in a foetal position, crying.'

By the time I met Dave, he had managed to stay off alcohol for several months, partly with the help of disulfiram tablets, which would make him sick if he drank. He had won a university place to study counselling and psychotherapy and was hoping he would soon be well enough to start a new career as a therapist after completing a course of in-patient therapy at Combat Stress.

'I'm just one man and I've got on my iMac sixty contacts of ex-soldiers who suffer from trauma,' Dave said. 'There's only a very few who have got treatment. The rest live in bars, gutters – there's a few homeless. They've lost their families. They've lost everything.'

Though Dave seemed to have a fighting chance of escaping the Spiral, he knew he was only one drink away from sliding back down.

The problems of Dave and the many other soldiers who turn to alcohol to try to manage their trauma symptoms become easier to understand when viewed from the perspective of changes in the brain associated with PTSD. Even though the trauma is long in the past, the sufferer is periodically hijacked by visceral feelings of anxiety or fear – as if they are once more in mortal danger. The neural circuits governing mood and emotion are scrambled, suppressing production of hormones that foster a sense of well-being. The brain is compelled to find new ways to generate the pleasurable feelings: some indulge in obsessional exercise or develop an addiction to caffeine. Drugs are sometimes used, but the method of choice for ex-forces is alcohol.

'People who take alcohol in that context are actually completely misunderstood, because they are regarded as people who could stop it if they wanted to,' said Professor Gordon Turnbull, one of Britain's top trauma experts. 'They are not. They are in fact doing it because they unconsciously need to make themselves feel reasonably normal.'

For those with an alcohol problem, finding support is not easy. As I would learn, the NHS is trying to improve its mental health services for ex-forces, but the health system is already struggling to treat alcoholism among the rest of the population. Only one alcohol-dependent patient in every eighteen will access treatment in any given year, according to one study, and in some areas the picture is far worse. In north-east England, for example, a big Army recruiting ground, the figure was one in 102. With budgets for alcohol services under pressure, treatment may become even harder to access.

Given the scale of the alcohol problem, it was striking that the issue seemed to be treated almost as an afterthought by many of the organisations set up to help ex-forces. Of the roughly 350 military charities in Britain providing welfare, mental health or other support, I came across only one – Tom Harrison House in Liverpool – that had been set up primarily to offer in-house addiction treatment to veterans. Within nine months of welcoming its first client in late July 2014, the organisation had received fifty-nine referrals and made twenty-eight admissions – a tiny fraction of the likely number needing help countrywide.

Those using alcohol to self-medicate symptoms of PTSD face an even bigger struggle. Sufferers cannot undergo therapy to address their underlying trauma if they are turning up to sessions intoxicated. But as soon as they stop drinking, their nightmares, insomnia and flashbacks return with renewed ferocity, making relapse much harder to resist. Such patients often find themselves bouncing back and forth between their GP, specialist NHS services and military charities, unable to find the kind of comprehensive care they need.

Dr Keron Fletcher, the consultant psychiatrist who specialises in trauma and addictions, believes the only effective way to treat ex-forces stuck in this cycle is to provide simultaneous detox and trauma therapy. Such work is delicate, requires experienced staff and often demands weeks or months in a specialist in-patient unit. Fletcher said Britain has no such unit.

'Many servicemen and women with PTSD and alcohol dependence have risked their lives for their country, and what they've been through is appalling,' said Fletcher. 'It wouldn't cost a huge amount to give them the combination of treatment they need and you would have thought that they'd have been given a degree of priority.'

Dave Salt summed up the stakes involved like this: 'When you hit that low, it's death. You're a dead man walking.'

6

'No Safety Catch'

Ex-forces and criminal justice

Though he spoke of events more than forty years in the past, the scene Jimmy Johnson described was stored in his mind as perfectly as a diorama preserved under museum glass. The setting was Lurgan, a town in County Armagh. The year: 1972. The occasion: a routine patrol. It was a spring evening and the men were returning to their base – they called it the Factory – hoping to make it in time to catch *Top of the Pops*. Without warning, a massive explosion erupted a hundred metres in front of Jimmy's vehicle, followed by an ominous crump. Then a twenty-six-year-old corporal in the Royal Tank Regiment, Jimmy saw people scatter as smoke billowed from an underground toilet. A man yelled at a policeman: 'My wife's in there!' The constable recoiled, his eyes full of fear, but Jimmy grabbed a torch pinned to the officer's jacket and made his way down the steps.

He felt his way through the rubble-strewn corridor, blinded by smoke and dust but guided by the sound of water rushing from burst pipes. Other soldiers followed and they began to comb through the wreckage until one of the men told them to hush. Jimmy paused and heard a sound that seemed to be coming from very far away. Somebody was calling his name – a policeman, shouting through a megaphone. A car bomb had been found parked in the street above, packed with 500 pounds of explosives.

The voice was insistent: 'Get out! Get out!' As Jimmy hesitated, one of his men found a shoe.

'Fuck it,' Jimmy said. 'She's under there – dig!'

The men began pulling away bricks with their bare hands, uncovering the prone form of a young woman – stripped almost naked by the force of the blast. Jimmy draped her with his combat jacket. Her face reminded him of his own wife, but her wounds were grave. In the half-light, he could see that all her toes were missing. Night had fallen by the time Jimmy carried her up the steps and placed her in an ambulance. He shouted at the medics to save her but a doctor took one look, shook his head and said: 'I'm sorry, son. She's dead.'

Jimmy began to shake and pour with sweat so a soldier led him into the back of a Land Rover and placed a cigarette in his mouth. Passers-by gathered near the vehicle – women Jimmy's mother's age. 'Poor thing,' one said. Jimmy assumed she was referring to the young woman, until another lady turned to him and said: 'Don't worry, son. She was only a Catholic.'

Jimmy burst out of the Land Rover, cursed them, then wandered down the street, leaving behind his men, their vehicles and his rifle. Soldiers quietly followed, taking up discreet positions in doorways to keep a watch as their leader's anger ran its course. Back at the Factory, Jimmy installed himself at the bar, his uniform still caked with grime and blood. The soldiers had missed *Top of the Pops*. While Jimmy and his men had been digging through the bomb site, families back home had been watching hits by Engelbert Humperdinck and Cilla Black. When the barman began to roll down the shutter, Jimmy wedged it open with his hand.

'It's time, Jim,' the barman said.

Jimmy demanded another pint. He was scared to go to bed, afraid of what would happen when he closed his eyes. Officers noted the commotion and he was escorted to his room. An Army doctor sedated him with a syringe.

A few days later, Jimmy was ordered to facilitate a covert mission to photograph mourners at the young woman's funeral. The IRA spotted the soldiers and boxed in their Land Rover by parking a tractor across a lane leading to the church. Residents from a nearby Republican estate swelled the ranks of mourners and the crowd engulfed Jimmy's Land Rover – it looked to him like a sea of fans heading home from a football match. Part of the crowd tried to block his vehicle – some leaning their shoulders against the grille while others began to rock it. Women pressed their hate-filled faces against the windows and hurled obscenities, globules of spit sliding down the glass. The vehicle proved too heavy to overturn, but Jimmy saw hands clawing at the door handles – and remembered that there were no locking systems on Army Land Rovers. As he steeled himself to fire, he wanted to cry out that he had tried to save the woman they had just buried.

'I cocked my weapon,' Jimmy told me. 'The first one through here is going to get it – straight through the head.'

The Land Rover eventually managed to forge a way through the human wall, but the bombings, shootings and street battles continued. By now, Jimmy's platoon was well schooled in the art of quelling riots. They threw aside their Army-issue batons – which broke too easily – and fought using improvised weapons passed on by the previous rotation of troops: hammers, baseball bats and lead pipes. Jimmy carried a blackjack that fitted down his trousers. No mercy was given, none asked.

During a riot in Lurgan, Jimmy spotted a man creeping up behind one of his troopers with a bucket. Jimmy feared his soldier was about to be doused with acid, but it was blue paint. As the liquid streamed down his shocked colleague's face, Jimmy flew into a rage and chased the paint-thrower into an estate. The man sought refuge by running through the front door of a house and Jimmy pursued him into the kitchen, as if on autopilot. It was only then he realised that he had made the potentially fatal mistake of cutting himself off from his men in a Republican stronghold.

As the occupant looked up from his bacon and eggs, Jimmy's quarry tried to clamber onto the sink, intent on wriggling through the kitchen window. Fearing the man would alert the estate and IRA sympathisers would converge on the house, Jimmy grabbed him and began battering him with his baton gun. Time seemed to slow down as blood spurted from the man's head like a jet from an oil well. Jimmy could not stop – he was in a panic, far from his unit, and the man would not stay down.

Another soldier burst into the house and yelled: 'Jimmy, he's had enough!' Panting, Jimmy stopped beating his prisoner, who slid to the ground, twitching. The two soldiers hauled the man out of the house and ran, chased by a mob of about 150 people. They managed to escape the estate and hand their prisoner over to the police. One of Jimmy's superiors later joked about how many stitches the man had needed: 'I'll tell you what, he's the only Paddy that I know that's got a head like a fucking piggy bank. You can drop five bob pieces in it.'

By the end of the tour Jimmy had had enough of Northern Ireland, but in career terms his deployment had been a great success. He earned a mention in dispatches for risking his life trying to save the woman in Lurgan, entitling him to wear a bronze oakleaf spray on his campaign medal and ribbon. His superiors viewed him as an experienced leader who would play an invaluable role on their return deployment in eight months' time. But as his unit trained to go back, Jimmy began to suffer night terrors and flashbacks. He wanted to buy himself out of the Army, but his colonel vetoed the idea, telling him: 'I need you to help the rest of us through this posting.'

When Jimmy's second tour ended, he was tormented by a recurring nightmare. He is standing alone on a damp, darkened road – a street light shining in the distance. All of a sudden, he is swallowed by a hole like a giant shell crater. He plunges into a submerged, cellar-like chamber lined with alcoves, and starts swimming, as if searching for something. He discovers a locked door, barges inside, and is trapped in an even smaller room. Jimmy looks down to see a body – bandaged from head to toe – surging up towards him from the depths. He tries to swim away, but the mummy-like creature is too fast, and he begins aiming kicks, desperately trying to drive the apparition back. He would wake to find bruises on his feet from the bedroom wall. It was not long before his wife broached the topic of single beds.

Jimmy, once gregarious, turned into a recluse. He could never bring himself to speak to his wife of what he had seen on tour. He felt so disconnected from his family that they seemed to him to resemble mannequins in a department store.

'She would scream at me: "When I married you, you were always laughing and joking. Now you just sit there, you don't say nothing,"' Jimmy said. 'You look at them as if they're in a shop window.'

Jimmy, who is sixty-nine years old, has a shiny bald head and expressive features. Intensely animated when speaking of Northern Ireland, he recalled his ordeals with a luminous clarity that outshone the drabber colours of his present life. I felt torn, keen to let his anecdotes run their course, but acutely conscious of time. My conversations with ex-forces generally unfolded over days, weeks or months. In Jimmy's case, I would have a maximum of ninety minutes.

We were seated in a very small room, painted cream from floor to ceiling. The only item of decoration was a functional-looking wall clock. The chairs we sat on and the small table between us – which Jimmy sometimes tapped with his palms for emphasis – were screwed to the floor. Outside, guards wearing short-sleeved white shirts, black clip-on ties and earpieces waited in a corridor. An officer had offered a word of advice before the meeting began. 'Any problems, shout,' he said. 'Simple as that.'

Our room was in the visitors' suite at HMP Frankland, a

maximum security prison in Brasside, just outside Durham. The Category A facility – reserved for the most dangerous criminals – had been Jimmy's home for the past twenty-nine years.

Sometimes, the road back from war leads to a cell. The spectre of jail was a common theme in the stories I heard of ex-forces fighting the hardest battles with the Spiral. Some talked of brushes with the law after drunken brawls. Others described fits of anger that boiled over into violence at home or on the street. A small number had followed a path to full-blown criminality, finding roles at various stages in the supply chain for Ecstasy or cocaine.

Jimmy Johnson had been jailed for murder – twice. Several months after he left the Army in December 1973, Jimmy was offered a lift by a former workmate who was then working as a security guard, who collected him in a van outside Middlesbrough. Some children had thrown something at the side of the vehicle, perhaps a piece of brick, and the crash had seemed to trigger something in Jimmy, plunging him back into the kind of blind rage that had gripped him in life-or-death situations in Northern Ireland. He pleaded guilty to the security guard's murder and was sentenced to life imprisonment. After serving nine years he was released on parole. Eighteen months later, Jimmy killed again. He again pleaded guilty to murder and this time was given a minimum thirty-year sentence.

Jimmy told me that during his trials and sentencing the court never assessed whether his traumatic experiences may have played a part in his crimes. In 1986 he befriended a doctor who had been convicted of killing his wife. The doctor asked Jimmy if he had heard of PTSD.

'I'm an ex-squaddie, not a brain surgeon,' Jimmy shrugged. 'You're talking double Dutch to me.'

But as Jimmy learned more, he began to wonder. In January and May 1994, he was assessed by Morgan O'Connell, the former Royal Navy psychiatrist who had accompanied the Task

Force to the Falklands. O'Connell was quoted by the *Daily Mail* as saying that Jimmy appeared to have committed his murders while in 'a state of detachment or flashback to conditions of severe stress while serving in Northern Ireland'. Jimmy became convinced that he – and many other ex-forces in jail – had offended because of undiagnosed symptoms of trauma.

As an ex-serviceman in prison in the 1970s, Jimmy said fellow inmates had looked at him as if he had 'two heads'. During his subsequent decades of incarceration, he began to meet more and more former soldiers, mostly veterans of Northern Ireland. In July 1990, Jimmy formed a 'veterans therapy group', which ran for a time at HMP Frankland. He had since written a seventy-five-page 'Veterans Survival Guide' aimed at raising awareness of trauma among ex-forces and their families and to encourage them to seek treatment.

'If they know what's going on, they can get help for it,' Jimmy told me. 'If they don't treat them for PTSD, it's like releasing tigers into a school playground.'

Some days after my visit, a draft of the guide arrived in the post. Among the many endorsements was a comment from a veteran of the Falklands, Northern Ireland and Bosnia who had received a copy in prison. 'I've read it about five times, it's "dead on",' he wrote. 'If I had known about it before my court case, I wouldn't be here now.'

Fears that warriors, unhinged by battle, will return to terrorise the societies that sent them to fight are an enduring theme in British culture. In 1824, concerns over threatening behaviour by veterans of the Napoleonic Wars led to the introduction of the Vagrancy Act. After the First World War, Sir Nevil Macready, the commissioner of the Metropolitan Police, warned of the appearance of murderous criminals 'grown callous by four years of fighting'. Similarly, in September 1945, the *Daily Mirror* told its readers that 'a crime wave usually follows a war'. As the historian

Clive Emsley has noted, there is scant evidence in the crime statistics to support such claims. 'The notion of the brutalised, violent veteran, created by war and at the centre of a post-war crime wave, was largely a fantasy,' he wrote.

When Britain wound down its operations in Afghanistan, such fears resurfaced in a new guise, fuelled by sporadic media reports of crimes committed by young men pumped up from combat. In May 2014, for example, the *Telegraph* reported that a judge in North Wales had warned he was seeing more cases of young men who had served in Afghanistan facing trial for assault. The report reminded me of Aaron Black, who took his own life a few days after appearing in court on charges of headbutting a friend.

Army officers tended to argue that focusing on the small minority of offenders obscured the military's wider role in keeping thousands of young men out of trouble on home-town streets. Among those who believed passionately that the military was a force for social good was Brigadier Greville Bibby, who had served in Northern Ireland, the Gulf War and Afghanistan during a career spanning more than three decades. In July 2014 he spoke at a 'Broken Soldier' conference on veterans and the criminal justice system held in the chapel at HMP Doncaster. Bibby told the audience that the Army provided a unique career opportunity for young people from deprived backgrounds – stating that the average reading age of an infantry soldier was seven. The Army was increasingly aware that the transition to civilian life could be difficult, he said, and had bolstered the amount of support for soldiers preparing to leave.

'That's why we are an absolutely wonderful organisation,' Bibby said. 'We're picking up misfits from society, we're turning them into something. A lot will tell you if they weren't in the Army, they'd be in prison. We turn them into honest and public-spirited citizens.'

Like so many of the issues involving ex-forces, the relationship between service and offending is a subject that stirs strong opinions, often in a vacuum devoid of hard facts. Nobody knows exactly how many veterans are in prison because the government does not keep a tally and attempts to count them are complicated by the fact that some are reluctant to disclose their service history for fear of being victimised. Others who might have had an unhappy experience in the military are keen to forget it.

Seeking to end the uncertainty, the National Association of Probation Officers published a report in 2009 that said there were more than 20,000 veterans in the criminal justice system – including 12,000 on probation or parole and a further 8,500 in custody – almost one in ten of the British prison population. The estimate suggested the numbers of ex-service personnel in jail had risen sharply during the Iraq and Afghanistan campaigns and that they were being incarcerated at a far higher rate than other civilians. The Napo research also featured 90 case studies of convictions, which included 39 for domestic violence and many involving alcohol. Though the report made for explosive headlines, some questioned the findings, pointing out that they were largely based on limited survey data and that no effort had been made to verify prisoners' claims of a military background.

A subsequent government-backed study painted a more reassuring picture, concluding that the true proportion of ex-military in prison in England and Wales was 3.5 per cent – less than half the prison officers' estimate. Rather than relying on statements by inmates, the authors had cross-referenced a database of prisoners with MoD personnel records, giving their findings more credibility among policymakers. The controversy did not end there, however. HM Inspectorate of Prisons subsequently published a survey that showed that 6 per cent of the prison population identified themselves as ex-servicemen, with the figure rising to 10 per cent in high-security facilities such as HMP Frankland. Several experienced probation and prison officers believed the correct figure for the system as a whole was probably about 7 per cent – which would still make ex-forces the biggest single group in the prison population by profession.

The reasons why former servicemen might run into trouble also defy easy generalisation – their experiences are diverse and the pathways to law-breaking many. The obvious place to start looking for answers was in prisons themselves, but various jails running programmes to support ex-forces seemed reluctant to admit a reporter. The breakthrough came at the Broken Soldier conference, where I met Mac McPherson, an avuncular retired lieutenant colonel, who invited me to visit a veterans' support group he helped facilitate at HMP Doncaster on Wednesday mornings. Sometimes the meeting swelled to more than twenty members, he said, but he could never be sure who would turn up.

The centre of Doncaster is dominated by the blocky exterior of the Frenchgate shopping mall and the more elegant spire of Doncaster Minster. The prison lies a few minutes' walk away, on the other side of the tree-lined banks of the river Don. From a distance, the complex resembles a generic industrial facility comprised of a cluster of red-brick warehouse-like buildings cloistered behind a high grey wall. The prison appears to be situated on an island – which accounts for the nickname 'Doncatraz'. Closer up, the exterior feels like an out-of-town business park, with flagpoles and a neatly mown verge. A sign says: WELCOME TO OUR PRISON.

At reception, a warder working for Serco, the contractor that runs the jail, gave me a locker key so I could deposit my phone, then took my picture from behind a one-way glass screen. A sign announced the headcount of inmates at the last roll call: 1,108. A series of transparent doors swished open to admit me into the prison proper. David Hesford, a criminology graduate working for Catch22, a company that runs social schemes in prisons and schools, led me through a series of corridors with floors polished to a squeaky sheen. Every so often, he would unlock a cage-like door with a formidable bunch of keys, then carefully swing it shut behind us. We passed an atrium where prisoners, mostly young men in tracksuits, milled around chatting. Our destination was a grey door bearing the sign: GROUP ROOM ONE. Styrofoam cups were laid out on a table with a flask, teabags and an industrial-sized tin of instant coffee.

First to arrive was Dave, a forty-six-year-old with a close-cropped beard and an earring, who appraised me with cool brown eyes. Dave had left the Army shortly after joining at the age of sixteen because his girlfriend had fallen pregnant. His life had been shaped to a far greater degree by England's underground biker scene – comprised of clubs with names like Devil's Disciples, Satan's Slaves and the Blue Angels. He said he had been jailed for jabbing somebody with a dumbbell bar to protect his elderly aunt when they had attacked his car.

'I've been brought up to stick up for myself,' he said, softly. 'It was enough to put him down.'

Dave seemed nostalgic for his Army days and believed his life might have turned out differently had he stayed in uniform.

'I'd sign up now,' he said, 'but I'm too old.'

Dave's story underscored one of the main obstacles to unravelling the links between military service and offending – the sheer diversity of the population who could qualify as a 'veteran'. The term is used by the British government to describe anybody who has served even a single day of basic training. In 2005 the Royal British Legion estimated this group at 4.8 million people in Great Britain and Northern Ireland. The word 'veteran' thus applies equally to a former infantryman who has served multiple tours in Afghanistan as it does to a pensioner who once did National Service, which was abolished in 1960. The complexity deepened when I met the next arrival in Group Room One, a middle-aged man named Stephen. An imposing figure who wore a white T-shirt, Stephen had wispy stubble and short, unruly hair. He marched over and offered a hearty handshake.

'If it wasn't for these guys I would have topped myself,' he said, gesturing towards Mac McPherson and the other facilitators, who were chatting with a couple of other prisoners.

'If I'd had someone out there helping me like Colonel Mac does now, I wouldn't have been in this predicament. He's been like a father to me in here.'

Stephen had never been deployed during his four years in the Army and had spent most of his time in a tracksuit, boxing. He said his problems began when he was medically discharged in 1992 after being diagnosed with schizophrenia. Stephen's platoon sergeant had predicted he would end up in jail and, sure enough, he had found it hard getting work in the declining steel and coal industries in his home town of Rotherham and had begun using heroin.

'There was no work to go to – ended up on the dole, trying to get by on nothing,' he said. 'That's how I ended up doing crime.'

Stephen was convicted of shoplifting, beginning a two-decade relationship with the prison system that has landed him in HMP Doncaster forty-seven times, by his own tally. He regretted the loss of his military career, which seemed to have exerted a protective influence.

'I was a good boxer, they loved me, but you couldn't be in with that,' he said, pointing to his temple in a reference to his mental illness. 'I wish to God they'd never found out.'

Stephen suddenly seemed anxious to leave and I fell into conversation with one of the facilitators. A solidly built man with a crew cut, Greg wore a polo shirt embroidered with the wings of the Parachute Regiment. He told me he had served for nine years, but had been thrown out when he failed a drug test after snorting lines of cocaine at a party. Greg was a qualified joiner, but he missed following orders and had begun submitting fake time sheets. He served three months of a year-long sentence for fraud in HMP Doncaster before being released on a tag. He quickly adjusted to life inside: the routine and clear chain of command reminded him of the Army. He had killed time by making picture frames out of matchsticks.

Since his release, Greg said he had been diagnosed with PTSD and was receiving therapy on the NHS. He kept himself busy by coaching junior rugby league and mentoring veterans at the Wednesday meetings.

'People would ask me: "Where've you been?" I'd say "Bosnia, Afghanistan, Sierra Leone," and then I'd stop,' he said. 'That's what triggers it: Sierra Leone is the biggie.'

While he was serving his sentence, Greg had befriended another Afghanistan veteran who had been jailed after a pub fight. At first, he barely ventured out of his cell, but he cheered up a little when Greg took him a few copies of *Soldier*, the British Army magazine, and he passed his sentence quietly.

'It doesn't matter what they've done, if they've been in the Army, there's just something there which means we can get on with each other,' Greg said. 'It's like a couple of hours away from all the shit.'

After the meeting, I was able to have a look round more of the prison, passing through a courtyard with a well-kept garden and goldfish pond guarded by a plastic heron. Tucked away in a less accessible corner of the complex was a special two-storey unit used to deal with the most violent inmates. It was known colloquially by staff as the 'Seg', short for Segregation Unit.

The Seg contained a series of pairs of specialised cells. One pair was adapted for easy hosing down to contain prisoners who launched 'dirty protests' by smearing excrement on the walls. Two more had been fitted with transparent doors to allow for easy monitoring of inmates on suicide watch. A motionless figure lay on a bed behind one of the doors, cocooned in a white sheet. As we passed, a guard warned: 'Don't stand too near the window.'

As a last resort for the most recalcitrant inmates, there was the 'Box' – a bare chamber painted green with no toilet and a wooden deck for a bed. Anybody locked inside was subjected to a continuous low-frequency thrumming sound. The guard said prisoners were only supposed to spend a maximum of two hours inside or the Box could be considered 'torture'.

Warders in the Seg said that there had been a steady increase in disciplinary problems due to staff shortages and prisoners experiencing psychotic episodes after smoking 'spice' – a potent synthetic cannabis smuggled in by visitors. The unit very rarely received ex-forces, who tended to do their time quietly.

'Nine out of ten times they're not even sure why they're in prison,' said the guard. 'It's just a one-off mistake and they just want to come out as quickly as possible.'

My conversations in Group Room One had suggested that there is no simple relationship between military service and prison. Indeed, one study by the Howard League for Penal Reform concluded that many of the offences committed by ex-forces had taken place some years after they had left, and appeared to have only a tenuous connection with their previous career.

'We need to be really wary of those popular assertions that all of these guys are coming back from Afghanistan damaged by combat trauma, ticking time bombs, and they're going to explode,' said Dr James Treadwell, a former probation officer and lecturer in criminology at the University of Birmingham. 'Actually they are more likely to explode because they were un-employed on the estate drinking in the pub. It's got nothing to do with their combat experience.'

Treadwell believes that many of the most powerful drivers of offending among ex-military personnel are not much different from the factors that foster crime in the wider population: poor schooling, a history of drug and alcohol abuse and troubled childhoods spent in downtrodden neighbourhoods. Serving in the Army may even have a 'pause effect' – delaying criminality until a veteran leaves.

This theory did not find universal favour among ex-forces serving time. Jimmy Johnson, the Northern Ireland veteran doing life in HMP Frankland, sent me a series of letters and documents arguing that the government should investigate whether PTSD could have played a role in large numbers of convictions of former soldiers.

'It will be like uncovering a mass war graveyard of wrongful and illegal convictions,' he wrote. 'Beyond a shadow of doubt, thousands of them will have been unknowingly suffering from this disorder at the time of their arrests and trials.'

In theory, following their arrest, veterans should be able to benefit from existing measures to ensure mental health problems are considered during sentencing. In practice, veterans often do not readily volunteer information about their service, and police, solicitors or others in the judicial system often do not ask. Certainly, courts could have difficulty assessing the possible role of PTSD in a violent offence, a task complicated by the subjective nature of the symptoms and the possibility a defendant might be exaggerating them to try to avoid prison.

In Jimmy's case, some might question whether the wife-killing doctor, in telling him about PTSD, had planted the seed of an idea that had allowed a double murderer to re-imagine himself as a victim. One former senior Army medical officer viewed Jimmy's claims with a degree of scepticism, arguing that in the vast majority of cases, ex-forces with PTSD posed a much greater danger to themselves than to others. But General the Lord Richard Dannatt, who had served as Chief of the General Staff between 2006 and 2009, was convinced the case was genuine. After visiting Jimmy at HMP Frankland, Dannatt had arranged for an assessment by a forensic psychiatrist who had confirmed a diagnosis of PTSD. In rare cases sufferers could experience the kind of immersive flashbacks and compulsion to re-enact life-or-death situations that appeared to have afflicted Jimmy.

'It's entirely likely the flashback experiences that some people get are what he got and probably explain why he murdered a man and then after doing a life sentence murdered another man,' Dannatt told me. 'He wasn't a natural candidate for criminal justice. He'd been a very successful soldier and family man for a large part of his life prior to that.'

While Jimmy's story might seem to belong to a different era, Dannatt said people tended to forget how intense the fighting was in Northern Ireland in the early 1970s, where he also served. In 1972, the worst year of the conflict, 148 members of the British security forces were killed – more than in even the bloodiest year of operations in Afghanistan. Dannatt believed a new generation of ex-forces could learn from Jimmy's experiences and had agreed to write the foreword to his 'Veterans Survival Guide'. But for one twenty-five-year-old former soldier, Jimmy's advice had already come too late.

On 3 November 2009, a group of Grenadier Guardsmen set out from an outpost in Nad-e-Ali district, Helmand Province. The soldiers had arrived two weeks earlier to train a group of Afghan police based at the checkpoint, known as Blue 25. When they returned from the joint patrol, the British troops stripped off their helmets and body armour and began to unwind in a courtyard. Some drank tea or read magazines while others played a game to see who could catch the most mice.

There was a shift system for cleaning weapons at Blue 25 and some of the men had started stripping down their rifles when a burst of gunfire shattered the calm. They frantically began reassembling their weapons as other soldiers shouted orders, bracing to repulse a Taliban attack. In fact, the shots were coming from inside the courtyard: one of the police, a man named Gulbuddin, had opened fire on his mentors. At an inquest, Liam Culverhouse, then a lance corporal, described what happened next: 'I then saw a flash of red in my eye. I didn't hear no gunfire but I knew I'd been shot. I covered up my face with both hands and screamed some swear words. I heard gunfire and I saw Gulbuddin standing right in front of me with an AK–47 assault rifle.'

Gulbuddin shouted what sounded like a war cry. Culverhouse lunged at him, intent on grabbing the barrel of his rifle and wresting the weapon away. But the policeman was too quick: he wheeled around and shot Culverhouse through his right forearm. As Culverhouse reeled from his second gunshot wound, Gulbuddin loosed off more bursts at two soldiers standing next to him, killing them almost instantly. As chaos erupted in the courtyard, Culverhouse dashed towards a nearby building for cover. Gulbuddin sprayed another volley and hit him three more times – in the left elbow, right hip and left hamstring – before he was able to crawl around a corner and play dead. 'All I could hear was gunfire, scream, gunfire, scream, gunfire, scream, and then it all stopped,' he said.

Gulbuddin was pacing the courtyard, firing into dead and dying British soldiers. He turned to Culverhouse and shot him yet again – this time in the lower left leg. Then the policeman began walking towards him, as if intent on reassuring himself the Guardsman was well and truly finished.

Culverhouse usually carried a 9mm handgun strapped to his leg, a close-quarter weapon for use in emergencies. During the shooting, he had instinctively reached for the pistol – only to remember he had handed it in for repairs a few days earlier. The damage had been minor – a crack in a component known as the 'top slide stopper' – but he had decided to err on the side of caution and have it fixed.

As Gulbuddin took another step, both men were momentarily distracted by a sound coming from one of the adjacent buildings. Apparently satisfied that Culverhouse no longer posed a threat, the policeman spun around and headed for the entrance, searching for surviving Guardsmen. By the time Gulbuddin eventually fled, Culverhouse had sustained a total of six gunshot wounds and been blinded in his right eye.

I remembered the attack well – having written about it from Kabul for the *Financial Times*. By the end of the day, the number of British dead had risen to five, with at least as many wounded, along with several Afghan police. Culverhouse was repatriated to Selly Oak Hospital in Birmingham, which received wounded from Iraq and Afghanistan. As he recovered from his physical injuries, his behaviour became increasingly erratic, characterised by heavy drinking, unexplained absences and aggressive outbursts, and he was diagnosed with PTSD. Superiors, concerned about the change in his behaviour, held a series of meetings with welfare and medical staff to discuss how best to help him.

As the first anniversary of the attack neared, Culverhouse told a doctor working for the Army that he had always struggled to control his anger, but his moods had become much worse since his return from Afghanistan: a mishap as trivial as breaking a cup could ruin his whole day. He further confided that he was worried about being left alone with his fourteen-month-old son for fear he might lose his temper if he did not stop crying. Culverhouse was referred to a psychiatrist at a mental health clinic at Woolwich barracks who recommended he attend an anger management course. He discussed his anger problems at several further appointments but then stopped attending sessions and was discharged from the clinic in February 2011. By then, his on–off partner was expecting their second child. He returned to Northampton for the birth and helped dress his newborn daughter, named Khloe, before he returned to barracks later that day.

On 8 May, when Khloe was seven weeks old, Culverhouse and his partner brought her to the Accident and Emergency department at Northampton General Hospital. Khloe was suffering from multiple injuries, including skull and rib fractures, and doctors described her as being pale and unresponsive. After weeks of round-the-clock hospital care, Khloe was eventually transferred to Rainbows Hospice in Loughborough. She died eighteen months after arriving at A & E.

In November 2013, four years after being wounded at Blue 25, Culverhouse was put on trial over Khloe's death. He pleaded guilty to causing or allowing the death of the child. The prosecutor, Sally Howes QC, told the court it was clear Culverhouse had been hyper-vigilant, irritable, angry and aggressive. David Howell, his lawyer, told the court that Culverhouse was horrified by what had happened and that the military mental health system had failed to provide his client with the help he needed.

'This is a young man who did say to many people: "I can't actually cope with the crying and I do get angry,"' Howell said.

The judge, while sentencing him, said it was clear that PTSD had contributed to the tragedy and that nobody who understood what Culverhouse had experienced in Afghanistan could have anything but profound sympathy. But he also noted that he had struggled with his anger before the tour and held him responsible for ceasing to attend mental health sessions. He sentenced him to six years, three of which would be served on licence. As the judgement was read out, Culverhouse bowed his head.

The Culverhouse case received a flurry of coverage and provided a stark illustration of the potentially tragic consequences of failings in the Army's mental health provision. It also exposed the lack of information-sharing among the many military and civilian professionals involved in his family's care. A review by authorities in Northampton found that Culverhouse had not been offered any follow-up care after he was discharged by mental health staff at Woolwich, nor were there any records to show that his chain of command had been informed of his failure to attend appointments. Despite his explicit warnings that he could not handle crying children, and the extreme trauma he experienced, Culverhouse had received only the most cursory care.

I wrote to Culverhouse in prison to see what further light he could shed on his case. He explained that he had missed some of his appointments partly because avoidance was a symptom of PTSD, and that in any case he had only been offered therapy sessions once a month by the military. Ordinarily, somebody undergoing treatment for PTSD could expect to be seen much more frequently.

'It was in fact the actual mental health department where issues arose,' Culverhouse wrote. 'The correct technology is there, if you like, but it is not used frequently enough. It would be like going to the gym once a month but looking for progress in the mirror every day.'

He said he had been provided with some antidepressants and 'face to face depression work' in prison after he demanded help, but he was receiving no trauma treatment.

By his own admission Culverhouse had been a difficult client to help – angry, irritable and withdrawn. Yet to blame him for missing appointments would seem to absolve the Army and NHS of responsibility for providing effective support to soldiers whose erratic behaviour was a symptom of their psychological wounds, not a reason to let them walk away. There was little public debate about how to improve mental health services in the wake of the case, which only seemed to reinforce damaging stereotypes around disturbed ex-soldiers – stereotypes Culverhouse was keen to dispel.

'Just because an individual has PTSD does not mean he/she is more likely to commit serious crime,' he wrote.

In his handwritten letters, Culverhouse denied he had harmed his daughter – saying he had agreed to plead guilty to avoid the risk of a longer sentence – a claim I was not in a position to assess. After all he had been through, I had anticipated the former Guardsman would have little good to say about the Army. But he voiced no complaints about his superiors, describing his regiment as: 'extremely understanding and equally just as professional'.

★

During the two years I spent meeting ex-forces, academics at the King's Centre for Military Health Research provided the most persuasive evidence yet of a link between serving in the military and committing a violent offence. Dr Deirdre MacManus published a study based on the police and criminal records of almost 14,000 randomly selected serving and ex-service personnel. The conclusion was stark: military personnel committed fewer offences than civilians when all types of crime were considered. But soldiers, particularly younger ones, were much more likely to have committed a violent offence than their equivalents in the general population. Of the sample surveyed, 20.6 per cent of military males under the age of thirty had committed a violent crime, compared with 6.7 per cent of their civilian peers. The risks were greater for those who had fought directly in combat, suffered PTSD or had an alcohol problem.

Professor Sir Simon Wessely, the co-director of the King's Centre, told me the study had revealed that 6 per cent of recruits had a conviction for actual bodily harm even before they joined the military, contrary to the Army's claim that it did not recruit people with criminal records.

'Probably the single most direct correlation with deployment in combat is violent behaviour,' Wessely said. 'But then, of course, is it a surprise? It isn't – chess-playing choirboys don't normally join the Marines.'

For ex-forces with PTSD who ended up in jail, prospects of receiving meaningful medical care were uncertain. In Wrexham, I met Mandy Bostwick, a consultant trauma psychotherapist who works with ex-forces in prison. She had seen a number with trauma symptoms who had never received a formal diagnosis or any treatment before or after their offence. One prisoner had found his symptoms growing steadily worse and had asked to be allowed to remain in his cell while other inmates were mingling for fear he might hurt somebody. At one prison, Mandy had met three veterans who had been confined to a segregation unit after lashing out at warders. After speaking to them at some length, she suspected that each had lost control due to PTSD.

'When I explained how PTSD works to them they were shocked, angry and upset, but relieved that they were not going mad,' Mandy said. 'In looking further into their case history, it was shocking to see that their trauma symptoms had not been taken into consideration during sentencing.'

With concerns growing over Afghanistan veterans ending up in the courts at a time when the prison system was already stretched to breaking point, the government conducted a review into the issue of ex-forces and criminal justice in 2014. It emerged that there was no national coordinator responsible for veterans' welfare, neither were there any policy guidelines on how to help them avoid re-offending. Efforts to form support groups like the one I had visited in HMP Doncaster were often ad hoc and depended on the goodwill of individual prison officers, many of whom had themselves served. Pilot schemes had been set up in partnerships between the NHS, probation officers and charities in several areas to try to steer ex-forces away from prison, but it was clear that some would have a hard time avoiding jail.

A few weeks after I attended the Broken Soldier conference at HMP Doncaster, a twenty-three-year-old former soldier named Ashley Clark was sentenced to twenty-one months in jail by Burnley Crown Court after a series of violent incidents. The court heard how Clark, a web designer, had found it difficult to cope with civilian life after being forced to leave the 2nd Battalion of the Duke of Lancaster's Regiment after suffering a brain injury in a blast in Afghanistan in 2010. Early one morning, Clark had lost his temper and verbally abused a taxi driver, ranting and swearing and calling him a terrorist. He then scuffled with police, biting a female officer on the arm and kicking her colleague in the shin. Three months later he was arrested again for being drunk and disorderly. Clark subsequently told me he had turned to drink to try to cope with his trauma symptoms.

At his trial, his barrister said he had recently attended an alcohol treatment course and had made good progress with the help of a counsellor.

'I recognise to an extent I am undoing the good work you have now started and it may set you back,' said Judge Andrew Woolman, as he sent Clark to jail, 'but you have only yourself to blame.'

7

'Life's Easier with Your Eyes Closed'

Searching for a way out

Smoke. Fire. Darkness. Caine Hansen is first into the ground floor of the building and somebody is firing at him. The sound, amplified in the confined space, is stunning. Other operators are making an entrance upstairs and Caine will later conclude that one of their targets had probably fled down some steps, shoved his weapon around a corner and emptied the better part of a thirty-round magazine in his direction. Had the shooter taken a breath and steadied his aim, he would have been a dead man. As it is, his assailant is half-lucky: Caine is hit four times.

Caine said: 'We knew they would fight. We knew that they were the remnants of a certain group of people. And as I went through, I was engaged at very close quarters – maybe five or six metres away, maybe even closer.

'I think he must have had severe cataracts, or he was just a terrible fucking shot. Because if he had settled himself down I wouldn't be here now. He didn't make the most of that opportunity.'

'I was pretty calm, and I was also pretty shocked, and I was also pretty fucking worried. And it doesn't matter what cap badge you belong to, or how hard you think you are, because you know it's over. That particular job's over, and you kind of know things are never going to be the same again. All of this comes crashing in.'

After the shattering sound, the pain. One round had missed

Caine's face by millimetres and smashed through his night-vision goggles. A fragment of the casing burrowed into his left wrist and it felt like a hornets' nest had erupted beneath his skin. Two other rounds slammed into his chest, leaving dents in his body armour. But by far the gravest injury was caused by a fourth round. Travelling at supersonic speed, it had ploughed through his right elbow, bulldozing forearm muscle, shredding nerves, stripping fasciae and severing an artery. Caine's weapon fell slackly to his side, suspended on its sling, and he staggered back.

'I backed out a couple of steps, walked through the breach, and said to one of the guys: "That's me. I'm done. I'm down. I'm outta here." I didn't quite know where I was going, but I wasn't going back in there.'

Despite being shot, Caine felt surprisingly calm – so much so that his team leader was at first unsure if he had been wounded. He steadied Caine with his arms and asked: 'Have you been hit? Have you been hit?' Caine nodded and the soldier began treating the arterial bleed: pressure, elevation, tourniquet. He was injected with morphine but the pain of the tourniquet biting into splintered bone was worse than the wound.

'We operated strictly within our rules of engagement, the rest of the guys engaged the threat that had just opened up on me,' Caine said. 'No one walked out of there that night.'

By then Caine, an experienced patrol medic who had once patched up a colleague under fire on a mountainside a few years previously, was bellowing orders as other colleagues half dragged, half lifted him onto a stretcher. Caine instinctively felt he would be better off walking and insisted on standing up so he could hobble towards the landing zone, where a helicopter had just touched down. And then he was hit again, this time in the back. Enraged, he turned around and shouted that it was not his turn, not again. It was not another bullet that had caught him, but a fragment of rubble from the blazing building.

★

When I first met Caine, I did not know the name of his organisation. Nor did I know where he had been, what he had done, or how he had been hurt. These were not facts he volunteered to strangers. We had been put in touch by a former soldier I had met while reporting from Kabul and we exchanged occasional emails for a few months before eventually he suggested we meet at Clapham Junction station. It was late on an autumn afternoon and we ducked into a quiet-looking pub. Caine led me to a table in the corner where he could sit with his back to the wall and keep an eye on the street through a plate-glass window. Occasionally, he went out for a cigarette. Though the bar was almost deserted, he shot me a hard glance whenever he deemed I was talking too loudly, which was more often than I had imagined. It was not a look easily ignored. There was an intensity behind Caine's deep-set eyes that conjured instant respect.

Caine possessed the pent-up energy of a powder keg. His attitude to his work life was summed up in a throwaway remark he made about the night he was wounded: 'If you're going on a job, why hang around at the back?' But as we spoke, I began to suspect that there was a deep well of sensitivity concealed behind his high-voltage outer persona. The most obvious clue was the creativity evident in his sense of humour. Caine had elevated the ribaldry common among ex-forces to the level of an art form and it was impossible to imagine that anybody, however prim, would be immune to his blunt charm. His eloquent profanity acted as a kind of universal solvent, equally effective at breaking down barriers with gun-toting militiamen in a far-flung desert as it was in disarming new acquaintances during breaks in Miami, São Paulo or Dubai.

The other thing I would soon learn was that although Caine's whereabouts were often unclear, you were never in any doubt where you stood. Caine could be impulsively generous – he once withdrew a large sum from a cash machine and gave it to a homeless man who had served in the Royal Artillery and needed money for a hostel. But he also knew how to speak his mind. I once left a coffee jar open on his kitchen worktop and he lambasted me like a sergeant chewing out a sloppy recruit who had left an ammunition pouch flapping open during a contact, albeit with humour in his eyes.

As we talked in the pub, Caine temporarily switched the beam of his charisma onto our Spanish waitress, enquiring about the meaning of the tattoos on her arm, which he called 'ink'. Yet as she returned to the bar it was clear he was far more intrigued by the prospect of helping me write a book about the troubles that can follow a soldier home. He was also wary. Men who have walked his path generally consider even meeting a journalist taboo – let alone affording them a glimpse into the darker recesses of their minds. It was obvious from the oblique manner in which he referred to his past that he moved in the veiled world of special forces. Yet quite which subset of this world only became clear later. Caine, it turned out, had served for fifteen years in the Special Air Service Regiment, better known by its acronym, the SAS.

With its winged dagger motif and 'Who Dares Wins' motto, the SAS, one of the world's best-known special forces units, has operated almost entirely outside the public eye since its origins during the Second World War. There have been the odd exceptions, notably the Iranian embassy siege in 1980, when images of hooded men in gas masks cemented the regiment's place in the public imagination. In more recent years, their skills in capture missions, surveillance and hostage rescue have been much in demand. Several ex-SAS men have, under pseudonyms, penned thrillers based on their experiences – a practice not universally admired in a regiment that prides itself on working in the shadows. It was this code of silence that gave our early exchanges the feel of a friendly game of chess.

Caine's instinct was to shun any kind of publicity in case people mistakenly concluded he was somehow seeking to take credit for his service. But he also believed that the mystique attached to his old regiment would give his story special weight in encouraging others to seek help. One day, after months of chewing over his dilemma, he called me, seemingly on impulse, and invited me to visit him for a few days. Caine was adamant he would not reveal any details about his classified past or say anything that might compromise his or anybody else's security – and indeed 'Caine Hansen' is not his real name. He also made sure to follow the requisite authorisation process so that what he told me was cleared for publication by the military. Had it not been for the demands of confidentiality, he would have asked me to write much more about the family, friends and colleagues who had been so central to his life.

Caine lived a life immersed in rock and punk music – he had prepared for his final mission with a session of Van Halen – and strains of Metallica, Soundgarden or The Prodigy blasted through his house from shortly after sunrise. When the time came for us to speak, however, the house was silent. He had warned me beforehand that I would probably see a grown man cry. He lit another cigarette, lay back on his couch, and returned to the night when everything changed.

Caine's memories of the shooting in 2007 were clear, but the procession of medical professionals who had cared for him at various stages of his journey to hospital in Birmingham had blurred. He could, however, distinctly recall asking a nurse whether he should prepare himself to wake up without an arm. She told him it might be a good idea, but his surgeon overheard their conversation and promised he would do everything he could to save it.

Less than a week before he had been shot, Caine had been out with his unit on another mission when one of his friends had been killed. The entire unit had felt the loss, but there had been no pause in the relentless pace of operations. When the day of the funeral came, Caine was still being treated at the vast American airbase at Ramstein in Germany. A nurse led him to a chapel, where he held silent vigil. As Caine well knew, grief had a similar texture, no matter who you were mourning. He was well aware that his oldest griefs, those dating to his childhood, remained dormant, kept at bay by a career of frenetic activity and danger. But the new loss resonated on the same frequency as the old. In constant pain, dependent on nursing staff, and far from those he loved, Caine's defences were starting to buckle.

At Selly Oak Hospital, the darkness deepened. Since the closure of most of Britain's military hospitals in the 1990s, responsibility for the in-patient care of serving personnel had been transferred to the NHS and soldiers were at first placed in wards with civilians. Caine underwent about a dozen operations over the course of seven weeks. At one point, a nurse gave him sponge earplugs to block out the cries of elderly patients. Caine managed a smile for the wives who had come to comfort injured husbands repatriated from Afghanistan or Iraq, but when his own family arrived he could not manage to maintain the facade and had to send them away. Friends visited him and his ex-girlfriend appeared at his bedside. He told her he wanted to rekindle their relationship. He felt manipulative, even selfish, but he knew he needed her support.

Next he was moved to Headley Court, a rehabilitation centre for wounded personnel in Surrey, on the southern slopes of the Epsom Downs. Though his arm would be saved, the damage meant his trigger-squeezing days were over. Nevertheless, Caine knew that he was luckier than most: he watched television with men who had lost arms or both their legs. The sight of the wounded struggling to perform basic tasks unleashed a new upwelling of sorrow. The shell that had protected Caine through-out his military career was starting to crack.

'What wasn't healing, what was becoming more injured and

infected, was my mind – made worse by being in Headley and so up close and personal with these guys,' Caine said. 'Some were just young lads, and it broke me.

'I'd dragged a lot of stuff into the Army, but I'd always managed to keep it at bay. Now, it didn't feel like I had a chink in the armour – I didn't have any armour at all. I was done. The hard drive was scrubbed. Use whatever analogy you like but that was it. I was pathetic in every sense of the word and I was broken and I was ashamed.'

Caine gathered what few possessions he had with him in a Tupperware box and was sent to a branch of the Priory Group. He could not help but question how he had ended up among well-heeled civilians battling depression or addictions while the rest of his unit was still fighting. And yet, for all his self-reproach, another part of him recognised that he had found a sanctuary, a place where he could stop pretending. In group therapy, a woman started to talk about her husband, who was dying of cancer, and Caine realised the moment had come to speak.

'I just thought she has to know that there's somebody in this room who knows what she's going through,' Caine said. 'And I did tell part of my story.'

His voice began to break at the memory.

'I looked at her and I told her about my family. I just thought: "I hope you can at least take something from that."'

Caine had, in certain respects, joined the Army at the age of eight. He had been sent to a military boarding school where the only way to survive the bullying was to contrive a steely mask – basic training in the Army would be straightforward by comparison. Coping at such schools was an ordeal for every pupil in the 1970s, but Caine's predicament was unique. Shortly before he arrived, he had lost his mother to cancer. His elder brother died later the same year of the disease, caused by a rare genetic condition that had claimed the lives of two other siblings before he was born. Five years later, aged thirteen, he was called into the headmaster's study to learn that his older sister had died the same way.

I had the impression that Caine had been running from grief, or perhaps propelled by it, ever since. He had poured every drop of his energy into his career, pushing himself to do hard courses – parachuting (which would leave him seriously injured in an accident), military diving, and then the punishing business of SAS selection, the Army's ultimate test. Passing marked the pinnacle of his career – a feat his eight-year-old self would have regarded with awed delight. A new family embraced him. Membership of the Regiment was not just a job. It was a career so all-consuming that it rendered the mundane considerations of everyday life irrelevant, overshadowed all relationships and fostered a special sense of destiny. Above all, it instilled a feeling – rare in the regular Army – that your opinion mattered, no matter what rank you held. It was, as Caine put it, 'a devotion' – 'a life lived among wretches and kings'. His stay in the Priory gave him his first chance since childhood to properly rest. Two weeks later, his respite was cut painfully short.

'I sat in my room one day, in the Priory,' Caine said, his voice flat, his eyes moist. 'My pay-as-you-go phone went.'

A close friend had rung to break the news: two of their younger colleagues had been killed on the same operation in which Caine had been wounded. Once again, the unit was left with a profound sense of loss. It had been less than two months since Caine had been casevaced to Germany, having lost another friend in action only a few nights previously. All he had wanted was for the rest of the unit to come home safely. Now there were three who would never return.

As we spoke, Caine bowed his head and seemed to be having trouble speaking. 'I'm not going to go into how, but we lost them. And it broke my fucking heart because all I wanted was for the rest of them to get home in one piece.

'So I went downstairs and I said to the nurse: "I'd like my

medication please and I'd like you to package it tomorrow. Because I'm leaving. And I want you to know now I'm not coming back here. I've just lost two of my friends and colleagues. I want to try and get back to the real world."'

The next day he returned home and began a new relationship: with tramadol, an opiate-based painkiller, prescribed after the operations on his arm.

'Life's easier with your eyes closed,' he said. 'Sometimes life's easier when you're stoned, be it through prescribed medication, or finding it somewhere else. And I did find it somewhere else.'

Caine could take up to twelve tablets a day along with a host of other pills. The ritual would compound his stubborn sense of self-loathing and he would suddenly decide to crash off all his drugs at once, going through a painful withdrawal, before restarting the cycle. For months, he wandered through his house, his mind whirring with plans or simply filled with a dull fog. Sometimes he would break things.

'At times I was very analytical. I used to drum up scenarios, and think about things, and think of "what ifs",' he said. 'Then the other times I didn't even know what to think – I was confused. You'd sleep and you'd wake up and you'd fucking bawl and get up again. And all of a sudden you'd maybe have a little bit of a spike and you'd think "cool" and it would be snatched away from you.'

The Regiment sent an Army therapist to see him but Caine turned him away.

He said: 'Did I cut my nose off to spite my face, and pride got in the way? Of course I did. Did I bat back all offers of mental health help? Yes, I did.

'There are some good people around me. They're respectful enough of me just wanting to be left alone, which is to my detriment at times.

'And the person who suffered the most was my ex-partner, and I think the second person that suffered the most was my dog.'

Some days, Caine would wish the bullet that had smashed his night-vision goggles had slammed squarely into his forehead. Or he would look in the mirror and be seized with a desire to grab a carving knife and slash his throat. He pushed the thoughts away, but the image of the knife would arise, unbidden, the plan would form, and the endgame would unfurl before his mind's eye.

'You know how many people you've lost,' he said. 'You know what this would do to people. Even though I didn't rate myself, I knew people cared about me and loved me as I loved and cared about them.

'I never liked myself – that's why I thought: "You don't deserve this counselling. You don't deserve x, y and z." It was pathetic.

'But the thoughts were very, very real. And I've had those thoughts recently, but not as bad. You kind of just don't want to be here.

'Then you start feeling guilty because you are here and there's family and friends of yours that would give anything to be back on this plane and in this life with their loved ones – people that grabbed it by both hands and picked it up and ran with it and made the most out of it.

'So there's a whole conflict of thoughts and emotions – a quagmire of grief: immediate grief, tangible grief, that's only happened in those months or days. Then the legacy griefs. And also knowing that eventually I was heading out towards those camp gates and not knowing what my future was going to be.'

On better days, Caine would sit in his kitchen, pop some tramadol from a blister pack, pour a coffee, light a cigarette and begin tapping out poetry on his MacBook. He had been writing verse for years, some of it about his family or his days at the military boarding school. In 2001, he had written a poem that was a manifesto of sorts for freeing himself of his burdens. But the reinvention he had promised himself never materialised. In the alternating phases of deployment and training there was never the time.

The first Christmas since the shooting arrived. It had only been a few years since Caine had spent a Christmas Day 'schnurgling around' as he put it, a euphemism for covert operations. Now back home, recovering from being shot some months earlier, he wanted to be alone.

He said: 'I thought: "If I do go anywhere, I'm not going to be good company." My Christmas dinner was three rashers of bacon and some scrambled eggs because that's all that was in the house.

'I couldn't drive of course. There's a shop nearby but I didn't like leaving the house. Life was bizarre. It was surreal. It was haunted by things. I was fucked. It's hard to describe.

'But listen – so I got my food in this bowl, and the phone goes off upstairs. It's my brother, wishing me a happy Christmas, seeing how I am.

'And I hobble upstairs, and as I'm on the phone all I can hear is the fork falling into the bowl, knowing that my dog's face is eating my Christmas dinner.'

It was Marsha, a big, woolly-haired curly-coated retriever.

'I end up roaring at her, and came down to find maybe half a rasher of bacon and a bit of scrambled egg left. And I just looked at her and she was just expecting verbal and physical Armageddon.

'I go: "I will let you off. Because it's Christmas Day."'

Some time later, Caine lost another friend. A fellow SAS soldier, who had visited him while he was recovering in Selly Oak, had been killed on operations. All Caine was authorised to say was that his loss was felt heavily by many. After all Caine had endured, grief seemed unwilling to let him go.

In the years before he had been shot, Caine had made sporadic attempts to tackle his dark moods. At one point he had tried hypnotherapy, but the therapist could not even get his name right and Caine had to check an impulse to wreck his office. Once, while stationed in the north of England, he had found a counsellor who was caring and helpful, but his life was too unpredictable to allow him to do any consistent work on himself. These abortive attempts had left him wary of the help the Army had offered in the aftermath of his injury, but as months turned into years, and he suffered more losses, he began to suspect that his grief and confusion might not disperse by themselves.

In January 2010, Caine lost another very close friend from the Army, this time due to complications following surgery. Within a week of that, news arrived of the death of yet another friend who was working abroad. With his world once more feeling like it was imploding, he contacted the military therapist who had visited him after he had been shot.

'Did I totally custard pie the mental health professional that was sent to my house and fuck him off for a year? The answer to that is "yes",' Caine said. 'Who called him back? He didn't just cold call me. It wasn't my partner that called him. It was me. And I was full of woeful dread at the prospect of even ringing him. But I thought: "There's no fucking way out. You've tried to be the big man for the year."

'I'd recently lost a dear friend of mine, not through active service, but post-operative complications. He was like a brother to me. That was a tipping point. The pint glass was just being tipped to keep it from spilling over and I couldn't do it any more. The tap was literally just on permanent send.'

We had been talking for a long time. Caine told me the story of his recovery would have to wait and the tension that had filled the room during the hardest parts of his retelling began to dissipate.

'I knew it wasn't going to be easy, I'm not ashamed to cry in front of you,' he said. 'You know I could dispatch you in a fucking heartbeat.'

I felt I had got to know Caine well enough by then to know with a reasonable degree of certainty that he was joking.

'I have to try and hold on to some of my masculinity by threatening you. Is that on "record" still?'

I glanced at my phone and nodded.

'You've got me threatening you? I can dispatch you? Scrub that. That will not hold up in a court of law. I was talking to my dog.'

There comes a point in the Spiral where it seems like there is no way out, when despair saturates the psyche, and when images start to crystallise: the noose, hanging from a branch; the box of pills; the carving knife. This is the time when ending your life can seem like not just a logical, but a necessary step – the only rational response to a future that seems to promise nothing but endless, intolerable pain.

Though I had deliberately sought out those who had struggled the hardest on leaving the military, it was striking how many spoke about their suicide attempts or about former comrades who had taken their own lives, sometimes many years after serving. There was a special poignancy attached to the fate of men who had survived encounters with enemies of flesh and blood, only to fall in a battle with their own minds.

Unlike in the United States, where an epidemic of military suicides has gained widespread coverage, the relationship between suicide and service has received limited attention in Britain. Investigating suicide is by its nature a difficult task, but with soldiers the issues are compounded by a lack of data. Just as the government makes no attempt to track the number of ex-forces in prison, so it keeps no systematic record of those who take their own lives, leaving ample room for dispute.

For example, it was reported in the *Mail on Sunday* in 2002 that some 264 veterans of the Falklands War had committed suicide – more than the 255 members of the Task Force who were killed during the campaign. The claim subsequently became a staple of media stories on military mental health. In May 2013, the MoD published a study that said the actual number of suicides among Falklands veterans was ninety-five – and calculated that their risk of dying as a result of suicide was no different from that of the general population. In fact, the veterans had been 36 per cent less likely to die over the thirty-year period of the study than their civilian equivalents. Not all Falklands veterans were convinced, however, believing some had taken a 'slow suicide' route by drinking themselves to death. It was also worth noting that the study had evaluated the 26,000-strong Task Force as a whole, rather than focusing on the subset who experienced the most intense combat.

In July 2013, the journalist Toby Harnden cast a new spotlight on the issue of military suicides with a BBC *Panorama* programme called *Broken by Battle* and an accompanying story in the *Sunday Times* documenting the cases of a number of Afghanistan veterans who had taken their own lives in 2012. Among those to feature was a lance sergeant in the Welsh Guards named Dan Collins, who, like Aaron Black and James Forrester, had served in Operation Panther's Claw. Collins was rarely far from the action in Afghanistan – having been shot in the back plate of his body armour, grazed in the leg by a bullet, blown off his feet by one bomb and showered with mud and shrapnel by another. He once tried to revive a mortally wounded colleague who had lost both legs and an arm and the next day lost a close friend, a lance corporal named Dane Elson, who was killed instantly by an IED.

When Collins returned to Britain, he was given intermittent treatment by the Army for PTSD then admitted to an NHS psychiatric ward after making several suicide attempts. After five weeks on the ward, he was released, but his flashbacks worsened and he started missing weekly NHS appointments. On New Year's Eve 2011, Collins dressed in his camouflage uniform and a bandana he had worn in Helmand, then headed to the Preseli Mountains in Pembrokeshire, and spent the night in the woods.

On New Year's Day 2012, he recorded a farewell video on his iPhone, addressed to his mother Deana Collins. With tears streaming down his face and the sound of rain in the background, he said: 'Hey, Mum, just a video, just to say I'm sorry, OK? Ever since I've come back from hell, I've turned into a horrible person and I don't like who I am any more. This is why I'm doing what I'm doing, OK? I know it's selfish but it's what I want and what I need. I can't live like this any more. One thing I'd like to ask is could I have a full military funeral if that's possible? That's how I'd like to go.

'Mum, please don't get too upset. You've got to understand this is what I want. I've tried all the help. There's nothing seems to be working, OK? I love you, OK, and I'll see you, I'll see you up there in a few years, well hopefully not a few years but you know what I mean. I love you. Bye-bye.'

He then called 999 and told the operator his name, rank and service number. 'I got shot twice in Afghanistan and I got blown up twice. I lost a lot of friends and I should have died out there and now is my time,' he said. 'There'll be a body up on the Preseli Mountains and it's me.'

Collins then climbed onto a pile of slate he had pulled out of a wall and hanged himself from a pine tree. He was twenty-nine.

As Dan Collins had been grappling with the legacy of Panther's Claw at his home in Wales, James Lindsay, another veteran of the operation, was fighting a similar battle in Scotland. In Dumfries, I met Nicola Howat, James's mother. She told me her son had joined the Royal Scots Borderers, part of the Royal Regiment of Scotland, at the age of seventeen as a way to make a break with peers drifting into trouble in their Lochside neighbourhood. James served a tour in Iraq and his 'Minden' platoon volunteered to accompany the Black Watch to Afghanistan in 2009, where he fought alongside Aaron Black and James Forrester. After the tour, the three young men marched in the same homecoming procession in Perth.

James Lindsay was a strapping young private and thus ideally suited to carry the platoon general-purpose machine gun, meaning he was typically central to the fighting. His section was often at the forefront of operations, clearing routes and compounds. James had been present on the day when Robert McLaren was killed in the grape hut and had been involved in the aftermath of several incidents involving dead and wounded.

James was a popular member of his platoon, and his leaver's certificate noted that he was enthusiastic about Army life and would often volunteer where others did not. Like Aaron Black, he had been awarded an 'exemplary' grade. He also had a sensitive streak, and had seemed upset when other soldiers concluded after a firefight that he had shot several Taliban fighters.

'James would be like: "I did not! I did not! I did not!" It was just a laugh and a joke,' said Kenny Leslie, who served with him and has since left the Army. 'I don't know if that wound him up or not.'

James had decided to leave the Army after his father died in March 2010. His mood had dropped since his return from Afghanistan, and he told his mother he was having suicidal thoughts. She told him he must tell his medical officer, but she never knew if he had followed her advice.

When James returned to Dumfries, he moved back into his mother's house. He would have nightmares of being captured and scream: 'Get off! Get off!' Sometimes he went for days without sleeping, and would walk the streets with the vigilance of a soldier on patrol. James told his mother that people kept asking him how many people he had killed and seemed to think his time in Afghanistan had been a holiday.

'Even I was asked a couple of times by some idiots: "Is that your son home now? How many people did he kill then?"' Nicola told me.

A doctor referred James for psychotherapy on the NHS, but he felt uncomfortable because the first session, conducted by a trainee, was recorded on video, Nicola said. He was given medication, but he stopped taking the pills as they made him feel disorientated and he abandoned the sessions.

Another ex-serviceman pointed James in the direction of First Base, the drugs and alcohol agency run by the novelist Mark Frankland, who had started a parallel service to help soldiers who were finding civilian life difficult. James once arrived at First Base fuming after a visit to a job centre, telling Frankland he felt the staff had been dismissive of his service and one of his greatest fears was that he would lose his temper and hurt somebody.

Things began to look up when Frankland lobbied the Dumfries and Galloway Housing Partnership on James's behalf and he moved into a flat in Closeburn, a quiet village outside Dumfries, where he lived with his dog. SSAFA, one of the main forces charities, provided some furniture and he assembled a multi-gym. Frankland had recently set up a project to offer ex-forces temporary jobs cleaning stairwells in blocks of flats. James began work on Monday 16 January 2012 with enthusiasm, telling his mother he could not wait to buy some new clothes. The following Saturday, Nicola called his mobile. He did not answer and she assumed he might be nursing a hangover.

When James did not turn up for work on Monday, his uncle put a note through his letterbox. By this point, Nicola was worried enough to phone the police. Then his uncle called her, screaming that he had seen James through the blinds. He had hanged himself in the stairwell. He was twenty-two.

'I think they should all have counselling before they leave. Nobody's going to feel any stigma if they do that,' Nicola told me. 'It would help if more things were explained to them – so they're not thinking they're just going mad.'

As part of his *Panorama* investigation, Toby Harnden wrote to coroners around the country and found that there had been a steady increase in the number of suicides among those who had served in Afghanistan and Iraq. There were twenty-one likely suicides of serving personnel in 2012, compared with fifteen in

2011 and seven in 2010. Of those twenty-one likely suicides in 2012, sixteen had served in Afghanistan or Iraq, compared with eight in 2011 and just three in 2010. Each case would have to be examined in depth to draw firm conclusions, but the numbers raised the question of whether the after-effects of the intense fighting in Helmand were taking an increasingly deadly toll.

Seeking to quell such concerns, the MoD issued a statement saying that suicide rates among personnel who were still serving in the military were significantly lower than in the rest of the population. The statement also pointed to a finding by the King's Centre for Military Health Research that there was no difference in the suicide rates among service personnel who had served in the Gulf War and those who had not.

The statement raised more questions than it answered. First, it was unclear what relevance the hundred-hour ground campaign to liberate Kuwait might hold for assessing the likely impact on suicide rates following from years of grinding counter-insurgency in Afghanistan. Second, it was not surprising that personnel were on average less prone to commit suicide while still in service since they were employed, generally in good health and looked after – problems tended to arise with much greater intensity when they left. Third, the statement did not acknowledge that the picture changed significantly when the age of service personnel was taken into account. Official data showed that suicides among males aged between sixteen and twenty who were serving in the forces were 82 per cent higher than in a demographically matched group of civilians during an almost twenty-year period ending in 2012. There was also no reference to the MoD-funded study by the University of Manchester that had revealed the elevated risks faced by young men aged twenty-four years or younger, like Aaron Black and James Lindsay, who had left the military after a few years of service. Members of this sub-group were two to three times as likely to take their own life as their civilian peers. The risks were greatest for those who had served in the Army, who were of low rank and who were single.

The studies' authors – Professor Navneet Kapur and Dr David While – floated a range of possible explanations. Could it be that the men who died had carried some pre-existing vulnerability into the Army? Or might younger men, who tended to do the bulk of the fighting, have suffered the most trauma? The study, published in 2009, provided little insight into the potential impact of the war in Afghanistan because its sample had stopped before British troops deployed to Helmand in 2006, heralding the most intense phase of the campaign. It would be years before it would be possible to determine conclusively the full impact of Afghanistan on suicide rates in the military, but Harnden's investigation had flagged a disturbing trend.

Statistics could only reveal so much, however. Some ex-forces were anxious to dispel what they saw as a widespread misperception that soldier suicides were caused solely by what they had seen on tour. It was not necessarily traumatic memories that proved intolerable, but often the strain of adjusting to civilian life – and the lost sense of purpose, the broken relationships and the hopelessness that could follow. Perhaps the clearest insights were provided by A.J., the former Royal Marine sniper, who knew what it meant to reach the brink.

On a crisp January morning, we drove down to the beach near A.J.'s home. A fierce storm had battered the sea wall the previous night, and scattered figures trudged across the beach, hoods up against the wind. Dogs raced over sand polished to a sheen by the receding tide. We passed a row of closed-up bathing huts painted red, yellow and blue and A.J. parked facing the sea.

Therapists embarking on trauma treatment sometimes ask clients to spend some minutes visualising a sanctuary which they can return to if they feel overwhelmed by the feelings that arise as they confront their worst memories. Ever since he was a boy, setting out with his father on the family trawler, A.J. had drawn comfort from the ocean.

'Good place to come,' he said. 'This is my little safe place.'

When the darkness returned, A.J. would imagine a summer's day on the shoreline – hear the cry of seagulls and the crash of waves, and feel the gritty softness of his toes digging into the sand.

'There were times when I thought about killing myself and I came down here,' he said. 'I physically couldn't put a smile on my face – it was that painful.'

Standing on the beach after dark, as Jen, his pointer, raced across the shoreline in defiance of her advancing years, A.J. would feel the breakers beckon.

'If you go down to the darkest depths with it – where it doesn't matter if you go forward or backwards – it's only then I sort of realised that suicide is actually really easy,' A.J. said. 'You get to that state of mind where actually walking out there' – he nodded towards the sea – 'and turning round and walking back to the car were almost equal.'

As an Army cadet in the 1990s, A.J. had been mystified by reports that Marines who had fought in the Falklands were committing suicide a decade later. He had assumed it must have had something to do with what the tabloids called the 'horrors of war'.

'Now I know it doesn't necessarily have to be that – it's just the extremes of stress that you've gone through that induce depression,' he said. 'For different people, that depression can be induced by different things: a school teacher getting it dealing with kids, doctors get it with patients.

'It wasn't about soldiering and the "horrors of war" – it was being depressed that was causing me to think like that. Had I been a different person, that depression could have been brought on by something else.'

As A.J. was making his way home from Afghanistan, he had

followed an impulse to order a guitar online while he was in transit at Kandahar Airfield. He had never been particularly musical, but he drew immense satisfaction from learning to form chords. He began to write poetry, and as his playing improved, his poems turned into songs – often written in the hours before dawn.

One day, A.J. composed a song called 'Ocean', dedicated to a fellow Marine who shared his love of the sea and who also battled suicidal thoughts, once taking an overdose on a beach. A.J. had sent him the song one night after recording it on his iPhone.

'Twenty minutes later he said: "You couldn't have sent it at a better time. I'm on the beach thinking about giving it up again, and that song's made me change my mind."'

A.J. scrutinised his iPhone.

'I think I've got it on here, but if it is it'll be a really embarrassing version, because I can't sing,' he said. 'The lyrics are brilliant, I think.'

A ripple of acoustic chords filled the cab, followed by his voice.

When you're feeling all alone,
And you got no place to go,
Call me, and I'll be there.
Watch you for a while.
I rise with you and my wave will make you smile.
A beautiful winter's day.
Do you hear, the waves cry, crashing.
Horses chase you as you pray.
Spend some time, Admire and smile.
Take a walk with sand beneath your feet,
Breathe your life in for a while.
Do you hear, what I'm talking to you friend
Do you see me when I'm sitting down beside you on the shore
Can you open up your eyes
And just smile

Let the ocean change you for a while
And just smile
Let the ocean change your life for a while

There was silence for a moment, then A.J. started to nudge the car out of the parking space.

'You're the only person that's ever heard it apart from that guy I sent it to.'

Despite all he had endured, A.J. was one of the fortunate ones. He had managed to find a way back from the darkest and most dangerous reaches of the Spiral. For many others, survival had seemed to be as much a matter of luck as of fate. One young man who had served in Afghanistan told me he had once taken an overdose but woken up the next morning after his best sleep in years: the pills had turned out to be herbal sleeping tablets. A.J.'s friend – considering another attempt to end his life on the beach – was saved by a song. A man in his sixties, haunted by guilt over an incident in Northern Ireland in the early 1970s, told me how he had been about to throw himself from a window when his toddler son crawled into the room. On another occasion he did manage to jump – somehow surviving a plunge onto frozen ground without a bone broken. A contemporary of his who had also served in Northern Ireland was not so fortunate and hanged himself in his garden shed.

For some, an encounter with mortality spurred a search for meaning that they would later look back on, if not with gratitude, then at least with a sense that their encounter with life had been profoundly deepened. But this was not a journey easily accomplished alone. I wanted to know what happened next. Where could ex-forces turn after hitting their lowest point? How do they begin to climb back up from the depths? And who is there to help?

PART II

8

'Maintaining the Assets'

How the military tends its psychological wounds

On the quay in Portsmouth, Britain's maritime capital, visitors can take a tour of HMS *Victory*, the 104-gun ship that carried Vice Admiral Nelson to his triumph in the Battle of Trafalgar in 1805. Though the victory cost him his life, Nelson's humbling of the French and Spanish fleets would be remembered as one of Britain's greatest feats of arms. Nelson's unflinching leadership style was distilled into a semaphore signal he sent as battle commenced: 'England expects that every man will do his duty.' The words captured the spirit of self-sacrifice that has long shaped Britain's martial culture, and prescribed a studied silence as the standard remedy for distress.

Portsmouth remains the host to a major Royal Navy base, where the grey silhouettes of modern-day warships loom above centuries-old docks. The complex is also home to one of a network of sixteen outpatient mental health centres located at military bases across Britain, known as Departments of Community Mental Health, or DCMHs. I had come to visit Surgeon Captain John Sharpley, defence consultant advisor in psychiatry. A consultant psychiatrist who had served for twenty-eight years in the Royal Navy, he bore ultimate responsibility for the care of the forces' unseen wounds.

I had first met Sharpley a few months earlier at a conference on military psychiatry at the Royal Society of Medicine in London, held almost a century after Myers had introduced 'shell shock' in the *Lancet*. A polished speaker, Sharpley had emerged as the public face of forces psychiatry in recent years. The role involved a constant battle to challenge public perceptions that the military was in the grip of an epidemic of psychological collapse.

In his keynote address, Sharpley showed a slide featuring a selection of headlines – TSUNAMI OF POST-TRAUMATIC STRESS HAUNTS OUR HEROES – the *Sun*; BRITISH TROOPS BACK FROM AFGHANISTAN ARE 10 TIMES MORE LIKELY TO SUFFER MENTAL ILLNESS, SAYS MOD – *Daily Mail*. Sharpley then quoted a survey that showed almost 60 per cent of the public believed that mental health problems were 'quite common' in the military – an impression he was keen to dispel. Though Sharpley did not make the point explicitly, there was a growing concern in the military that damaging stereotypes could create a self-fulfilling prophecy by making it harder for ex-forces to find jobs, or even foster a kind of psychological hypochondria among the more suggestible. But the most harmful misperceptions around mental health occurred among service personnel themselves: the stigma attached to breakdown, familiar from Myers's day, was stopping many seeking help.

'We know there's a lot of unmet need, a lot of people out there with symptoms, who need treatment, who are not getting it,' Sharpley told a packed hall of psychiatrists and therapists. 'We need to get the message out that treatment does work.'

I had a brief chat with Sharpley during the coffee break and some months later the MoD arranged for me to meet him in Portsmouth to speak in more depth.

The DCMH was located a few minutes' walk from the *Victory*, in a converted building in the historic part of the dockyard. Antique maritime charts decorated the walls of Sharpley's office and a ship in a bottle rested on a shelf of psychology texts, next to a model of a head used in phrenology – the Victorian pseudoscience of divining personality traits by measuring bumps on the skull. Sharpley wore a Royal Navy jumper with gold-trimmed epaulettes formed of four circles – denoting his rank as a naval captain – and trimmed with red lines to signify his role as a medical officer.

Sharpley had joined the Royal Navy as an officer cadet while studying medicine at Guy's Hospital in London, but his journey into military psychiatry was the result of a chance encounter when he first went to sea. Sharpley had boarded the frigate HMS *Campbeltown* as a surgeon lieutenant for a voyage to the Falklands, part of the commemorations for the tenth anniversary of the war. The captain lent him a copy of *Regeneration*, the Pat Barker novel based on the encounter between the psychologist W. H. R. Rivers and the war poet Siegfried Sassoon. Sharpley read the book, then immediately started it again – his new career path charted.

As the military's chief psychiatrist, one of Sharpley's main tasks was to oversee the network of DCMHs, designed to allow personnel rapid access to psychological assessments. The military provided twice as many mental health staff per capita as the NHS did for the civilian population, primarily because it needed to be able to ascertain rapidly whether somebody was fit for duty – a priority task when jobs might involve operating sophisticated weapons or leading troops in battle. Personnel were also trained to varying standards to offer treatment – medications for depression or anxiety, for example, and some psychotherapy – but the core function was a military version of occupational health. In that sense, the words of Lord Moran, writing in 1945, still have a ring of truth today: 'My job as a medical officer was to value the assets of the battalion – to take stock – to guard against depreciation.'

For PTSD, the military employed the same two treatments recommended by the National Institute for Health and Care Excellence for use in the NHS. The first of these is a trauma-focused version of cognitive behavioural therapy, or CBT, a form of talk therapy in which a therapist aims to help a client improve their mood by learning to identify and change negative patterns of thought and behaviour. CBT has occupied pride of place in a government drive to expand access to psychotherapy for common problems such as depression and anxiety in recent years. The trauma-specific variant involves repeatedly revisiting a painful memory to try to gradually weaken its grip on the present – a process known as exposure.

There is, however, growing concern in the psychotherapy community over CBT's effectiveness for a number of disorders, including the most severe cases of PTSD. Though research suggests that the technique may work for otherwise healthy people who may have experienced a one-off traumatic event, far fewer studies have tested its impact on people with ingrained PTSD symptoms stemming from multiple shocks suffered over many years – the kind often presented by soldiers.

The other recommended PTSD treatment is eye movement desensitisation and reprocessing, or EMDR, which A.J., the former Royal Marine sniper, had been offered, and which works through a process of bilateral stimulation of the eyes. The approach has not enjoyed the same level of state support as CBT, though many trauma specialists argue that it can sometimes prove remarkably effective at rapidly resolving symptoms and it has gained a number of converts within the military. But EMDR also has risks attached, particularly if it is started too early in the therapy process, when recipients may feel it is reopening their wounds rather than healing them.

Sharpley's staff had no shortage of opportunities to put both approaches into practice. In the year to 31 March 2014, 396 service personnel were diagnosed with PTSD, an increase of almost 20 per cent on the previous year, according to an analysis of MoD data by the *Telegraph*. There had also been a 12 per cent increase in the rate of mental disorders diagnosed as a whole, including depression and anxiety. Some believed the figures pointed to the accumulating strain of operations in Iraq and Afghanistan. Others thought there had been no overall change in the burden of mental health problems and the numbers were only rising because people were seeking help earlier. The picture was further complicated by the fact that these official statistics might only capture a fraction of the overall burden of illness, since many personnel feared that asking for help might damage their careers. One therapist said he saw clients from Catterick Garrison who drove for hours to see him rather than visit a DCMH. Service personnel were not alone in their reluctance to seek help – stigma is also a major problem in the civilian world. But despite the best efforts of the Don't Bottle It Up campaign, many were still keeping their troubles to themselves.

When I asked Sharpley why the stigma remained so entrenched, I was caught off guard by the frankness of his response. Though attitudes are changing, he said, there was still a view in the military that some stigma around mental health is essential to bind the organisation together.

'The military operation is dependent on small groups, not individuals,' he said. 'And stigma is bad for the individual, but good for the group.'

He gave the example of a unit of ten soldiers ordered to assault a hill and destroy a machine-gun nest. Since they would all be risking their lives, they would ostracise anybody showing signs of weakness.

'If they've got a person in that group who's not functioning properly, what are they are going to do?' Sharpley said. 'Get rid of them and get another one who's OK. That's why stigma's good for the group.'

The idea that 'some stigma is good' was certainly not the message of Don't Bottle It Up – but Sharpley was simply being honest enough to acknowledge the dynamics that have always been at work in the military. It was only in more recent decades that attitudes had begun to shift in wider society, forcing the services to play catch-up.

'In the Second World War, it was OK to shun someone with a mental health problem – it's not OK now,' he said. 'That creates a lot of conflict in the military. It's an interesting conflict we have difficulty managing.'

It was notable that neither Sharpley nor anybody else I spoke to in the military could point to a single senior serving officer who was speaking out publicly about overcoming their own mental health problems. The official message was Don't Bottle It Up – but the hierarchy seemed reluctant to demonstrate that suffering from PTSD, or a bout of depression or alcohol misuse, did not have to wreck your career.

Such taboos have complicated the task of assessing the scope of the psychic wounds suffered by British troops. The military relies on figures from the King's Centre for Military Health Research, which has conducted studies of large cohorts of personnel by asking them to fill in questionnaires about their symptoms, supplemented by some follow-up interviews. The King's Centre has consistently found that the rate of probable PTSD in the forces is about the same as that in the civilian population – at around 4 per cent. The figure rises to 7 per cent among those who serve in combat roles. The data were widely recycled by the MoD and the media and in official reports on military mental health services.

Though the King's Centre enjoyed a near monopoly on the statistics used to inform public debate, some questioned whether its questionnaires captured the full extent of the military's symptoms. Among them was David Gee, an independent researcher who co-founded Forces Watch, a pressure group campaigning for the recruitment age to rise from sixteen to eighteen, when personnel can be legally deployed on front-line duty. In October 2013, Gee published a wide-ranging critique of the King's Centre methodology entitled 'The Last Ambush' which was widely quoted in the media. The eighty-page report drew a stark conclusion: the King's Centre might only be identifying less than half of those with PTSD. 'In effect, the studies deal with the tip of an iceberg of mental health issues, most of which remains hidden beneath the waterline,' Gee wrote.

Gee's argument turned partly on the issue of stigma. Research should ideally be conducted in anonymous conditions because personnel might otherwise be wary of admitting the full scope of their symptoms for fear of harming their careers. Although the King's Centre assures its respondents of confidentiality, it has to ask them for identifying information so it can follow them up over time. But Gee pointed out that one of the King's Centre's own studies of just over 600 personnel deployed in Iraq had found that respondents significantly downplayed their PTSD symptoms when they had to give their contact details.

'That study's finding is one of a number of indicators suggesting that King's are substantially underestimating the rate of PTSD in British veterans,' Gee told me. 'The natural next step would be to follow up the study with a larger one in order to test the effect of anonymity on reporting more thoroughly. Would King's do that? Would the MoD fund it?'

Professor Sir Simon Wessely, the co-director of the King's Centre for Military Health Research, rejected the suggestion that his studies might be missing large numbers of possible PTSD cases, and advanced several arguments against drawing broad conclusions from the stigma study, which he co-authored. If there was a small degree of under-reporting, he said it was a price worth paying for the advantage of being able to monitor cohorts over time. 'Such a result [from the stigma study] could mean that our identifiable but confidential data collection method underestimates the prevalence of PTSD but this is a trade-off against the advantage of being able to carry out prospective follow-up of the same sample,' Wessely wrote in an email.

Research by the King's Centre – often used to underpin assertions that the military suffered from 'low' rates of mental disorders – had rarely been subjected to such an overt challenge. At the minimum, Gee's report was an important reminder that assessing rates of mental illness in large populations is a complex task fraught with limitations that the MoD did not tend to explicitly acknowledge when quoting King's Centre data. If Gee was right, then mental health problems might be far more wide-spread than the MoD assumed. Sharpley acknowledged that no one could ascertain the number of cases with absolutely certainty since most personnel with symptoms never came forward to DCMHs for treatment.

'Ten per cent of the visible stuff we see,' Sharpley said. 'Ninety per cent we don't see.'

The uncertainty over the precise scope of PTSD fed into another source of controversy: the origins of the traumatic reaction itself. In the United States, the debate around military mental health has moved full circle from the days when Myers's contemporaries had wondered whether 'shell shock' was a result of microscopic lesions on the brain caused by explosions. The Pentagon has spent large sums on neuropsychological testing programmes to investigate whether shockwaves from roadside bombs in Iraq and Afghanistan may have caused thousands of hard-to-detect cases of what is known as Mild Traumatic Brain Injury, or MTBI, whose sufferers can exhibit some of the symptoms found in PTSD. Though British troops have been subjected to many similar blasts, the MoD has taken a more passive approach, encouraging people to come forward if they think they may have symptoms of MTBI, fearing that actively screening for cases might inadvertently lead to the creation of a new 'signature injury' from the recent conflicts. Though Sharpley did not say so explicitly, it seemed a safe bet that the MoD was eager to avoid advertising the existence of a new and mysterious condition that might emerge as a catalyst for controversy in the same way that Gulf War syndrome made headlines in the 1990s.

'What'll happen,' Sharpley said, 'is people will focus on it, other people will say: "I'm like that too," and the more it gets talked about the more you see of it.'

In Sharpley's view, the locus of distress remained firmly in the psyche – and in particular in a sense of loyalty breached. He was keen to dispel what he saw as a widespread misperception that the mere fact of witnessing a horrific incident or experiencing a life-threatening event would inevitably cause chronic symptoms. In his experience, the active ingredient in many apparent cases of trauma was a sense of broken trust. Sharpley reeled off a list of hypothetical examples. Perhaps you felt betrayed by a partner when a relationship broke down after a tour. Or perhaps you felt you had betrayed yourself when you realised you were not brave enough to run out under fire to save your friend, whatever you might have seen in the cinema. Sharpley gave the theoretical case of an Apache helicopter gunship crew who might have fired at some figures highlighted on their screens.

'They kill them. They see this splat. They have to play their video to their commanding officer. It's not unreasonable to think if they were a bit iffy they might be a bit nervous,' he said.

'Then, say, command decides they hit the wrong target and killed civilians – and the pilot receives a reprimand. For two months, he is known as the idiot who made the mistake and his marriage starts to crumble when he returns.'

A year later, the pilot may present to a mental health nurse, saying he was haunted by images of the targets turning to 'red mist', though as Sharpley says: 'It isn't the case at all – the trauma was possibly being ticked off by his commanding officer for doing the wrong thing.

'He may well have been very cohered to the group; his loyalty to the CO or the system is then shattered. It isn't necessarily war that rots people per se. It's people that rots people.'

One task of therapy, Sharpley said, was to help a soldier to embrace reality: the trauma and its aftermath had torn away a filter to reveal a glimpse of a more frightening yet truer version of the nature of things.

'Normality is looking at the world through a veil – you see what you want to see,' Sharpley said. 'It's safe. Rosy future. People around you are generally pleasant. Then trauma happens, and the veil is lifted. The re-experiencing and symptoms of PTSD are the intermittent lifting of the veil.'

The key, Sharpley said, was to persuade people to embrace their new perspective, however uncomfortable it might feel, rather than shy away.

'Sometimes you have to accept that you can't put the veil back, and you have to get the person to adapt to seeing the world as it really is,' he said. 'Otherwise you're trying to tell them: "You're ill, you're going to stay ill, and I as a doctor am powerless to stop it."'

Our meeting had overrun and I still had to speak to a member of Sharpley's team – the closest modern-day equivalent I would meet to the 'shell shock' doctors of the Western Front.

Sigmund Freud is said to have likened the role of the military psychiatrist to that of a machine gun behind the front line, 'driving back those who have fled'. It would have been hard to imagine a less machine-gun-like figure than Chief Petty Officer Craig Zdrodowski, an ebullient thirty-five-year-old Royal Navy mental health nurse and cognitive therapist. Having served four-month deployments in Afghanistan in 2008 and 2012, Zdrodowski was well qualified for his new job running the Portsmouth DCMH. When I visited his office, he radiated a genuine enthusiasm for his work, and an evident compassion that bore little resemblance to the hard-boiled attitude of his First World War predecessors.

Zdrodowski had started out as a mechanic repairing Royal Navy helicopters and jets, but he decided his skills would be put to better use in the less-predictable business of fixing minds, and the Navy retrained him as a mental health nurse. His first job in Afghanistan was to ensure that soldiers knew support was available through the TRiM system, in which personnel in each unit were trained to spot colleagues who might be showing signs of distress.

'One of the things that's really helpful for people is to talk,' Zdrodowski said. 'That's what unit commanders are becoming more attuned to – engaging with their guys – rather than "stiff upper lip, let's forget about it and move on, they're dead, there's nothing we can do about it". Those days are gone – thank God.'

As Zdrodowski promoted TRiM, soldiers began to turn to him for help. Some were young combatants who had suffered 'acute stress reactions' – characterised by blank stares, trembling and numbness. If the symptoms persisted for four weeks, these patients might be diagnosed with PTSD. When such cases were admitted to hospital at Camp Bastion, Zdrodowski would encourage their commander to send one of their friends to come and sit for a while by their bedside.

While relatively few soldiers suffered a full-blown breakdown in combat, a larger number were fighting secret battles. One serviceman felt an intense burden of guilt because his friend had been killed by a roadside bomb on an earlier tour and he had not been there to save him. Using the techniques of CBT, Zdrodowski led the soldier through a kind of Socratic dialogue that challenged his assumption that he was to blame.

'His conclusion: it wasn't even the enemy's fault,' Zdrodowski said. 'So therefore the blame dissipates and there was no blame. He was able to come to terms with his loss, the guilt disappeared, his mood lifted and he was able to carry on.'

Sometimes, Zdrodowski would have to challenge the well-meaning but counter-productive advice of commanders. For example, a thirty-four-year-old serviceman had been reluctant to return to his armoured vehicle after he struck a mine and suffered minor injuries. His superiors had allowed him to continue working in the relative safety of camp, but Zdrodowski feared the driver's temporary anxiety would solidify into a permanent phobia. He gently suggested he might try driving around the base. The mechanic agreed and within three days he had overcome his 'spike of anxiety', as Zdrodowski put it, and was asking to resume full duties. It had been a little like using gradual exposure to cure a fear of spiders. I asked Zdrodowski if he ever felt conflicted. After all, there were IEDs in Afghanistan and the driver probably was safer in the camp.

'It's not a therapist's job to try and somehow do some psychological trickery so the person misinterprets the risk,' he said. 'It's to get somebody to a point where their distress has reduced to a degree where he can make the decision for himself.'

Zdrodowski used a similar approach with another soldier who was badly shaken by a blast, suggesting he calculate the statistical odds of being hurt. His client felt better after doing some sums and arriving at a figure that was a fraction of a percentage point. In rapidly helping front-line troops, Zdrodowski and his colleagues were implementing the classic principles of PIE – proximity, immediacy and expectancy of return to duty – championed by Myers. The difference was that Zdrodowski encouraged a soldier to seek help long before he broke down.

'People are beginning to hold their hands up and say: "I'm scared, can you help me with this?"' he said. 'Good, effective leaders will recognise that having some fear in that situation, especially in a combat station, is pretty healthy – it keeps people alert.'

In rare cases, soldiers were sent to see him not because they were suffering, but because their commanders were baffled by their behaviour. One had said he wanted to be a physical trainer when he left the Army and therefore could no longer run the risk of being wounded by going on patrol. Zdrodowski found no evidence of pathology: the soldier was making a rational decision that he would rather face military discipline than continue to fight.

Then came the moment when Zdrodowski put the TRiM system to the test for himself. Early one morning, he had finished giving a stress briefing and was about to grab a coffee when a rocket slammed into the ground. Zdrodowski felt as if he had been shoved hard in the back and fell. In the confusion of smashed furniture and disoriented men, his mind registered the strangely beautiful sight of a ruptured pipe spraying droplets of water. Patting himself down, Zdrodowski realised he was bleeding from his right leg, but he shrugged off the injury and helped medics to hand out packs of field dressings and morphine. Two people had been killed and eight wounded, including him. When the all-clear sounded he made his way to a shelter and slapped on a field dressing to staunch the wound in his thigh.

Zdrodowski said the shock stemmed not so much from his injury, but from visions of the anguish such a scene would cause his parents, wife and children. He went through a TRiM debrief, but his greatest solace came from colleagues who could not resist the satirical opportunities presented by the spectacle of a Navy man being wounded in the backside. They bought an inflatable rubber ring shaped like a giant doughnut for him to sit on as he convalesced – a gift accompanied by sniggers. Zdrodowski keeps his get-well cards, exemplars of trench humour, in a filing cabinet in his office.

Plenty of other personnel were grateful for the progress made since the days of 'shell shock'. One was a thirty-one-year-old combat medic named Danny Smart who had joined the RAF at seventeen and was deployed multiple times with the RAF Regiment, the air-force ground-fighting unit.

In 2007 in Iraq, Danny had led a medical team treating casualties from hundreds of rocket attacks. He went on to serve two tours in Afghanistan, where he once treated a young child who had suffered a severe head injury after teenagers pelted him with stones. He briefly considered calling a helicopter to airlift the child to hospital, but that would have been a serious breach of the rules – such call-outs were only permissible to treat friendly casualties or civilians hurt by coalition fire. Danny did what he could to patch him up and his commander reassured him the unit would return in a few days, but plans changed and Danny later learned the child had died. On returning to Britain, Danny was sent to a quiet post in Wales, where he lay awake at night, tormenting himself over the child's death, and replaying scenes of the many casualties he had treated in Iraq.

'Obviously, when you've heard that somebody's died, you question everything you do – did you stop the bleeding quick enough in a catastrophic haemorrhage? Did you move quick enough? Were you stunned in any way?' he said.

'When these things happen, you feel the clock is moving tremendously slow or tremendously fast. It's remarkable how much thinking you can do in what is only a few seconds, when you've got a casualty screaming in front of you whose leg has been blown off. And you're trying to get into the first field dressing – the plastic's going everywhere – you start to shake because the adrenalin's going through you at a rate of knots.

'Afterwards, the aftermath – the patient's gone, they're off to hospital – to definitive care somewhere. You ask yourself: "Was that just a fumbling mess or did that go the way it was supposed to do?"

'It's all right when somebody's able to say: "You did well. You followed the drills." Without feedback, you can find yourself asking the same questions about the same patient over and over again for the rest of your life.'

When Danny eventually sought help, he was referred to Major Cormac Doyle, a mental health manager stationed at the DCMH at Donnington, near Telford. Doyle made an assessment and offered him sessions of EMDR. Danny wrote a description of their work:

> EMDR scared me; there is no other word for it. In the days leading to my first session, I was restless, always fidgeting. Inanimate objects seem to cause me offence. I had been given a leaflet to read. My girlfriend read it also, and I could see the concern in her face.

As I arrived at Donnington for my first session, I felt afraid and angry. I largely kept it inside, only to complain to the Major about the aesthetics of the building – the barbed-wire fence made it look prison-like. 'Not ideal for mental health,' I said. I complained about the spotty pattern on the carpet and the fact the doors were numbered, instead of bearing practitioners' names.

In the time between appointments, I re-read a Wikipedia article and began to hear about positive outcomes from patients. It all sounded good – they were happier, their issues seemed almost entirely resolved. People had described how they saw their memories dissolve in their mind, how they became less 'hot' or 'painful'. I was sceptical: I felt that perhaps I would have to 'manufacture' this to get it started.

Major Doyle called me through – with a shake of the hand and a genuine exchange of pleasantries. He moved his chair in front of me, asked me to rest my hands on my knees – sitting straight but comfortable. He held up his right index finger, before explaining that I was to follow the movement throughout. I was to recall an image – a traumatic incident from my past.

For a second, I could think of nothing. Then suddenly, as if my unconscious had taken over, a memory of Iraq entered my mind: a rocket fired by the enemy at the Contingency Operating Base in Basra had triggered the early warning system. A newly fitted weapon system, codenamed Phalanx, targeted the incoming munition: cannons fired bursts, destroying the shell entirely but the same could not be said for the warhead.

Now tumbling toward the ground, it impacted between two lines of 'Corimecs' – prefabricated metal buildings used as temporary accommodation. The explosion was terrific. The accommodation was surrounded by a

HESCO barrier, which caused the force of the blast to bounce back. Many sleeping RAF Gunners were injured; three were killed.

Thrown from my bed in the neighbouring lines, dropping the book I had been reading in my stand-down, I ran outside. Flames, smoke, shouting. Heading for the impact area, just metres away, I began stepping over debris – pieces of broken Corimec and miscellaneous items. It seemed like minutes before I began to register individual items or objects. Longer still: the realisation that some of what I could see was the poor souls of men amongst the wreckage.

As a medical commander, I needed to switch on and take control. I found an area to coordinate a response – 'game face' on. Two ambulances arrived and would be ferrying the injured to the Field Hospital. Now followed the sad task of transporting the dead to their temporary place of rest. The chaos had faded and a cloud of emotion enveloped those still present, dealing with the mess.

Time began to slow down again; the noise level had dropped and as each soul was brought out and laid to rest in an ambulance, each physical movement seemed amplified. If what had happened so far had been surreal, the atmosphere here now was beyond what the brain could comprehend.

As just a few firemen were left to hose down the wreckage, a sergeant caught my eye: a medic come to help. He found a piece of wreckage to sit upon. He curled his feet inwards to release the strain on his ankles. Taking off his issue hat, he wiped his brow; his face was solemn – the sight of a man truly weeping inside. This sergeant was over six feet tall and built like a brick, and yet at this moment he seemed small and shrunken.

It was at this moment the true nature of what I had

just encountered that afternoon set in – the images burning in my mind. The image of the sergeant had lived with me ever since, and I recalled it in the office in Donnington.

The finger began to move. How does this work? I paused – for a few moments I did nothing but follow the silent left and right movements and then a calm descended. The moving footage – once violently playing in my mind – seemed to be in the background, like ambient noise, barely audible. Calmer still, my mind seemed to start throwing up lessons learnt. A pause – the Major had stopped his wagging for just a split second. He would pause often – it served to keep me anchored and focused – and before long he stopped completely.

'How do you feel, what do you see?'

I felt calmer and as I recalled the memory an almost black and white, still image appeared. Bordered in white, this picture seemed ready for the album: one image, one memory resolved.

'On a score of one to ten, how did you rate that image, that memory, at the start?' the Major asked.

'Ten.'

'And how does it feel now?'

'Two.'

Previously that image had been in perfect High Definition. Now it was a faded, still picture that would remain with me forever, but – now processed – one that would serve to build my character.

I left the consulting room that day and felt the fresh air on my face as I walked across the car park. How did it work? I have decided it needs no explanation.

That was my first EMDR experience, and it paved the way for more memories to be processed and added to my photo album. It wasn't always so easy – some required more work than others – and some were filed with a higher number on the scale to reflect the need to learn from the experience.

Now, all but discharged from care, I can appreciate that all of my experiences have shaped me. Was I unfortunate to have had them, to see what I have seen? It certainly felt like it at the time. Now, I'm not so sure, because it is only having had them all that I am the person today who appreciates the good things in life. I can identify people who hurt inside; those with issues who for many years have done so well to hide it. Previously easily angered, today I find there is an answer to every situation.

I was asked by the good Major at the end of our sessions, some months on, how I feel now. 'Like a buoy, once anchored in the sea, bobbing precariously in the same strained place, I am now free to float calmly over the waters of life, enjoying the setting of the sun and the sounds of gulls, but ready for anything the ocean can throw at me,' I said.

He paused, and then he wrote it down.

Danny ended his note with the RAF motto: *Per Ardua Ad Astra*, or 'Through adversity, to the stars'.

Danny's decision to seek help had paid dividends. So too for Caine Hansen, the SAS operator who had been shot on operations overseas. After he was wounded, Caine had refused offers of help from his regiment, preferring to work through his pain alone. Yet as time went by he realised he was going round in circles, wearing the grooves of self-blame ever deeper. Eventually he picked up the phone and the Army therapist returned to see him. They talked about his injury, but then delved deeper, mining the layers of grief that had accumulated in his life like a sediment, forming a submerged inner landscape where his relationships had often foundered. One afternoon I sat with him in his living room as he reclined on a sofa, smoking cigarettes, and reflecting on his sessions.

'He helped me because he won my trust,' Caine said. 'And I'd set some of the conditions as well. I said: "You've got to be hard over on me." And there were times when he was hard over on me – even a bit too hard over – and I felt like getting up and slapping him in the mouth. But there was method in his approach. I was being counselled, and I didn't even know it at times. That's talent.'

Caine's therapist encouraged him to talk, dropping in the occasional comment or suggestion that challenged his ingrained assumptions. He soon realised the weekly sessions would not be a quick fix, but he stuck with them: 'When you start the process you feel like you're in a Marianas Trench of treacle. You don't know how many metres are above you. You don't know how many metres are below you. You don't realise your own progress: he would just drop something in or challenge something and it would make me think about it in a slightly different way. There were no big revelations, there was no blinding light, but you're making progress. You have to allow a lot of the counselling to run its course retrospectively.

'I didn't need to be a rocket scientist to know that I had trust issues, derailment issues in relationships to women. I'd lost my mum and my sister in the space of five years. It manifests as mistrust: testing, testing, testing. Push, push, push. "Don't get too close." You're almost brainwashing them into disappointing you and you hate yourself for it. Then you think about the reasons why you're doing it.'

Caine lit another cigarette.

'Did I turn a few corners? Yeah I did. Did he help? Of course he did. He's been key in many ways to my improvement.

'I think I'd have carried around that burden of grief and guilt and disdain and bitterness and darkness – which hasn't totally dissipated, of course not – but I'm more adjusted. You're always going to have the memories and the feelings and the emotions, and the effect of it in your mind, but the analogy is it's not in a folder on my desktop any more – it's in the back of that hard drive somewhere.'

Caine still struggled at times. Since leaving the SAS, he had developed various new strands to his career, mainly training others in aspects of tactical medicine or occasionally collaborating with fellow ex-forces running management-training programmes for executives. But the next phase of his life – his 'line of march' as he would say – had yet to snap into sharp definition.

He said: 'I go everywhere I go – so does the contents of my head. Change your environment, change your pay scale, change your girlfriend, change your underpants, change your car, change everything about yourself, get a facelift – full nip and tuck – change your sex if you want, but unless you get a brain transplant, you ain't changing fuck all, really. You're just changing appearances.'

Above all, Caine wanted other soldiers to realise that anybody could have problems, regardless of their background.

'You don't get some sort of "hard pill",' he said. 'They don't take your innards out and galvanise them. Your mind doesn't become granite, or steel. Your heart – it still beats. You're a sentient being.

'If anybody thinks for one minute that you just brush it off, that it doesn't affect you, you're very much mistaken. You've got to grab the odd lifeline, if it's afforded to you. And if you don't get a lifeline then go find one. If you don't even get help for yourself, try and be selfless – go and get help for the people that are severely affected by it around you. If you can't count the people who are affected by your condition, you're a very lonely person, and you're in a dangerous place. Those are the people that need to be found first.'

9

'Failing Your Soldiers'

Left to fight alone

When I first visited June Black, her living room had the feel of a shrine. A scented candle burned on the sideboard next to a framed photo of Aaron, decorated with a Black Watch tartan ribbon and a poem entitled 'Angel of Comfort'. His medals hung in a frame by the mantelpiece with his crucifix medallion placed in the centre – just as he had arranged them on his kitchen counter. In the corner stood an altar of sorts bearing keepsakes: a lucky horseshoe given to June by a woman whose daughter had been killed on duty in Afghanistan, and a swan-shaped pendant pressed into her hand by one of Aaron's friends – a token of his nickname, the 'Black Swan'. A wooden lion Aaron had bought in Kenya and a figurine of a Black Watch trooper decorated nearby shelves. June had once adorned the model soldier with feathers from the garden. 'See, Aaron, they're angel feathers,' she had said. 'Nah, Mum,' came the reply. 'They're from seagulls.'

One Sunday, June retrieved a set of clear plastic crates she used to store Aaron's papers. Among them were his confidential medical records, which the Procurator Fiscal Service had obtained from the Army as it deliberated over whether to launch an inquiry into his death. June had been told that the files might not contain much more than dental records. Though well intentioned, the advice turned out to be wrong. The documents, which reached June almost a year after Aaron's death, offered a series of snapshots of her son's state of mind as he prepared to leave the Army, and an unvarnished inside view of forces' mental healthcare. Though they did not make for easy reading, they provided an insight into how one young man, and perhaps many others like him, might slip through the elaborate net that Surgeon Captain John Sharpley had described during our meeting in Portsmouth.

June carefully lifted the documents from their container and began to spread them over the carpet. She seemed reluctant for me to touch them, as if the papers contained a riddle that she alone was entitled to decipher. Though she had parsed the files many times, the crisp sentences of the men and women who had recorded the full extent of her son's distress still seemed imbued with a raw, revelatory power. June had made a set of copies and highlighted key passages in fluorescent marker, which she read out loud. It would be some months before June would trust me enough to let me comb through the papers for myself.

Aaron's journey into the military mental health system had begun in November 2010, when his superiors, increasingly concerned about his bouts of absence, referred him to the Department of Community Mental Health at Kinloss, a forty-minute drive from Fort George. June read from the notes typed by a mental health nurse after his initial consultation: "'He disclosed to me today that he has been experiencing increasing suicidal ideation and has acted on these thoughts by taking tablets on three occasions. These have been whilst under the influence of alcohol. He informed me that he had stood on top of a bridge and wanted to jump off this whilst drunk but couldn't find the courage.'"

Though Aaron had experienced low moods before Afghanistan, he told the nurse that he had never before attempted to take an overdose. He spoke of setbacks in his personal life, and confessed that he had spent half the savings he had accrued while serving in Afghanistan on alcohol. It had been six months since he had handed in his year's notice to the Army and he had begun to regret his decision to leave.

'"He maintained good eye contact, but was tearful when he had spoke about the shame he felt about having suicidal ideation,"' June read out. '"Reports biggest fear was that 'he would turn out to be the "mink" who hangs around the town centre drinking all day'."'

June explained that 'mink' was a slang term used in Blairgowrie for a 'down-and-out'.

'"My impression is that in the short to medium term, Private Black is [at] high risk of acting impulsively, especially if he continues to use alcohol. There was some evidence of helplessness and hopelessness but today I encouraged him to think of the impact this would have on his family and ex-girlfriend if he took his own life."'

Aaron declined an offer to admit him to hospital and the nurse concluded their session by handing him leaflets on self-harm and alcohol and a diary to record his drinking. In a letter to his medical officer, the nurse said Aaron had insisted that his problems did not stem from Afghanistan, but he felt the last year had been 'pointless' and that 'he has just made a mess of everything'.

Three days after this initial consultation, Aaron was arrested and charged after attempting to run from police in handcuffs following the altercation at a pub in Blairgowrie. He drank solidly for six days, returned to Fort George unshaven and still intoxicated, and slept in a bathtub.

Aaron attended several more mental health appointments in the weeks before Christmas, before being referred to one of the military's consultant psychiatrists in February. During a fifty-minute session, he explained that his biggest problems were alcohol and depression. Though he had previously downplayed any link with Afghanistan, the psychiatrist noted that there appeared to be evidence of trauma: '"His presentation is of moderate depressive symptoms and trauma symptoms from Afghanistan; he is still jumpy with dreams and flashbacks. He continues to have suicidal thinking, accepting it is worse when he has been drinking."'

When June had first read the phrase 'trauma symptoms', it was as if a bulb had been switched on in the dark. In the immediate aftermath of Aaron's death, her impulse had been to blame herself for not being a better mother. It had never occurred to her that her son might have been affected by his experiences on tour. She had felt a particularly sharp pang over her decision to encourage Aaron to stand on his own feet by helping him to find a council flat. The files cast Aaron's death in a new light. June believed that if she had known as much as the Army had done about her son's fragility – the dreams, flashbacks and suicide attempts – she would never have let him leave home.

With hindsight, June began to discern a pattern in what had seemed at the time like isolated, unrelated events. The first warning sign had occurred during Aaron's mid-tour leave, when he had spoken about the horror of the explosion in the grape hut. There had been an edge in her son's voice that June had never heard before. *Mum – there's nothing left.* The notes showed the military had been far more intimately acquainted with the nature of Aaron's despair than she had been. In that case, June wondered, why hadn't the Army done more to save him?

June returned to the file. The psychiatrist at Kinloss had concluded the assessment by recommending that Aaron be offered a course of CBT for his mood and trauma symptoms and an alcohol education course – with a possible admission to hospital to dry him out if he went on another binge. "'I have reassured him that we would be able to complete whatever treatment we start,'" the psychiatrist wrote.

The planned therapy never happened. Two months later, another mental health nurse noted that Aaron had not managed to attend sessions regularly due to his enduring alcohol misuse and sporadic periods of absence. As a consequence, his treatment had made 'little headway'.

Nevertheless, as Aaron had prepared to leave the Army, he appeared to be doing better. He seemed physically well and told the nurse that his drinking was back under control. He also said that his relationships had improved and he was less troubled by disturbing dreams and intrusive thoughts. The nurse recommended that the Army consider extending Aaron's service to allow him to complete a course of CBT.

In May, Aaron once again missed a mental health appointment. The nurse telephoned and Aaron told him he was 'continuing to do well but felt he would still require some support on exiting'. The nurse wrote to a military mental health social worker the following day to request further support for Aaron after he left the Army on 17 May 2011. There the trail ended.

'Aaron had an expectation of being followed up,' June said. 'It never came.'

Slowly, she began to tidy away the papers.

June was not alone in her anger. The most common grievance I heard among former or serving personnel who were unhappy with the military mental health system was that superiors had not taken their condition seriously enough – that a diagnosis had relegated them to an 'awkward squad' of individuals who were treated as at best a burden, and at worst with thinly veiled disdain. Others complained of being neglected by their units during periods of sick leave, or being offered only cursory attempts at therapy for their PTSD, suspecting that the chain of command had decided to get rid of them as soon as they were diagnosed because it would be too much trouble to help them recover.

These anecdotes were not always possible to verify with the kind of paper trail and multiple sources I was able to consult in the case of Aaron Black. The events unfolded over years, and involved many different units, as well as a host of commanders, welfare officers, psychiatrists and others. In such a large organi-sation as the forces – comprised of almost 200,000 people – I could only speak to a tiny sample. I was mindful, too, of several stories I heard of ex-forces deliberately exaggerating symptoms in the hope of securing payouts. Even with such caveats in mind, the testimony of a number of ex-forces and their loved ones raised questions for the military.

In Scotland, others shared June Black's disappointment with the MoD's mental health services. In September 2014, the *Daily Record* featured a story about Robert Edgar, who had served in the Black Watch alongside Aaron Black in the 2009 tour of Afghanistan. He said he was planning to sue the MoD over the way he had been treated, saying the Army had sent him on a firing range with a machine gun after he had reported feeling suicidal. 'I could easily have ended up like Blackie,' he said.

In Lochmaben, a village outside the town of Lockerbie, I visited John Christie, who said he was diagnosed with PTSD after serving a tour in Iraq in 2006–2007. John said the Army had offered him the chance to leave within two months – rather than complete the usual year-long notice period – if he forfeited his resettlement package. Depressed and disillusioned, he accepted the offer – but he later regretted giving up the career he had once loved. In the final weeks with his battalion in June 2009, John said he was made to stand guard without a weapon, clean stairs and work in the stores. He was given an empty four-man room to sleep in, leaving him feeling isolated and alone.

'I felt forgotten,' he told me. 'I was just basically put in a room to rot.'

John, who had grown up training and flying birds of prey, sought refuge from his memories of Iraq on long walks in the countryside around Lochmaben with Elinor, his Harris' hawk, circling in search of rabbits and pheasants. He later found a job breeding falcons.

In West Sussex, Clare Blatchford-Hanna, a manager at a web design company, said her ex-partner was diagnosed with PTSD ten years after serving a tour in Afghanistan. One of the staff assigned by the Army to look after him – known as a personnel recovery officer – had been excellent, but others had been less than helpful. Her partner had been referred for treatment at a DCMH located a five-hour round trip from where they lived and transport often failed to materialise. He left the Army having never completed a course of treatment and Clare had dipped into her savings to pay for private therapy.

'He felt like they'd broken him and then they'd just left him,' Clare told me. 'If he'd had actual welfare, competent and consistent support from staff, and treatment, he might have been able to turn it around.'

Others said they had had to fight the Army for years before medical staff had been willing to acknowledge the severity of their condition. In Durham, I visited Jason Wilkes, a former corporal in the Royal Engineers, who had been medically discharged with PTSD after serving for twenty-one years. He said his troubles had started when his patrol was attacked by a suicide bomber in Iraq in April 2006, leaving him with severe burns to his hands and shrapnel injuries to his arm and jaw. As the burns slowly healed, Jason suffered flashbacks, irritability and depression, and was haunted by an image of the bomber's face. In 2009 he was among the first at the scene of the fatal shooting of two off-duty British soldiers in Northern Ireland – an incident that aggravated his sense of paranoia. He would wake at the slightest noise and reach under his bed to grab the curved kukri knife he had carried on patrols in Iraq.

'There came a time when I wished I'd been killed in the suicide bombing incident. My career, everything with the military, had just gone down the pan,' Jason said. 'People knew things were bad for me but they weren't helping me. There's not only the stigma from yourself, there's the stigma from your bosses.'

The core of Jason's complaint was that he had not been properly assessed and treated in the aftermath of the Iraq bombing – and had to wait six years before he was diagnosed with PTSD by an Army consultant psychiatrist. He believed that had he received proper treatment sooner he would not have suffered the same severity of symptoms and could have earned a promotion instead of losing his career. Though he spoke highly of some of the mental health staff he had encountered, and acknowledged the system may have improved in more recent years, he felt his experience was indicative of a reflexive instinct in the Army to try to discharge people with trauma symptoms rather than help them to get better.

Jason went through four rounds of tribunal hearings before he was awarded the top tariff compensation for PTSD – which included a lump sum and monthly payments. As part of a campaign to put pressure on the military to improve mental health services, Jason handed his veterans badge back to his MP to return to the then veterans minister, Anna Soubry, and spoke to the *Mirror* about his experiences.

Four months later, in Liverpool, a decorated sniper staged a more dramatic protest – launching a one-man pitch invasion at Anfield Stadium during an international match. As thousands of Liverpool fans looked on, Luke Huskisson, still a serving soldier, unfurled a white banner daubed with a slogan in red and black paint: THE MOD ARE FAILING YOUR SOLDIERS. Stewards wearing bulky orange overalls tackled the twenty-eight-year-old but the pictures made the *Liverpool Echo*.

It emerged that Huskisson had been diagnosed with PTSD after returning from his second tour of Afghanistan, where he had won a commendation for risking his life trying to save colleagues from the blazing wreckage of a fatal helicopter crash in January 2012. His solicitor said he had suffered a breakdown a year later due to his 'inadequate' treatment from the military. Huskisson had also complained about the lack of out-of-hours mental health support and had felt 'threatened and harassed' when he sought help from the NHS. He believed the MoD was trying to cut his career short by medically discharging him from the RAF Regiment rather than helping him to recover.

A spokesman for the RAF told the newspaper it was offering

the 'full scope of medical support' to Huskisson and was committed to providing all serving personnel with the help they needed. I put the other cases to the MoD but it declined to comment.

Leaving the military can be tough for any soldier – but the prospect of coping as a civilian while still grappling with the symptoms of trauma is even more daunting. For those forced to leave the Army after suffering psychological wounds that were far from fully healed, the future could sometimes feel very uncertain.

One day I received a text from Michael, a sergeant in the Royal Military Police who had been medically discharged with PTSD. He invited me to meet him at his home in a new estate of red-brick houses on the outskirts of a village in Lincolnshire, where he lived with his wife Karen, who had served in the police.

Michael was thirty-five years old and had grown up in North Shields, in a family with a long tradition of military service. He first joined up as a teenager but dropped out of basic training, not feeling ready for Army life. He began a new career as a master butcher but decided to give the military another try when he turned twenty-two. Michael progressed into a specialised intelligence role, training in police-style skills needed to investigate the types of weapons used by insurgents. On tour in Iraq and Afghanistan, he was part of a team that gathered forensic evidence from the scene of bombings.

Michael's face showed the anguish he felt over the loss of his thirteen-year career as he talked me through his tours in Iraq and Afghanistan, steadying himself every hour or so with a cigarette smoked on his garden step. A stout tabby cat named Walter, who luxuriated on Michael's lap, exerted a calming influence as he rehearsed a seemingly limitless store of anecdotes of gun battles, close calls with IEDs and harrowing scenes in the aftermath of explosions.

He said of his time in Afghanistan: 'You just could not detect these devices – people were getting blown up left, right and centre. It was just constantly getting shot at, blown up, recovering body parts – sticking them in a Bergen and taking them back so nothing was left on the ground.

'You see some burned flesh, you think nothing of it. Then when it's recognisable as somebody's head – somebody's flipping uniform with a name tag on – then it kind of hits home. You've got to put a name to it, you've got to write a report at the end of the day.'

One time, Michael was blown off his feet by a mine triggered by a Viking, one of the tracked armoured vehicles used by Royal Marines. As his hearing returned and he began to hear muffled screams, he thought he could feel his own blood on his combats – then realised it was hot oil spattered by the blast. A Marine squirted water into his eyes to wash away the oil and bring him round, shouting: 'You're all right, you're not bleeding.'

'It got to the point where we were scared to go back on the ground because every time something happens,' he said. 'We lost three engineers on that tour – they got blown up, basically had their bones turned into gravel. It was like losing close friends all the time.'

When Michael returned from his first tour of Afghanistan, he was diagnosed with depression and prescribed tablets. After his second tour, he was barely able to cope. He drank heavily and in November 2011 he was treated at a medical centre in Bulford in Wiltshire after badly hurting his back on a training run. The injury served as a trigger for a psychological collapse and he was diagnosed with PTSD. Michael was given EMDR (eye movement desensitisation and reprocessing), a technique that could sometimes yield near miraculous results, but in his case the sessions made him feel worse. Scenes from Afghanistan would return so vividly as he drove home that he would be unable to remember how he had arrived at his front door.

'I took the lid off the box – uncontrollable shaking, fear,

nightmares, crying, anger, flashbacks, hyper-vigilance – just everything flipping hit us in one go,' Michael said.

'I went from being relatively unwell to being extremely ill. I'd come home, open a bottle of wine, then cry for three or four hours, then square myself away before Karen came in from work – pretend I was all right.'

Like many military spouses, Karen initially found it difficult to grasp the gravity of Michael's situation, until his symptoms became impossible to hide. One day he was sitting on the back doorstep, smoking a cigarette, when she brushed against his back.

He said: 'I had some sort of mini-flashback. I turned round to Karen and said: "Don't ever do that again."'

Later, he reasoned that the sensation had evoked his days bursting through doorways in Iraq, where his team might sometimes communicate by touch. Karen caught another glimpse of his distress when they went for a walk on a wild stretch of shore. Michael found himself compulsively scanning the treeline for gunmen and the ground for hidden bombs. By the time they reached the car he was trembling, seemingly unaware that he was standing in a car park on the Lincolnshire coast.

One day, Karen called him from work to check he was OK.

'I said: "Yes, I'm all right. Gaz is here." She knows Gaz is dead. She was just like: "What?" I said: "I'm all right, I'm with Gaz." She got panicked and drove home and came back to find me with a carving knife in my hand, lying prone on the ground, crawling across the sitting-room floor, prodding my way through a minefield.

'What I remember is looking up and seeing my wife, and she's in complete shock shouting at us: "What are you doing?" She thought I was going to kill her.'

Michael had never threatened or harmed his wife in any way, but she worried about leaving him alone in case he tried to kill himself.

'She was scared to be in the house with us because she didn't know what I was going to do,' he said.

Both felt his regiment had handled him badly. Michael said that he received his first welfare visit eight months after he was diagnosed and that some in his chain of command seemed dismissive of his problems. Karen wrote a detailed complaint to his commanding officer. Michael showed me a copy of the correspondence: the officer had written back to apologise over their 'appalling treatment'.

'Nobody from my unit speaks to me now,' Michael said. 'They think I'm a failure. People would discuss it in the Sergeants' Mess: "He's off work, he says he's got PTSD, he's just weak blah, blah, blah." Comments on Facebook, things like that. That's people's perception of PTSD.'

He bitterly recalled a conversation he had had with a sergeant major from another regiment: 'Clearly, he didn't know I was suffering from PTSD. He said: "We've got nearly a full platoon of weak people who say they've got PTSD – they need to man up and get on with the job."'

As the day of Michael's medical discharge approached, he wondered whether he might find work on a North Sea oil rig, a popular option for some ex-forces, but he feared his mental health problems would prevent him obtaining the requisite insurance. He had considered resuming his career as a butcher, but a doctor had advised him to think carefully.

'With the blood and guts and meat, they think it might trigger something.'

It was dark by the time we finished talking, and Michael drove me back across the Lincolnshire flatlands so I could catch my train. I had been keen to visit him again, but long periods passed with my texts or emails going unanswered – a common occurrence among many of those I interviewed who were still battling with their symptoms. It was more than a year before he emailed to suggest another meeting.

Michael came to collect me from the station driving a new vehicle: a white van emblazoned with a logo of a blue flame. He wore a grey fleece and many-pocketed trousers – the uniform of his new trade as a self-employed gas fitter. The haunted look he had worn when we first met had lifted, though it was clear his battle was not yet won. When we went into a cafe, there was a slight tremor in his hand as he spooned sugar lumps into his tea.

In some respects, Michael had been fortunate. Unlike ex-forces who had struggled for months or years to find help on the NHS, he had been quickly referred to an experienced therapist, who took the EMDR process more gently. The therapist had suggested that he assemble a grab bag of calming images for use in emergencies. Michael had placed a picture of his cat Walter in a ziplock bag, accompanied by a tartan handkerchief scented with Karen's perfume. He kept his 'trauma kit' tucked under the sun visor in his van.

Though he was doing better, Michael still felt sad at the attitude shown by some of his former colleagues.

'You're called "weak". You're told "man up". People ignore you, avoid you,' he said. 'I've always got the impression that the Army knows there's a problem but doesn't want to admit the size of the problem.'

At his house, Michael produced a handful of photos from his study. One showed him standing in a row of soldiers posing smartly in front of the sleek fuselage of an Apache helicopter, its rotor blades drooping. Michael wore stubble, dark glasses, and cradled a rifle with a tanned forearm. The sun was so high there are virtually no shadows – the picture seems to radiate desert heat. Though Michael was still angry with the Army, he also grieved for his lost hope of serving a full twenty-two years. The photo evoked a touch of nostalgia, and the image of his younger self made him smile.

A few weeks later, Karen emailed to explain that Michael had taken a turn for the worse after his compensation claim was finalised, based on a directive saying he could be expected to make a substantial recovery within five years. Michael felt the time frame was unrealistic and the award did not come close to reflecting the full extent of the psychological injuries he had suffered.

Karen wrote: 'We just wanted you to be aware of this outcome as it now truly exhausts our personal attempts to challenge the military's neglect of duty with regards to Michael's welfare.' She said Michael had been admitted to a psychiatric ward overnight as he was deemed to be a suicide risk.

Michael wrote back some time later to say he was in better spirits, and he wanted his story to be told. His goal, like so many of the ex-forces who spoke to me, was to help others realise they were not alone.

The common factor in all these stories is that people felt the Army had failed to take their suffering seriously enough. Though attitudes had evolved considerably since the days of 'shell shock' or 'Lack of Moral Fibre', they had still not reached the point where mental health problems were universally regarded as legitimate conditions. The climate of opinion was shifting, but too slowly. James Forrester had been serving on his second tour of Afghanistan when Aaron Black and James Lindsay had taken their lives in the weeks either side of Christmas 2011. Not long afterwards, he said a senior non-commissioned officer had gathered three platoons into a patrol base for a talk.

'He called everybody over and gave a brief about how PTSD doesn't exist, and you can overcome it with sheer willpower, things like that,' James said.

Several officers had stood and watched, arms folded, nodding in agreement. James went on: 'I was thinking I wanted to go and punch him right in the face. I was going to say: "So you're telling me after all the years of trying to break down the stigma, you've just reinforced it in one sentence?"

'I was actually raging. He pretty much said that it's all in your head, that if you've got enough willpower you can overcome it, all this kind of stuff. That annoyed me. That's why I know that when there's guys like that in positions of responsibility, nothing will change.'

Despite such incidents, it was also clear that the years of hard fighting in Afghanistan were having an impact on attitudes throughout the chain of command. Captain Rob Colquhoun, who had commanded James Forrester and Aaron Black in Afghanistan while still a lieutenant, said that young, less-experienced privates might seem outwardly dismissive of the likelihood of suffering from PTSD. Nevertheless, anybody who had fought in Afghanistan would have since heard of somebody affected.

'There's a fatalistic hubris amongst young soldiers – no one believes it will happen to them and instinctively won't admit it if it does,' Colquhoun said. 'But the widespread education of recent years has led to an awareness of what to look for in yourself and others and this has helped to remove the stigma. It hasn't gone completely but we have made significant progress.'

When the procurator fiscal began looking into Aaron's death, the military launched its own inquiry, conducted by the Defence Inquests Unit. It concluded that Aaron had been offered fourteen appointments with a community psychiatric nurse in the seven months before he left but had attended only five. It had been unable to confirm whether or not the Black Watch had placed Aaron on a suicide risk vulnerability register the Army maintains for soldiers who may be in distress. However, Aaron had been seen regularly by a captain serving as the Black Watch welfare officer. Shortly before he left the Army, Aaron had told one of the nurses that he did not feel he needed any further treatment. He was concerned that engaging with mental health services would harm his prospects of working in the private security industry.

10

'Veterans Champions'

The NHS on a war footing

Hilary Horton knew just the place for us to meet: the Royal Air Force Club, a private member's club in Mayfair. A plush sanctuary for retired flying officers, its corridors are decorated with oil paintings of Lancaster bombers, Spitfires and Tornados. I should perhaps have anticipated the dress code, and felt the weight of disdainful eyes as I crossed the carpet wearing a leather jacket. A waitress told me I would be allowed to stay provided I did not take it off. Hilary had chosen a discreet spot in a corner of the Cowdray Room lounge by a window overlooking Green Park. She had no time for stuffiness and violated a rule banning talking on mobile phones with abandon.

Unlike many of the ex-forces I met, Hilary had entertained no childhood ambitions to join the military. A carefree, tearaway teenager with big hair, she had grown up on a council estate in Basildon and managed to talk her way into a job as a trainee nurse at the age of eighteen, while still moonlighting as a go-go dancer. She spent more than twenty-five years in the NHS, working in senior clinical leadership roles and later serving as the head of women's health in the prison system. Hilary's journey to Iraq began when an NHS physician who served as an air commander in the reserves invited her to visit RAF Lyneham in Wiltshire. Hilary, whose marriage was breaking down, was looking for new horizons. Though she was not a natural candidate for military discipline, her colleagues soon learned to respect her no-nonsense medical professionalism and she rose to the rank of squadron leader.

When the Armed Forces mobilised ahead of the Iraq invasion in 2003, Hilary was stationed at RAF Brize Norton in Oxfordshire, where she organised the transfer of casualties to NHS hospitals. She was soon asked if she would be willing to deploy to a small British base at Al Amarah to run a medical outpost. Hilary jumped at the chance.

As the deployment date neared, the words of the sergeant who put her through her paces with a handgun acquired a new edge: 'Ma'am you've got to get it through your thick fucking skull that these men don't care about "nursey nursey". They want to rape you over and over and split you in pieces. So you won't hesitate to use this weapon.'

Hilary never had to use the gun, but when she came home from Iraq, she put her not-quite-right feeling down to fatigue. Like the other returnees, she had been debriefed by a mental health team before boarding her flight. One of them had asked if she had seen anything out of the ordinary. 'No, nothing in particular,' she had lied, anxious to see her three sons. Back at RAF Lyneham, Hilary had told one of her superiors that she was feeling a little odd. She recalled the response: 'Don't be daft, Horton, you're as tough as old boots. Time will heal. All you need is to get back to your family and you'll be fine.'

Five years later, Hilary found a job as an occupational health manager at a railway company in Crewe. When a welder working on a nearby line suffered a flash burn to his eye, his colleagues brought him to Hilary. She was not employed to treat injuries, but she instinctively flipped into nurse mode, reassuring the patient and rolling up his sleeve to take his blood pressure. It was then that she saw the welder's Celtic tattoo.

When Hilary looked down, she was no longer wearing a pinstripe suit – she was clad in desert-pattern fatigues and combat boots. A wave of suffocating heat engulfed her and she began to sweat. She could smell cordite and hear the roar of Chinooks. Then she noticed her combat boots were stained scarlet. She was standing in a spreading pool of blood.

'Are you all right, Hilary?' somebody asked.

'I'm going to have to go,' she replied. 'Got to sort the nurses out.'

'What? What are you talking about?'

Hilary dashed to the bathroom and barged into a toilet cubicle, where she slid down to the floor, sweating. And as she stared into space a film began to play – a film she had no choice but to watch. Hilary was back in the field hospital in Al Amarah. A Land Rover had just pulled up to a kitchen area that served as a makeshift staffroom and storage area.

'Ma'am!' a soldier shouted. 'The bodies are here.'

Hilary stepped into the kitchen. The contents of the Land Rover were lying on the white-tiled floor.

The sound of knocking brought Hilary back from Al Amarah to the cubicle. A doctor had come to check on her. He was a former Army officer and said he thought she might have a touch of PTSD. Hilary was annoyed at the very idea.

'You're just tired,' she told herself. 'You've just been working too hard.'

She drove home and poured herself a whisky.

Of the hundreds of service personnel who are treated for mental health problems every year, the military says it helps about 60 per cent to recover and continue with their careers, while the rest are liable to be medically discharged. The upshot is that about 200 people leave the forces each year due to mental health or behavioural problems, while many others may be discharged primarily due to a physical injury but also carry a psychological wound. Responsibility for their care reverts to the NHS. The health service, created in 1948, was largely a product of social and political changes unleashed by the Second World War. As the impact of a decade of intense operations in Iraq and Afghanistan reverberates across Britain, the organisation will be at the fore-front in dealing with the fallout.

As I crossed the country the newspapers were full of stories about the enormous pressure the NHS is under: accident and emergency units in crisis, costs running out of control and mental health services frequently overwhelmed. It was perhaps no won-der, then, that many military families felt betrayed. Some of the most heartfelt complaints came from partners (sometimes known in the Army as S.W.A.G. – Soldiers' Wives and Girlfriends), who often played a vital role in steering their husbands through the healthcare system. The following comments were gathered by Combat PTSD Angels, a Liverpool-based support group:

- Phoned 999 for emergency help on New Year's Eve when my partner pinned me down due to the fireworks taking him back into combat and was told they couldn't help as it wasn't life threatening and for me to drive him to A & E.
- First and last trip to GP was told: 'There's no such thing as PTSD, it's work related stress – he needed to relax more.' Won't seek help from anyone else now.
- Husband mentioned got PTSD, GP reply: 'It's all in your head.'
- 'We don't know much about PTSD, never mind combat PTSD. How do you think we can help you?' – soul destroying 'you're stuffed' comment from a community psychiatric nurse.
- 'Why haven't the Army done anything for him?' [says] just about every NHS doctor we have seen. Answer is: 'He was discharged over 15 years ago. We have no contact with the Army.'

The NHS is increasingly alive to such concerns. In 2010, the government commissioned a report into military mental health by Dr Andrew Murrison, a Conservative MP and former Royal Navy medical officer. In response to his recommendations, and building on an earlier pilot project, it allocated £1.5 million per year over four years to pay for a network of 'veterans champions' across England, comprised of clinicians or medical managers who either had served or were familiar with military culture. Their role was to support GPs to ensure ex-forces received the right kind of help, or in some cases to provide treatment themselves. The NHS had also worked with the Scottish and Welsh governments to set up specialist services, including Veterans First Point, based in Edinburgh, and Veterans' NHS Wales, based in Cardiff. I met several ex-forces who were happy with their treatment, but as managers freely admitted, it was hard to know how many had yet to reach out for help, making it difficult to plan sustainable services.

'There's an awful lot of support available, but for whatever reason we need to be able to engage better with ex-forces to ensure they are actually managing to access it,' said Wayne Kirkham, national lead for the Veterans Mental Health Network for NHS England.

After years in the services, personnel were often not registered with a civilian GP, and military medical records had a habit of going astray. Although the MoD had taken steps to streamline the transfer of such notes to GPs, it was still up to ex-forces to register at their local surgery, and many did not. The MoD had further sought to soften the abrupt switch between the military and civilian health systems by introducing a new rule allowing service leavers to continue attending their DCMH for a further six months after discharge. It also offered mental health assessments to veterans who had deployed since 1982 at the DCMH at Chilwell near Nottingham. The service was equally open to reservists, who had been shown to suffer higher rates of PTSD than peers in the regular military, probably because of the additional pressures of oscillating rapidly between war zones and their homes without the all-encompassing support of full-time forces life.

But as the military well knew, it was far from easy to persuade those suffering from psychological scars to come forward. After years of immersion in a macho military culture, many were loath to confess their problems to a civilian doctor. Some even fretted that they might be in breach of the Official Secrets Act if they spoke about their problems, especially those who participated in murkier episodes in Northern Ireland. This was a myth – there was nothing to stop ex-forces talking about their traumatic experiences provided they did not touch on classified security information. They were, however, sometimes correct in assuming that an overworked GP might not have time to build the level of trust they would need before sharing their worst experiences.

Among those who had found it difficult to open up to his doctor was Jason Burns, a former sergeant major in the Royal Marines, who had suffered depression and anxiety after leaving the forces following a twenty-six-year career. I visited Jason and his wife Andrea at their home in South Shields. Andrea said Jason had found it difficult to be open about his problems with NHS staff. 'They didn't understand, he was embarrassed to explain,' she said. 'He sees it as a failure, because a Marine definitely doesn't get depressed.'

More than a year later Jason emailed me and told me he had since been diagnosed with PTSD. He said he had spent more than twelve months trying to find help through the NHS, but the complexity of his symptoms had defeated medical staff. He had found more support at Phoenix House Recovery Centre at Catterick Garrison. The modern residential building is one of four similar centres across Britain that form the backbone of the MoD's Defence Recovery Capability, set up to improve the facilities on offer for the influx of wounded service personnel from Afghanistan and Iraq with the support of Help for Heroes and the Royal British Legion.

'I'm somehow staying alive due to the dedicated, unwavering love of my wife, children and family,' Jason wrote. 'I feel let down by the NHS system where some work is needed in making them "veteran aware". I know I am not alone.'

For somebody suffering from the hyper-vigilance and anxiety characteristic of PTSD, simply summoning the courage to get on a bus to the nearest surgery and then sit in a waiting room packed with strangers can make visiting a GP an excruciating ordeal. A disappointing first encounter can be devastating as it only takes one bad experience to discourage a former soldier from ever coming back. I heard of one who turned around and walked out of a surgery because his appointment was ten minutes late – he interpreted the breach of punctuality, prized in the military, as a personal insult. Such mishaps are often compounded by the cultural gulf that can separate soldiers from NHS staff. One woman despaired at the attitude shown at a psychiatric unit, where her spouse had casually been asked: 'So how are you feeling about the war and killings and stuff?' Another woman called Faye, who I met in the reception area at Combat Stress, said the diazepam a NHS doctor had prescribed her husband had aggravated his PTSD symptoms, making him angry and abusive. 'I had one week of Hell,' Faye told me, as she waited for her husband to emerge from an assessment. 'That's a perfect example – the NHS has no idea.'

Doctors with little experience of the military face another potential pitfall: the task of spotting a small number of impostors who pose as ex-forces or embroider their experiences in the hope of winning greater sympathy. Peter McAllister, a former Army chief psychiatrist, offered the following advice for GPs at a conference: genuine soldiers will instantly be able to reel off their service numbers, drummed into them from their days as a recruit. A study published in 2012 concluded that 10 per cent of 150 veterans referred to an MoD clinic had fabricated or significantly exaggerated their accounts of traumatic experiences. In some cases, this can happen when an ex-serviceman genuinely needs support, but fears that an ordeal such as being shot at might not qualify as 'traumatic' enough to be taken seriously.

Assuming a struggling former soldier manages to cross all these hurdles and speaks openly, doctors often lack the experience to help. The NHS has not traditionally placed much emphasis on trauma treatments, with psychiatric services more geared towards severe, enduring mental illnesses such as schizophrenia, bipolar affective disorder, depression or obsessive compulsive disorder, and clinicians often miss a trauma history altogether. Clinical psychologists responsible for dealing with PTSD may have treated survivors of childhood abuse or sexual assault, but have little experience of the particular varieties of gruesomeness that occur in war zones. Conversely, there is also a danger that some doctors might sprinkle PTSD diagnoses too liberally when patients believe the label confers a greater legitimacy on their distress.

'It's almost a little bit like the argument we have had on antibiotics – everybody prescribes it and then the public ask for it when actually they've got a virus,' said one NHS manager. 'People get very defensive if you don't give them the diagnosis of PTSD. Turn around and say: "I had temporary onset psychosis," then everyone assumes you are mad. Turn around and say: "I had PTSD," people assume you have seen some horrible things because you served.'

For genuine cases, GPs might not be able to do much more than put a former serviceman or woman on a waiting list for CBT, which may not be of much help for ex-forces with a trauma history spanning many years. The problems faced by a man I will call Steve Townsend, a former Special Forces soldier, illustrates precisely the kind of hurdles that many ex-forces face. Steve said his first disappointment came when he told his doctor his PTSD symptoms were becoming so hard to bear that he had begun saving up his medication so he could take a fatal overdose.

Steve said: 'I explained this to the GP, who basically shrugged his shoulders and said "not sure what I else I can do for you".'

At this point, many ex-forces would have given up – especially those who do not have a friend or relative to act as their advocate with the medical bureaucracy. Steve persisted, largely for the sake of his wife, and was eventually referred to a young woman psychologist who began a course of CBT.

'There were things that I desperately wanted to talk about with somebody who had an understanding of where I was coming from,' Steve said. 'I looked at this woman and thought: "There's no way this is going to work."'

Steve stuck with the therapy for more than a dozen sessions but his symptoms persisted. He was eventually referred to Dr Alastair Hull, who ran an NHS traumatic stress clinic in Perth and is one of Britain's leading specialists in treating PTSD. Hull said many other veterans do not show Steve's persistence, however, tiring of having to repeat their stories at seemingly endless rounds of assessments.

'I came to the conclusion that the people who managed to get to me did it either because they had a very persistent sponsor who was sailing them through the hoops or it was serendipity,' Hull said.

For those ex-forces whose flashbacks are so acute that they might pose a danger to themselves or others, the NHS has little to offer apart from admission to a secure psychiatric ward alongside people suffering from severe disorders – itself a potentially traumatic experience. The role of such units is to provide a place of safety, not to treat trauma. Often the best a veteran in the midst of a crisis can hope for is to be sedated until they are stable enough to be discharged and then once more seek help from their GP.

While many ex-forces and their families I met felt badly served, it was also clear that there were a number of psychiatrists, doctors and managers working hard to improve their services. In the north-west of England, for example, the NHS commissioned a specialist psychotherapy service for veterans, starting in July 2015 after a successful four-year pilot by the Pennine Care NHS Foundation Trust, based in Greater Manchester. The trust had sought to encourage ex-forces to come forward by sponsoring the production of a film called *Unload*, which tells the fictional story of 'Eddie', a former soldier undergoing therapy for PTSD. Mersey Care in Liverpool had taken steps to make emergency psychiatric admissions more comfortable – including switching to plastic refuse containers to spare ex-forces the clatter of dustbin lids that might trigger flashbacks to Northern Ireland, where the sound was used on Republican estates to warn of the arrival of British troops. At the South Staffordshire and Shropshire Healthcare NHS Foundation Trust, which handles the contract for in-patient psychiatry for the military, managers had produced a veterans' mental health app featuring video interviews with ex-forces who had made successful recoveries – including Hilary Horton.

Though it took time for her to find the right help, Hilary would ultimately experience the NHS at its best. As we talked at the RAF Club in Piccadilly, she told me more about her journey home from Iraq – a journey that is still only partially complete.

In the early days of the invasion, the British base at Al Amarah was not a particularly welcoming place. Hilary recalled how the Camp Officer had greeted her with casual hostility: 'Oh, the RAF is here – we'll have to get covers for the toilets and serve afternoon tea.' She pointed out the tents and the toilet blocks and told Hilary: 'You'll get diarrhoea like everybody else.'

Hilary took charge of a makeshift hospital with a team of fifteen nurses. They converted a white-tiled kitchen area with shower stalls and drainage gullies into a staffroom, where they would store medical supplies and nurses would tidy their hair between shifts. The hospital served as a staging post for treating minor injuries or stabilising casualties to be flown by Chinook or driven to the main British base in Basra. As desert temperatures soared,

Hilary treated heatstroke, sexual health problems aggravated by the unsanitary conditions of the camp, or counselled homesick soldiers. The men went on patrol in soft caps, still hoping to play a policing role. It did not yet feel like a war.

Hilary rarely had a chance to leave the base, but some days she would hop in a Land Rover with the troops to buy big blocks of ice they used to make ice packs for patients, or chill fruit and cans of Coke. On one of these expeditions Hilary was chatting to some locals when one of them reached out towards her neck. A corporal shot out his arm to hold the man back. Hilary was incensed: the Iraqi had been innocently gesturing at a tiny cross she wore – as if to acknowledge they were both God-fearing people. She fumed during the drive back to camp, though she knew deep down that the corporal had only been trying to protect her.

On another ice-buying mission, Hilary's Land Rover ran into a makeshift roadblock manned by a tense group of militiamen. Hilary and four of her colleagues began talking to the gunmen, trying to calm them. Then she heard a soldier step out of the Land Rover behind her and there was a ripple of clunk-clicks as the men at the roadblock cocked their weapons. For a few seconds Hilary thought they were about to start shooting.

The hospital could not remain insulated from the tensions building in southern Iraq for long. One day, Hilary treated an Iraqi interpreter, beaten almost to death for helping the British. She had sought to shield the man behind a curtain but word reached the ward and patients began to shout: 'Ma'am, you got a rag-head in there? You got a rag-head?' The interpreter pleaded with big brown eyes. Hilary spent much of the night nursing him before he was sent to Basra. She never found out if he survived.

On Tuesday 24 June, Hilary arrived at the hospital early to find the nurses abuzz: the hospital had finally acquired a stable electricity supply. Lights flickered into life and fans whirred. She made an upbeat note in her journal about 'The Day the

Electricity Arrived' but as the sun climbed above the desert, an unusually large number of British casualties was brought in. There were gunshot wounds, screams. A sergeant approached Hilary.

'Ma'am, you're getting six bodies. We want them processed, we want them moved out. You've got a window of two hours.'

'What do you mean *six*?' Hilary asked. 'Where have they come from?'

'Military Police,' the sergeant said. 'They've just been killed. You've got to deal with them.'

Soon Hilary saw a Land Rover driving with unusual haste up the long, straight road that led to the hospital.

She told me: 'I thought: "these are the bodies coming". I watched it, it slowed a bit, came near, and then it went to the back. I said to the nurses: "You guys stay here, let's get ready. I will go and assess."

'I just heard this voice shout: "Right, ma'am, the bodies are here." And before I could blink the Landie's disappeared. And I see all the blood in the back of it. In fact it was dripping as it left.

'I went into the kitchen. There I stood. I can smell it and see it now.'

Hilary paused, and her gaze drifted through the sash window, across Piccadilly and over to the chestnut trees in Green Park.

'In nursing, I always thought that blood clotted,' Hilary said. 'But there were rivers of it. I remember that question in my head: "How come this isn't clotting?" There was this red, just flowing in the heat.'

The six men had been trapped at a police station when it was attacked by an enraged crowd. They had no personal radios and had been unable to call for help. Eventually gunmen had entered the building and shot them multiple times at close range, leaving them with horrific injuries. Every detail of the murdered men remains engraved on Hilary's mind.

'My first thought was I can't let the nurses see this. So on my own I moved all of the bodies. I couldn't bear anybody else to see the indignity of it.

'I don't know what happened. All of a sudden I just had this robotic strength: I'm going to lay them all out, I'm going to put them all in a straight line, and we're going to do this properly. And the nurses were banging on the door.'

As she worked, Hilary spoke soothing words, reassuring the men that she would do her best for them.

'I sent over a message that there's no way this is going to be done in two hours – these men deserve more than this. I'm a hospital nurse, and patients are sacrosanct. They're everything to you. And these beautiful men – I remember all their names, even now.'

When she admitted her colleagues to the room, Hilary noticed one of the nurses could not bear to look and was washing one of the men with her eyes closed. She took her off the duty. Another woman gave a scream of such desolation that Hilary could still hear it clearly as we sat in the Cowdray Room, taking our tea. After the job was done, Hilary felt disconsolate and angry – upset as much by the abruptness with which such tasks had to be performed in a war zone as by the terrible wounds she had seen. As the tour progressed, questions kept returning that her mind could not resolve.

How come the men weren't saved from the crowd at the police station? How come I was left to look after the dead?

And an answer began to coalesce: *They must think I'm not a good enough nurse.*

Hilary had been divorced before she deployed to Iraq. When she returned to her home in Stafford, she pushed her new partner away. A sense of guilt would intrude whenever she felt the stirring of desire and a leaden, unnamed sense of failure cast a shadow over her days. Her relationship ended, but she continued to work and see her sons. For her fiftieth birthday, they organised a canal trip with champagne. Hilary reflected on what a full life she had lived, and told them that when her time came, under no circumstances should they mourn. She was able to maintain her outward show of normality until the day she glimpsed the Celtic tattoo and the partition between past and present dissolved.

'Nothing happened for a while,' Hilary said. 'I kind of brushed it off as just a one-off. Then it happened again. And again and again, and in the end the film was nearly every day.'

Sometimes the dead men would visit Hilary at work. She would silently plead with them to leave, promising to watch the film as soon as she returned home. If she was reprimanding a subordinate, they would admonish her, saying: *That's not the way. You're kind. You've always been good to us, come on – this isn't you.* At night, the six would crowd into her room. In the morning, she would wake to find them lying in her bed. She began a daily ritual of reciting their names.

Hilary said: 'I'd be talking to them, saying: "Hello, what a shit day I've had – if there was any way I could bring you back, I would." When the film ended, I was always crying – really, really crying. Sometimes angry crying, sometimes just sadness.'

One night she was at the theatre in Birmingham when she was gripped by panic: she could not remember one of the names. Hilary had to make an excuse and rush home to look it up. She began to withdraw from friends, unable to reconcile the life of the living with the company of the dead.

'The minute there was any kind of emotion demanded of me, it would destroy it. I've got to go, got to watch the film – it's part of my life now.'

When she was a child, Hilary's father had taken her swimming in rivers or in the waves at Clacton-on-Sea. In later life, Hilary returned to the water alone, seeking solace in dawn dives into the Blackwater, Derwent, Dart and Lune. The icy jolt of the water made her feel alive and she savoured the magic of a swan gliding past through the early-morning mist. But the men would follow her into her sanctuary – their shades hovering over the surface.

The visitations seemed to exhume older images that Hilary had buried many years before. Once, when she had worked as an Intensive Care sister, an abused child had been brought into the ward with horrific injuries and burns.

'I remember looking at this child and thinking: "You are so wounded and so injured I want you to die,"' Hilary said. 'I was ashamed of these thoughts. He did die, that child.'

In her visions, the child returned. Memories bobbed up, too, of Hilary's years working in prisons. She remembered a time in her early days on the job when a teenager had been found hanged in a cell. She had rigged up a noose with her bra.

'The images were sometimes out of control – would make me completely not myself, not able to function. I couldn't drive sometimes for seeing dead all over the place,' Hilary said. 'I knew after a couple of years this was serious, I knew something terrible was happening to me.'

Hilary eventually decided she had to tell someone.

'I went to my doctor and said: "I think I'm suffering." I was off for about four weeks from work. If I could just take some space, I thought, take a break, I'll be all right.'

The doctor referred Hilary to an NHS psychiatric nurse. Hilary remembers her as a 'lovely, rosy, plump' woman, but she began to censor herself when she realised the nurse was overwhelmed by her story – such self-censorship being a common pattern among ex-forces.

'She couldn't deal with this military stuff, she was horrified,' Hilary said, with a wry smile. 'I told her I was better.'

The nurse did offer one helpful insight, however: she told Hilary the six were not hers to mourn. She suggested Hilary take six balloons, write one of their names on each, and release them. Hilary performed the ritual on a hillside in Wiltshire. She said a prayer, watched the balloons float away and bade them farewell.

Hilary gave another sad smile.

'It wasn't long before they were back in the bedroom again.'

One day, Hilary's job as an occupational health nurse took her to a pizza company in Lincolnshire. She left its premises at about six o'clock in the evening.

'Next thing I knew, there was a policeman in Iraq with me. I said to him: "What are you doing here?" He said: "What?"'

'"How have you come out to Iraq in that uniform?"'

'He said: "Are you all right, madam? We've driven past here several times, and you've been crying."'

'I said: "You need to get out of here."'

It was ten past one in the morning and Hilary was parked by the side of a field. She had spent seven hours trapped in the film. A few months later Hilary left her house to catch a train to make a presentation to a potential client.

'I remember leaving the house. The next thing I was sitting in a park in Stafford, a taxi driver saying: "Are you all right, you've been here a while now."'

'That was it then. I knew it was over. It was about ten o'clock. Should have been on the train. My car was in the station car park. I don't remember walking to the park. I do remember seeing the film, again and again.'

Hilary had been too scared to turn away.

'If you stop watching it, something bad will happen,' Hilary told me. 'You've got to watch it to the end.'

Hilary returned to her GP and he referred her to the local community mental health service, where one of the NHS 'veterans champions' sent her to see Dr Shirley Timson, a consultant psychologist at St George's Hospital in Stafford who specialised in helping ex-forces.

After an initial assessment, Timson led Hilary into a room and asked her to sit down opposite a row of lights used for sessions of EMDR. The bulbs began to flash in sequence and Timson told Hilary to follow the trail with her eyes as she led her step by step through her ordeal in the white-tiled kitchen. Hilary laughed and joked but deep down she felt ashamed and afraid.

'The first two or three were exhausting,' Hilary said. 'When I got back to the house, I'd lay on the couch – often just drift into a sleep.'

At the start of the therapy, as can happen to people undergoing EMDR, the flashbacks began to intensify as memories Hilary had suppressed in Al Amarah returned. The six, normally full of affection, spoke to Hilary in harsh tones, and began to demand: *Why are you leaving us?* Hilary worried the treatment was making her worse.

While the precise way in which EMDR works remains a mystery, Hilary gradually felt a shift. Something about the combination of the bilateral stimulation of the brain caused by the flashing lights and Timson's gentle coaxing began to help Hilary consolidate the fragmented images, sounds and smells from the kitchen into a coherent story and release the frozen vestiges of fear and sadness. Her sense of failure began to abate and her compulsive questions about why the men could not have been saved were tempered by a new realisation that perhaps there were no answers. The six visited less often, until eventually they seldom troubled Hilary at all.

By the time I met Hilary at the RAF Club, she was living an outwardly normal life. She still recited the names of the men each day – and sometimes visited the National Memorial Arboretum near her home in Staffordshire, tracing out the letters of their names carved in the stone. No longer haunted, Hilary nevertheless felt a lingering numbness – 'not 100 per cent part of society' as she put it. She had dabbled with dating websites, but was always worried she would have to tell the story of the six. Perhaps, she wondered, living a life with meaning was more important than the pursuit of pleasure.

'I keep thinking I might meet the man of my dreams, I don't know. I don't know if I'd recognise him if I saw him,' Hilary laughed, as we finished our tea and she disappeared into the Mayfair rush hour, en route to visit one of her sons.

11

The Pinball Machine

Into the maze of military charities

Combat Stress occupies a converted country house and adjoining complex of modern buildings outside the town of Leatherhead in Surrey. The building, known as Tyrwhitt House, has a smart, businesslike feel. Copies of an in-house newsletter placed on a coffee table in reception featured inspiring stories of beneficiaries, including a veteran of the Falklands War who had survived the firestorm that engulfed the *Sir Galahad*. Although I was unable to speak to clients undergoing therapy at Combat Stress, a media officer arranged for me to meet a soft-spoken art therapist named Jan Lobban, who had been working at the charity for twelve years and had laid out some of the hundreds of paintings and sketches produced during her sessions.

The first, called *Prisoner of Time*, featured a wooden mannequin painted blue and draped with melted clocks – reminiscent of the surrealism of Salvador Dalí. Lobban said the imagery evoked the soldier's sense of still being trapped during his tours in Northern Ireland in the late 1960s and early 1970s.

'One of key things about PTSD is that it doesn't fade with time,' Lobban said. 'The memories get stuck. Rather than being stored in words and understanding, they're stored as physical sensations and emotions. In this image, he's saying how part of his life is very frozen.'

Another participant had filled a page with an outline of a

keyhole. Symbols of everything he valued – people, mountains, a palm-fringed beach – were visible through the aperture but out of reach. Sculptures and models stood on another table. One man had fashioned a prison cell from a shoebox, then placed a clay figurine inside – shackled to the wall with string. Next to the cardboard dungeon lay an even more formidable container: a black box bristling with spikes. Lifting the lid, the viewer discovered a smaller box hidden inside and wrapped so tightly with twine it would be impossible to open.

'Often they describe being two people,' Lobban said. One of these personalities is typically cut off from their feelings. This is the part of a man's mind that harbours guilt, say, for feeling so numbed that he barely reacts when his mother dies. The other persona is buried deeper – and full of rage. Lobban gestured to a sculpture of a prisoner squashed into a tiny cage and groping a hand through the bars.

'If they open Pandora's box what's going to come out?' she said. 'Will they be overwhelmed or will they contain it?'

In reception, a more conventional piece of art was on display – a portrait of Sir Reginald Tyrwhitt, a patrician-looking First World War admiral who later served as one of the charity's most distinguished presidents. Medals jostled for space on his chest and his white glove was clasped over the hilt of a downturned sword.

Since the Armistice in 1918, the British state has left much of the care of former soldiers, sailors and airmen to charity. The poppy appeal, which today raises more than £40 million a year, was launched to support veterans facing hardship and handicap during a post-war recession. Public concern over the lasting impact of 'shell shock' also spurred the creation of a lesser-known charitable enterprise, the Ex-Services Mental Welfare Society, first established in Putney by a group of well-to-do women. Though the Society was founded to provide lifelong support in recognition that broken soldiers may never fully recover, its patrons placed much faith in vocational rehabilitation – a forerunner of occupational therapy – and before long the charity was a significant producer of electric blankets. In the late 1980s, the organisation came to be known as Combat Stress and it is Britain's biggest mental health charity for veterans.

In the last decades of the twentieth century, the core constituency of clients were men who had served in the Second World War, including a number subjected to the extreme privations of prisoner-of-war camps in the Far East. They were gradually supplanted by a younger generation bearing scars from Northern Ireland, the Falklands, Bosnia and other conflicts. Combat Stress welcomed these men year after year for residential stays funded by war pension payments. The admissions allowed them to reconnect with long-standing therapists and provided a few weeks of much-needed respite for their families. A degree of drinking was tolerated in local bars for many years and the smoking room was an incubator for the mix of military one-upmanship, incessant banter and halting confidences exchanged whenever old soldiers gather. For those ex-forces who could not open up easily to a civilian doctor, the quasi-military atmosphere rekindled a sense of belonging. Staff prided themselves on their pledge to deliver open-ended care to men who seemed beyond hope of making a full recovery.

By the time I paid my first of five visits in the summer of 2013, Combat Stress was in the throes of a revolution. With growing numbers of psychologically wounded soldiers returning from Afghanistan and Iraq, the charity had lobbied the government for millions of pounds to fund an ambitious new programme to treat PTSD. The financial injection meant that Combat Stress, though still 60-per-cent funded by charitable donations, had become a central pillar of the government's official strategy for tending to the invisible wounds of war. With the money came profound change.

Dr Walter Busuttil, a former RAF psychiatrist and Combat

Stress's director of medical services, had replaced the old model of lifelong support with a flagship six-week programme of intensive in-patient therapy designed to set beneficiaries on a path to lasting recovery. Gone were the days when men would keep coming back. The goal was to help them get well and stay well.

For Busuttil and the men he was treating, the stakes could not be higher. If his experiment worked, then he would save thousands of veterans bearing psychic wounds from Iraq and Afghanistan from the decades of suffering that had afflicted their predecessors. When I met Busuttil, his revolution was already well under way – and he believed that many had already reaped life-changing benefits. Yet in my travels around Britain, meeting mental health professionals, visiting smaller charities and attending conferences on veterans' issues, I met plenty of people who questioned whether the new regime was doing enough to help ex-forces with the worst cases of PTSD.

Busuttil was receptive to my plan to write about his work and granted me three hour-long interviews in his office at Tyrwhitt House. A model Spitfire, assembled and painted by one of the charity's beneficiaries, stood on a shelf and I spotted a copy of *A War of Nerves*, the study of military psychiatry by Ben Shephard, where I had learned about the work of Dr Charles Myers.

An unassuming physician who spoke with a consultant's precise tones, Busuttil had devoted much of his professional life to treating trauma. After joining the RAF at 21, he had served as a medical officer before qualifying as a consultant psychiatrist, specialising in PTSD. After a sixteen-year air-force career, he retired at the rank of wing commander, then worked for a decade in private hospitals with adult survivors of sexual abuse, before taking over at Combat Stress in 2007, where he became the organisation's first full-time clinician. I met a number of ex-forces and their partners who described him as a compassionate and skilled physician who had thrown their families a vital lifeline.

Busuttil explained that he had begun by looking abroad to see which models worked best for treating veterans with PTSD. While serving in the RAF, he had acted as an adviser to the Australian military when it was setting up a residential treatment programme and the outcomes had compared favourably with equivalent initiatives in Israel and the United States. Busuttil decided to reimport the Australian model to Britain and turn the thinking at Combat Stress upside down. Rather than offer the men regular periods of respite, Busuttil wanted to teach them to look after themselves.

The core of the model was based on delivering individual trauma-focused CBT in a series of one-on-one sessions, in parallel with group therapy. Although some therapists cast doubt on the efficacy of CBT for resolving entrenched trauma symptoms, Busuttil was confident the therapy was supported by a robust evidence base. The programme included workshops on anger and well-being and the occupational therapy used since the charity's inception. A parallel two-week version was launched for people who required a shorter burst of therapy.

'We had a philosophy before I arrived that: "Here you are, you're a veteran, we'll look after you for ever,"' Busuttil said. 'Many of the people who were getting stuck here were the illest people who couldn't or wouldn't do trauma therapy. The system colluded with them. The easiest thing to do with PTSD is: "Hi, let's have a cup of tea and talk about the football." As soon as you try to confront it, it's an issue.'

As his plans took shape, Busuttil began lobbying authorities for funds, anticipating that demand for clinical services would grow in the wake of the campaigns in Afghanistan and Iraq. Combat Stress also sought to raise the profile of military PTSD in the media and petitioned senior officers for support. Busuttil believed his approach would not only do a better job of helping men to get better, it would also be cost-effective – a key consideration for health service commissioners under pressure to save money.

'Government and NHS were very anti the funding of veterans,' Busuttil said. 'I don't think people realise the eyeball-to-eyeball fighting that's been going on in Afghanistan.'

As that fighting intensified, concerns over the potential for psychiatric fallout began to gain more attention. In February 2009, Johnson Beharry, then a lance corporal and the Army's most decorated serving soldier, launched a broadside against the government's response to PTSD in the military in a frank interview with the *Independent*. Beharry, who been awarded the Victoria Cross for repeatedly risking his life to save comrades under fire in Iraq, said he was still tormented by anguish, excruciating pain and nightmares more than four years later. Although he acknowledged receiving first-class care, he said it was 'disgraceful' that some ex-forces were struggling to find treatment for trauma, breakdown and depression. A further spotlight was thrown onto the issue by the publication the following year of the government-commissioned 'Fighting Fit' report recommending ways to bolster support.

In March 2011, Busuttil's lobbying paid off: the NHS awarded Combat Stress a special contract to fund the new six-week programme, which was launched at Tyrwhitt House in September then subsequently rolled out at the charity's two other centres – Audley Court in the Midlands and Hollybush House in Scotland. The influx of government funds, coupled with support from members of the public and corporate donors such as BAE Systems, a big player in the arms industry, fuelled an increase in income from £8.7 million when Busuttil took over to £17.4 million in 2014. Salaries also rose. The best-paid member of staff drew an annual salary of about £160,000, according to the charity's accounts – more than double the highest pay packet drawn prior to 2007. The organisation employed almost 180 key staff providing care across the country, including about forty psychologists and CBT therapists and seven consultant psychiatrists – more than the RAF.

The new team had its work cut out. When the six-week programme opened its doors, veterans of Northern Ireland still comprised the biggest single group of new clients – a stark reminder that it can often take more than a decade for ex-forces with PTSD to seek help. The charity has since seen a surge in enquiries from younger men who are coming forward much earlier. In the year to April 2015 the number of referrals rose by 26 per cent to 2,264 – most of them veterans of Afghanistan and Iraq.

I was keen to hear about the new treatments from the participants. Combat Stress told me it would try to find somebody to speak to me, but eighteen months after I made my request, reiterated on multiple occasions, it had not put me in touch with any of the more than seven hundred people who had been through the six-week programme since its launch. A media officer explained that it had been difficult to find people ready to share highly personal experiences and the organisation was wary of turning clients into spokesmen. In search of second opinions, I canvassed a wide range of NHS mental health professionals, independent therapists and several people who had once worked at Combat Stress in a range of roles, as well as a number of its former beneficiaries.

The most outspoken critic of the new approach was Dr Keron Fletcher, who started working as a consultant psychiatrist on a freelance basis at the Audley Court facility in the mid-1990s, seeing clients several times a week. He told me he had resigned in September 2013 over the way the organisation was being run. Fletcher said he had feared that the management was seeking to boost the uptake of the new clinical services by admitting candidates who might ordinarily have been deemed borderline for the six-week programme and he no longer felt able to take clinical responsibility for their well-being. He showed me an email he had written to Busuttil raising some of his concerns about the way Audley Court was being managed shortly before he left but said he had received no reply.

Fletcher questioned whether the six-week programme, though it might appeal to cost-conscious NHS commissioners, might not be based on wishful thinking about how rapidly people with the most deep-rooted cases of PTSD could make lasting improvements – particularly the many clients who had complex problems dating back to early childhood. He was particularly concerned that the standardised, time-bound nature of the pro-gramme meant that some participants might be abruptly sent home after finally managing to confront some of their most traumatic material.

'Guys would complete the six weeks and say: "You've just opened Pandora's box and you haven't put the lid back on,"' Fletcher told me. 'This was the story so frequently: "I'm just at the end of my six weeks, I've told you about bayoneting this poor Argentinian in the eyeball and now you're sending me home and it's the only treatment I can get?"'

He added: 'For a long time, I'd been explaining to the organisation: this is not right, we're harming people, not helping people. It fell on deaf ears.'

I put Fletcher's concerns to Busuttil, who firmly rejected his allegations. Busuttil said there was no evidence to suggest any patients had been harmed by any of the programmes and that inspections by the Care Quality Commission had not identified any problems. He also said management would never have allowed unsuitable candidates to attend the six-week course.

Further, Busuttil cited an in-house study of 246 veterans published in the *BMJ Open*, an online medical journal, in March 2015, which showed an overall significant reduction in PTSD symptoms in the group that was still visible six months after the programme finished. Many had been able to return to work and the low dropout rate suggested participants felt the programme was helpful.

The study had its limitations, however. Busuttil acknowledged that it had not been set up to verify whether the beneficiaries had improved to the extent where their symptoms would no longer meet the criteria for a diagnosis of PTSD. Yet this was an important question – key to ascertaining whether clients had made a genuine recovery or were simply coping better with chronic symptoms. There was also no comparison group, so it was impossible to know whether the treatment had worked, or whether the men had simply felt better after six weeks away from home, mingling with other ex-forces and avoiding alcohol, which was banned during residential treatment. Though the study was externally monitored, some questioned why there had been no truly independent assessment, given the millions of pounds of public money involved.

Fletcher was not alone in voicing scepticism over the likelihood of resolving the most hardened cases of PTSD with a six-week shot of therapy. Leigh Skelton served as director of clinical services at Combat Stress from 2001 to 2007, before Busuttil took charge. He was still supporting some of the Falklands and Northern Ireland veterans he met during his tenure, leading them on hill-walking trips in the Peak District. Some of these long-standing beneficiaries had felt angry and abandoned when the charity switched from its old model of continuous care.

'They've put a lot of focus into six-week blocks of intensive therapy for people that are first referred to them – for some people that has a very good effect,' Skelton said. 'But my experience is because it takes so long generally for ex-service personnel to disclose their problems they're often deeply ingrained, and therefore it is difficult to fix them quickly.'

There were concerns, too, about the scope of follow-up support. Growing demand for Combat Stress's services meant that even Busuttil's expanded network of dozens of community workers was thinly stretched. Smaller charities wanted to complement Combat Stress's work by supporting men returning from the six-week programme, but it was a frequent complaint among such organisations and some NHS managers that Tyrwhitt

House seemed reluctant to cooperate or share information. Combat Stress did not accept this criticism, saying that it liaised closely with the NHS 'veterans champions' Network and had seen a significant growth in referrals from GPs. The charity also worked with big forces' charities such as SSAFA, Help for Heroes and ABF The Soldiers' Charity. The media officer added that Combat Stress referred clients to at least ten other smaller charities offering activities such as woodland outings, fishing trips or opportunities to work with dogs.

Despite these partnerships, Gillian Taylor, who worked as an occupational therapist at Combat Stress from 2008 to 2010, believed gains from the six-week programme might prove short-lived unless the organisation made a much bigger effort to liaise with a wider range of groups capable of providing lasting support on a community level.

'It doesn't matter how wonderful the programme is – that person still has to go home and manage his day-to-day living. If for the rest of the year he's bunkered down in a flat and daren't leave the house you might as well not bother in the first place,' said Taylor, who now works independently with ex-forces in North Yorkshire. 'For the really poorly ones, we're talking years of ongoing support before they even start to get somewhere. It's about gradually learning to live again.'

Busuttil was confident that a series of planned studies would vindicate the enduring benefits of his programme for ex-forces with PTSD and believed that many of the questions raised about his strategy represented the kind of grumbling inevitably triggered by any major organisational shake-up.

'There have been a few disappointed that the old respite regime has gone, but I don't think that's a bad thing,' Busuttil said. 'I'm sorry they're upset.'

Beyond the concerns over the six-week programme, there was another complaint I heard about Combat Stress among other military charities and from within the NHS – that the organisation was 'cherry picking' the easiest clients to treat – a contention Busuttil also rejected.

The argument sprang from a belief that Combat Stress was not doing enough to help a potentially large and hard-to-treat group of ex-forces: those who had developed drug or alcohol addictions while self-medicating symptoms of PTSD. Drinking was prohibited during residential treatment because therapy would not work if patients were intoxicated. This raised the question of what would happen to men trapped in a cycle of alcoholism and trauma who could not contemplate going six weeks without a drink.

Combat Stress was alive to their plight and had deployed specialist outreach workers to steer such clients through NHS detox services to the point where they would be sober enough to attend the six-week programme. To the organisation's critics, this seemed like an abdication of responsibility since it was widely accepted that the NHS generally lacked the expertise or facilities to provide integrated trauma and alcohol treatment, especially to those ex-forces who might be wary of confronting their past in a civilian setting. In addition, detox services might refuse to admit clients suffering from the worst cases of combat-related PTSD if they were prone to aggressive outbursts.

'They'll turn up at Combat Stress and Combat Stress will say: "We've assessed you, you're suitable, but you've got to be clean and sober to come in,"' said Jacquie Johnston-Lynch, founder of Tom Harrison House, the veterans' detox charity in Liverpool. 'So then they'll pack them off to the GP or another service and that other service won't take them because they've got active mental health symptoms. It's like a pinball machine.'

Some questioned why Busuttil had not lobbied for money to set up an in-house detox service to provide a more comprehensive 'one-stop-shop' solution for those dependent on alcohol. Similarly, some therapists also lamented the fact that Combat

Stress lacked the kind of secure unit capable of admitting the relatively small numbers of ex-forces whose trauma symptoms were so severe they might pose a danger to themselves or others. When such men went into crisis they tended to end up in NHS psychiatric wards where they would be sedated until they stabilised enough to return home – until their next breakdown.

Among those concerned about the level of care available to the most vulnerable ex-forces was Dr Martin Deahl, a consultant psychiatrist and colonel in the Army Reserves. Deahl had been responsible for bringing in-patient psychiatry for serving personnel into the NHS from the Priory Group in 2008 and had since led initiatives within the organisation to improve mental healthcare for veterans. He believed the hybrid system of dividing responsibility for veterans between the NHS and the charity sector had led to a frustrating and at times infuriating degree of politicisation, duplication and competition for resources that had wasted a great deal of time and money.

'We in the NHS have tried to work with service charities and complement their efforts,' Deahl said. 'Most of them, however, simply don't want to know. They perceive us as a threat and would simply like to be given a pot of money by government to provide services for veterans themselves. Frankly, this is never going to happen, not least because of the enormous numbers involved.'

Deahl shared concerns voiced by many that the current system was failing large numbers of ex-forces suffering from alcoholism or at acute risk of self-harm.

He went on: 'Service charities can be quite selective and understandably wary of more challenging patients. There is a lot of talk and grand intention, but we see too many veterans contacting service charities and their calls are either never returned or they are redirected to other organisations on a merry dance before finally being told to see their GP or ring the Samaritans.'

Combat Stress roundly rejected any suggestion it was 'cherry

picking' its clients. The organisation had earmarked £2 million
to expand its efforts to help candidates for its residential
programmes access NHS addiction services using a grant
from the government's Libor fund, set up with the proceeds
of fines levied on banks who attempted to manipulate interest
rates. Equally, Busuttil said he and other psychiatrists regularly
helped to stabilise clients suffering from the most severe cases
of PTSD to the point where they were ready for the six-week
programme.

The frequent criticism Combat Stress faced within the
veterans' mental health community was partly a result of the
special status it had acquired since it began to receive millions of
pounds from the state. In the 2013/14 financial year, for example,
NHS England and NHS Scotland provided a combined total of
£4.5 million to fund the organisation's residential programmes
– a quarter of its annual income. In the eyes of many smaller
charities, Combat Stress's unique role as the biggest officially
sponsored provider of psychological interventions for veterans
outside the NHS meant it should be doing much more for the
ex-forces they saw struggling to find help all over the country.
From this perspective, Combat Stress – which described itself as
'the veterans' mental health charity' – had effectively been co-
opted by the government as a fig leaf for a broader failure to
provide adequate care to the most vulnerable.

And yet, while I heard many barbs directed towards Tyrwhitt
House, it was also clearly unrealistic to expect Combat Stress to
provide all things to all people at all times. Though there might
be differences of opinion over the best way to treat ex-forces
with PTSD, the organisation could argue that it was doing the
best it could within the scope of its expanded yet still finite
resources. It had never been commissioned by the NHS to offer
in-house detox services or facilities to handle patients at high risk
of harming themselves, which would have required substantially
more funds. Busuttil acknowledged that the charity might only

be reaching a fraction of potential beneficiaries because nobody could say for sure how many ex-forces might be grappling with problems but feel reluctant to come forward. By setting up the six-week programme, he had established a new way to deliver therapy to those who did seek help.

Ultimately, the controversy around Combat Stress reflected deeper concerns about whether Britain had the political will to meet the full cost of both the physical and the psychological wounds of war. Some feared that the increasingly prominent role played by big forces' charities would serve as an alibi for the government to sidestep its duty of care to those who were suffering. Others believed on principle that the state should meet the cost of looking after those it sent to fight, rather than try to split the bill with corporate donors or sympathetic members of the public sponsoring fun runs or skydives. Busuttil was aware of such concerns and wondered aloud during one of our interviews why the government had been content to allow Combat Stress to take on so much responsibility for providing clinical services.

'Why aren't we a national service appointed by the state? Why aren't veterans properly recognised?' he asked. 'We don't mind closing the charity and handing over to a thoroughbred service.'

With growing numbers seeking help, a host of much smaller organisations had sprung up across Britain offering a kaleidoscope of support. While many were quick to criticise Combat Stress, some faced questions of their own.

When I began speaking to ex-forces, I had no idea of the sheer scale of the military charity sector. I soon began to feel like a Victorian butterfly collector – delighting in discovering a new species. Organisations with 'for Heroes' occupied by far the biggest branch in this taxonomy – dominated of course by Help for Heroes, which in the space of six years had moved from a standing start to raising an annual income of more than £30 million. Much smaller organisations have since proliferated:

Rugby for Heroes; Fishing for Heroes; Hosties [air hostesses] 4 Heroes; Holidays4Heroes; Hounds for Heroes; Hire a Hero and Heroes on the Water, to name but a few.

The ecosystem had traditionally been dominated by several large and long-standing incumbents with significant annual incomes (shown for 2013) – the Royal British Legion (£125 million), SSAFA (£58 million) and Combat Stress (£15.6 million). In 2011 an investigation by British Forces News found that more than 2,000 armed services fund-raising groups have a joint income of £800 million, though most are not directly involved in providing welfare. While overall donations to charity fell during the recent recession, contributions to military charities rose considerably – a sign of the depth of public affection for ex-forces.

In some cases, this pool of generosity proved a temptation too far. In 2013, a fund-raiser named Christopher O'Neill was sentenced to three years in prison after lying about his own very brief military career to win a £125,000 grant from the Welsh government ostensibly to fund a home for veterans with mental health problems. He used the money to buy speedboats, fund hotel stays, pay gambling bills and wine and dine three women, the *Daily Mail* reported. The following year, police warned of a sharp increase in the number of reported frauds by 'charities' trading on the reputation of Help for Heroes and similar large organisations without their consent.

The success of Help for Heroes stemmed in part from an outpouring of sympathy for the roughly 310 soldiers who lost one or more limbs in Iraq and Afghanistan, though it has also donated £6.7 million to Combat Stress. In addition, the charity has provided a £400,000 grant to allow service personnel and their families free access to the Big White Wall, an online support network and counselling service for people who are anxious or struggling to cope. Help for Heroes has also begun to develop 'Hidden Wounds', a helpline and psychological well-being service of its own.

The Iraq and Afghanistan campaigns have also spurred a proliferation of smaller organisations, some set up by grieving parents in honour of their sons – including the Mark Wright Project, Welsh Warrior and the Ben Hyde Memorial Trust. Many others had been set up by ex-forces themselves. In Warrington, I visited Blue Apple Heroes, a newly formed organisation founded by Mark Smith, a veteran of Northern Ireland. He had opened a drop-in centre and gardening project and had organised outings for ex-forces, including a trip to Aviemore for about twenty men seeking an escape from firework night.

In Cornwall, I spent a week with Surf Action, a charity that runs surfing outings for ex-forces and has a particular focus on PTSD. The group was founded by Rich Emerson, a Gulf War veteran, who captured something of his own struggle in the tattoo on his forearm – a man crucified on a cross formed of two surfboards. One sweltering August afternoon, Surf Action held an open day on the Great Western Beach in Newquay, joined by Mark Ormrod, a former Royal Marine who had lost three limbs after stepping on an IED in Afghanistan on Christmas Eve 2007. Ormrod, whom children had nicknamed 'Iron Man' for his high-tech prosthetics, had launched a new career as a motivational speaker and Emerson and other volunteers helped him and his daughter ride surfboards for the first time. The day ended with a sense of camaraderie recaptured and raucous singing on the minibus home.

In Bournemouth, I met Sarah Bennett Thurston, the founder of a charity called Garrison Girls. A sparky woman married to a serving soldier, she founded the group to raise funds for PTSD and welfare support by producing calendars of forces wives posing nude. When we met she was hoping to secure permission to organise the next shoot around one of Britain's vintage Vulcan bombers. (Garrison Girls is not to be confused with Hotties Helping Heroes or The Daffodil Girls – other groups producing similar calendars.)

One of the more prominent of the smaller organisations is called PTSD Resolution, co-founded by Tony Gauvain, a former colonel who served for thirty-two years in the Army, and who runs the charity from his home in a farmhouse in Surrey. The goal is to raise funds to enable veterans to access a 200-strong network of therapists practising Human Givens psychotherapy, developed in the 1990s, which hinges on helping clients access their 'internal guidance system' to meet their emotional and physical needs. Raising funds is a constant battle, but Gauvain managed to find multiple donors, including an arcade games company which pledged a share of takings from fruit machines.

To help me better understand PTSD Resolution's work, Gauvain arranged for me to join a week-long retreat at a villa in the Algarve region of Portugal where Joy Gilson, a Human Givens therapist, planned to build on previous one-on-one sessions with three ex-forces. One of them was Tom Sawyer, a former Army driver who had been forced to leave his job after being injured in a vehicle accident in Saudi Arabia during the build-up to the Gulf War.

Tom was haunted by a memory of a day in Northern Ireland in 1985 that he would never speak about. Drifting from job to job, he retreated from the world behind biker-style clothes, a formidable beard and a ponytail. Tom said that it had only taken Gilson five sessions to help him lock his memory in a box where it could no longer rule him. The trip to Portugal was the first time he had boarded a plane since being flown home injured from the Gulf more than twenty years earlier. Before meeting Joy, even leaving his flat was an ordeal.

'If I hadn't have had the therapy off of Joy I would be dead now,' Tom told me, as we strolled through crowds of tourists in the seaside town of Lagos. 'It's like being reborn.'

Tom had marked his inner shift by cutting off his beard and ponytail to raise money for PTSD Resolution at a benefit at his local in Newhaven. Gauvain cited Tom as one of the prime examples of how PTSD Resolution had played a vital role in reaching ex-forces who were reluctant to engage with their GP or Combat Stress. He said the charity had treated more than a thousand people in its first six years, including a number who were homeless or in prison, and referrals were growing in frequency. Other small charities made a similar argument and I came across a number of cases where volunteers and therapists working outside official channels had provided the first listening ear for men who might have struggled in silence for years.

Yet for all the good intentions, there were clearly potential pitfalls. While many of the bigger organisations belonged to a loose military charity confederation called Cobseo, there was no system of accreditation or independent oversight for the many new players in veterans' mental health. There seemed to be an obvious risk that ex-forces dealing with serious trauma symptoms might end up being seen by people with little or no clinical experience, specialist training or formal supervision. Treating PTSD is an extremely delicate task – akin to opening a pressure cooker – and mistakes can do lasting harm.

Such concerns were flagged by Lord Michael Ashcroft, the Conservative peer, entrepreneur and philanthropist, after his ap-pointment as the government's special representative on veterans' transition in 2012. He addressed the problems in the military charity sector as part of a wide-ranging report on the transition published in February 2014. Focusing on 350 organisations with objectives relating to welfare and mental health – a group with an annual income of about £400 million – Ashcroft reached a blunt verdict: a maze of overlapping, competing organisations that range from 'very competent to the (frankly) ineffective . . . While individual charities may believe they are making the best use of their funds as an organisation, collectively they are not.'

Ashcroft recommended greater cooperation and consolidation, publication of a directory of accredited forces charities and the creation of a single twenty-four-hour contact point for veterans who need help. In a follow-up blog posted a year later, he said the government had committed to most of his recommendations for improving the transition and, despite some resistance from within the military charity sector, his proposal to create a register of accredited organisations looked likely to happen.

Despite Ashcroft's assurances, there was anger and frustration at the slow pace of reform. Mandy Bostwick, the Wrexham-based consultant trauma psychotherapist, said she had encountered several charities offering to treat PTSD that she believed risked putting ex-forces in danger.

'We've got charities which have been set up who are putting programmes together to treat this and have no idea what they're dealing with,' she said. 'This has been allowed to happen because the government has abdicated all responsibility. These veterans have no voice right now.'

I made repeated requests for an interview with Anna Soubry, the Conservative politician who was serving as veterans minister during my two years of research. The MoD said she was unavailable because she could not respond to all the media requests she received.

Among those who sought help outside the services offered by the NHS and Combat Stress was A.J., the former Royal Marine sniper. While he was serving his last few weeks in the Marines, somebody pointed him to a charity in Bath called Save Our Soldier. The organisation was founded by Lee Hayward, an emotional coach, and a team of practitioners offering approaches including hypnotherapy and neurolinguistic programming, a technique developed in the 1970s for exploring thought processes and behaviour. Serving soldiers are not allowed to seek help outside official channels, but once A.J. had left the Marines, he punched the charity's address into his satnav.

As A.J. navigated winding country roads with his wife Karen, he felt a growing sense of apprehension. The feeling deepened when they found themselves driving through a seemingly deserted village. The satnav kept urging A.J. onwards but road-works blocked his path. They were only ten miles from Bath but he felt the same mortal fear that had gripped him when mortar shells rained down around his sniper tower in Sangin. His tension proved contagious and soon Karen was also close to panic. Deciding to abort the trip, A.J. yanked the car around, fighting a wild urge to ram into a tractor approaching from an opposite lane. He reached a service station and fell into a fitful doze as Karen calmed down by walking their dog Jen. At a second appointment A.J. talked through the journey with Lee Hayward and had a flash of insight.

'We kind of related it all back to the day we drove into an ambush,' A.J. told me. 'He just pointed out all these triggers. He made me realise that the whole day's events were very similar if not identical to stuff that happened out in Afghan.'

The journey had unearthed a suppressed memory of a day when A.J.'s convoy had run into an ambush, then turned around under mortar fire. The satnav had evoked the voice of the commander, urging them onward, even when A.J. could sense they were heading into a trap. The hot day in the Somerset countryside parallelled the heat of Helmand. Driving through the quiet village, A.J. had been struck by the absence of people – a common 'combat indicator'. Hitting the roadworks had served as a proxy for the Taliban attack. A.J. began to see that his bouts of anxiety were not spontaneous products of his mind, but closely mirrored events in Afghanistan that he had not had a chance to process.

As his sessions at Save Our Soldier progressed, A.J. was asked to draw three imaginary circles on the floor and fill the first with the worst of the 'Big Five'. He was told to imagine the second as a receptacle for the best things in his life: A.J. thought of his wedding and the birth of his children. A third circle was neutral. Unlike in most standard therapies, A.J. was not asked to recall the

'Big Five' in detail – rather, he was shown how to kill the feelings in the 'bad' circle using emotions from the 'good'. A.J. began to shake, as if some long-pent-up energy was leaving his body.

'It worked – I had a total emotional outburst. A big man hug with another man,' A.J. told me. 'No problems driving since.'

They returned for more sessions. Hayward taught Karen relaxation techniques and performed hypnosis on A.J. – an echo of the treatment Myers tried on 'Case One'.

'I'd be asleep, snoring on a bench, with a headset on, listening to his voice,' A.J. said. 'Have I been hypnotised? Have I just had a good kip?'

Hayward established that A.J. found the colour red relaxing and asked Karen to make various red objects visible at certain times of day. During their sessions, A.J. realised his anxiety around crowds stemmed from a fear of suicide bombers, and his faith in Hayward grew when he managed to attend a concert in Hyde Park. Hayward was available at all hours and A.J. would sometimes call him for help to manage the anxiety that could strike as he tried in vain to sleep.

The case presented a dilemma familiar from other smaller charities. Hayward had no formal clinical training and some medical professionals might regard his techniques with a high degree of scepticism, even concern. Yet A.J. was certain that Save Our Soldier had helped him manage his panic attacks and he began to refer other former Marines who approached him for advice to the charity.

After leaving the Marines, A.J. had felt inspired to order three industrial-grade embroidery machines, almost on a whim. Working for himself appealed to his independent streak and would allow him to take time out if he was feeling overwhelmed. He set up a sportswear embroidery business with Karen and started landing contracts from Royal Marines teams. The crossed sniper rifles I had noticed on A.J.'s jumper when we first met were not a regimental badge, but his company logo.

Like many of the ex-forces who had survived the grimmest reaches of the Spiral, A.J. had been determined to pass on what he had learned to others. He had set up an organisation to help other former Marines battling with PTSD or the transition to civilian life to find a goal that would harness their energies and give them a sense of purpose – what A.J. called a 'Rock'. It could be something as ambitious as learning to play an instrument or as simple as running regularly. In August 2013, he joined a group of ex-forces climbing Mount Kilimanjaro in Tanzania. On the snow-capped summit, high above the clouds, he once again had a fleeting taste of peace – the 'meeting God' feeling he had discovered while running on the beach after his darkest day.

The Kilimanjaro climb struck A.J. as an apt metaphor for the step-by-step process of recovery and he incorporated the peak into his organisation's logo – a man with a guitar climbing a mountain. He emphasised that the work of coming to terms with trauma would rarely yield the clear-cut ending of a successful trek. Nevertheless, eight years after leaving his tower in Sangin, he had discovered depths within himself that he had never known, and a new-found realisation that there was more to life than he could always see or understand.

'I like to think the reason I had a breakdown is to make sure nobody else does,' he wrote. 'You have changed and you must manage that change. It is a long and exhausting journey of self-discovery.'

12

'Living with Mr Grumpy'

When your partner has PTSD

A decade ago, Merseyside police set up Matrix, a specialist team dedicated to tackling Liverpool's spiralling rates of gun crime. Marksmen were put on stand-by while officers served warning letters to anyone suspected of links to armed criminals. Sue had never been in trouble with the police, but she came to know Matrix well. Officers clad in riot gear and equipped with Taser guns had repeatedly deployed in her front garden.

One time, her husband Joe clambered onto the roof of their semi-detached house and began flinging tiles into the street. On another occasion, he donned combat gear and dug a trench in the back garden, his collection of laughing Buddha statues watching serenely from the shrubs. Joe was never armed with anything more than a kitchen knife but in the midst of his flashbacks he felt twenty-one years old again – as if the incident more than two decades earlier in Northern Ireland that had injured his back, and possibly his brain, had never happened.

There was little doubt that the greatest danger Joe posed was to himself – once he had grabbed a chopping board and tried to cut off his trigger hand. But of all the many crises that Sue had faced, the one that was engraved most deeply occurred when she had come home to find Joe had locked himself in the house, convinced he was under siege. Sue gave the police permission to break in by smashing a window. There was a tinkle of breaking

glass and Joe charged down the stairs shouting: 'IRA bastards.'
Assembled officers heard the sound of the knife drawer rattling
and alerted Matrix.

'About ten police cars rocked up, they just came from
everywhere,' Sue told me as we drank tea in her living room.
Joe, a bald, heavyset Glaswegian, sat next to her on their sofa. He
wore a solemn, moon-faced expression as Sue recalled how one
of the officers had called out to a comrade who had served in the
forces to try to reason with him through the front door.

'It was only when the guy opened his mouth, I was like:
"Get him away from there!"' Sue said. 'The guy had a Northern
Ireland accent.'

Convinced he was in mortal danger, Joe grabbed the fridge in
a bear hug, barricaded the kitchen door then ripped the cooker
from the wall. Gas filled the house – Sue could smell it from the
garden. The police would not dare to use their Taser guns for fear
of igniting a fireball. The stand-off lasted eight hours until Joe was
eventually persuaded to drop the knives out of a kitchen window.

'I just can't remember nothing of it,' Joe said, his eyes downcast.

'He was in hospital for about two days before he recognised
me,' Sue said, casting a sidelong glance at her husband.

Sue wanted a cigarette so we went into the garden. Their
Yorkshire terrier, Arwen, scampered back and forth on a lead
attached to their washing line. Arwen had become so attuned
to Joe's moods that she could sense the onset of his interior
storms even before he could, and would bolt for the door in
anticipation.

Over the past three years, the family had faced a constant
battle to find anybody who seemed capable of helping Joe to
bring his flashbacks under control. Medical staff seemed at first
not to understand that his experiences were not like ordinary
memories – in his mind he really was back in Northern Ireland,
fighting for his life. During such episodes – known in trauma
survivors as 'dissociation' – the real world of his home and family

did not exist, and his body pulsed with waves of the fear, anger and disgust that had gripped him in combat, and that had never been fully discharged. Joe had thus developed a revolving-door relationship with mental health services: he would suffer a flashback then spend several weeks in a secure psychiatric ward, where he would be given tranquillisers and left to watch TV – a strategy of 'cope and dope' as he and Sue called it. Eventually, Joe would be sent home, only to suffer another flashback and return to hospital. Nobody seemed to know how to break the cycle.

'You feel abandoned,' said Joe. 'You feel the military's abandoned you onto civvy street. You feel the NHS has abandoned you because they don't know how to treat you.'

Sue nodded – she felt particularly let down by the military charity sector.

'There's a lot of big money to be made in curing veterans, lots of people making a good living out of it – and very little curing going on,' she said.

For most ex-forces, it is not the Army, or the NHS, or charities that provide the bulk of their support when they enter the Spiral – it is their partners. Across Britain, hundreds of women, and some men, face an agonising choice: walk away from a loved one who may have become abusive or violent as a consequence of war trauma, or adapt to life as a carer for someone who bears scant resemblance to the person they married. The duty can feel as demanding as looking after an adult child.

In many cases, the strain of living with a husband plagued by symptoms of PTSD, anxiety, depression or alcohol abuse becomes too much and the relationship dissolves. But there are some who refuse to accept defeat, displaying more heroism than many soldiers have shown in battle. Such women soon find they must confront their own version of the Spiral, a mirror image of their husband's encounter with grief, guilt, anger and despair – with the added burden of having to fight on their behalf to obtain the right care.

Sue, who had married Joe before he joined the Army, became my unofficial guide to the parallel world of military wives. As she began her battle to find help for her husband, she realised she was not alone, and co-founded the support group called Combat PTSD Angels. Members could swap information or simply vent on a members-only Facebook page. The group started with six women – within two years it had more than 200, with dozens more waiting for Sue to approve requests to join.

Queries might include: 'My husband has started carrying a knife – should I tell the police?' To which Sue's response would be: 'Not unless you want him Tasered' – followed by a discussion on how best to try to resolve his potentially dangerous behaviour. Another might report that their husband had popped out to the shops and been found hours later, apparently lost. Sue's advice: 'Google "dissociation".' Christmas posed particular problems: the enforced jollity could stir profound feelings of guilt over lost comrades. Even the sparkle of decorations was a hazard. Sue Tweeted a tip: 'Christmas tree lights a trigger for your veteran? Try static white or blue lights instead . . .'

One technique she shared with new 'Angels' was to devise a family safety plan by agreeing a codeword, such as 'Scramble'. On hearing it, the children would know to rush to the front door so their mother could rapidly remove them to a prearranged sanctuary, at a friend or relative's house. It helped to keep a packed bag handy and a list of emergency numbers. Sue also advised women to ensure dangerous items such as medication or knives were kept in one place so they could easily grab them on their way out. Though I was not admitted to the discussion page, a member called Faye, whom I had met at the reception at Combat Stress, sent me a post she had written. She had fallen in love with her soldier husband when they were both still teenagers. Fifteen years later, he had been diagnosed with PTSD sustained while serving in Kosovo, and his explosive bouts of anger had begun to make her feel like she was living in a war zone.

'*Through sickness and in health! I meant every word!*' she posted. '*What if the sickness is a rage redder than red that tears thru our house, our home leaving a trail of devastation and terror! Two years into full blown military ptsd and I'm asking myself where do I draw the line? When do I say enough is enough? Will my children grow up nervous wrecks, scared of their shadows and too afraid to speak up? How many more times do I have to work through tears trying to stop shaking as I fold clothes or wash up? I'm done! I'm tired!*'

Later, she explained she had devised strategies for coping with her husband's anger – including leaving a red bath mitt on the back-door handle as a warning to her children that their father was cooling off in his den in the garden, which was equipped with a punchbag, and was not to be disturbed.

Though the Combat PTSD Angels Facebook group sometimes served as an echo chamber of wearyingly similar complaints about the latest outrages committed by 'OHs' – 'Other Halves' – its members provided each other with a source of comfort that friends with no experience of military marriages could rarely offer. Almost a year after our first meeting, Sue confided something of the sense of the loneliness she had felt as Joe's conditioned worsened.

'At the very beginning of our PTSD journey, it was soul-destroying. I felt so abandoned, I felt so alone, I felt like I was the only person on the planet who was dealing with this,' she said.

'I'd lost contact with most of our military friends at that point, I was surrounded by our civilian friends who had less clue about PTSD than I did. Unless they had prior experience with mental health issues, their response was generally: "You don't need that, leave him."'

Sue had a tattoo on her forearm of an English rose stem entwined with a Scottish thistle – a symbol of her determination to preserve her marriage even in what she called the 'harsh soil' of Joe's illness. She quietly resolved to do whatever it might take.

'You either cope, you sit in a corner rocking yourself somewhere, or you "do one", which is what 99 per cent of spouses do with PTSD – they leave them, they don't understand,' Sue said. 'I had two choices: educate myself, forewarn and forearm myself as much as I could, or watch my marriage crumble. And I wasn't having it.'

I was curious to know how representative Sue's experience might be, and asked her whether I could attend one of the monthly meetings she organised in Liverpool – usually strictly only for carers.

'I'll have a chat with some of the girls and see if anyone's interested in meeting you,' Sue said. 'Don't take it personally if they say no.'

Some days later she sent me a Facebook message. I had received an invite to the first of three of the gatherings I would attend of Combat PTSD Angels.

Liverpool Carers Centre occupies an unprepossessing block next to a roundabout on the edge of the city centre, not far from Liverpool University, and within sight of the Radio City Tower, a futuristic structure built in the late 1960s that dominates the urban skyline. Cages guard the ground-floor windows and the front door is protected by a metal shield fitted with a spyhole.

The door swung open to reveal a more welcoming interior. In a meeting room, half a dozen Combat PTSD Angels were seated on sofas. The wall was decorated with soothing photographs of English landscapes and a coffee table was strewn with bags of nachos, hunks of chocolate cake served on paper plates and mugs of tea. As the women began to swap stories, an Angel whose husband had served in Northern Ireland, whom I'll call Dee, was suddenly overcome with the strain of living with his unpredictable moods.

'I just want my old life back,' she said, wiping away tears and turning to Sue for a hug. 'You don't realise how much you've changed.'

Dee explained how she could be curled up on the sofa with her husband watching the news when a Sinn Fein politician would appear and he would form a pistol shape with his thumb and forefingers then slowly take a shot at the screen. Or he might wake up in the middle of the night and mime washing his hands while shouting: 'Don't touch me! I'm not clean!'

'It's only in the last few years that he's met me that he's let it out – his first wife never knew anything about it,' Dee said. 'He just suffered but didn't know why.'

Susan, whose husband George had served in Northern Ireland, said: 'When we first met everything was hunky dory, beautiful, lovely, happy, then *Bang.*'

A woman wearing a striped top nodded, recognising the pattern from her own husband: 'He was fine for about twelve to eighteen months,' she said. 'When he had his full-on breakdown I just freaked out, I thought he's completely lost his marbles. From that day on, everyday normal life just completely went out the window and I never got it back.'

Denise described how her husband, Mark Smith, founder of the local charity Blue Apple Heroes, insisted on sleeping with a combat knife within reach.

'If he hears a noise, the knife's out straight away,' she said. 'What if the kids are going to the toilet?'

'What I don't understand is how he can keep it bottled up all these years and what in me brings it out?' said Dee.

'You're "the One",' said the woman in the striped top.

'Still now the house is very regimented, the meals are a set time – and dare not be five minutes earlier,' said Dee.

Sue remonstrated with her – 'You've got to start opening your mouth – supper's ready when it's cooked.'

'The worst possible crime is kids coming home early and leaving stuff on the stairs. Then I think: "Why should it be such a big deal?"' Dee said. 'Then I'm making sure there's no scene when he does come in.'

Sue cut in: 'But it doesn't matter – even if you're hiding the school bags, if he's in that mindset he's going to do it.'

'I've done that loads of times – purposely lost an argument so he can get all that anger and rage out,' said the woman in stripes.

'I've given up going out, I've given up friends – it just leads to more arguments,' said Susan.

'Being punched, being screamed at, being called all sorts of names, having them in your face – they don't see you,' said a woman in red. 'What he was saying is that it wasn't me he was talking to – but it still hurts.'

'Well obviously, we love our husbands,' said Dee. 'What happens when you don't love them any more? You stay with them out of pity? Fear of what they'll do if you're not there?'

Sue offered more advice: 'You reach a point where you have to accept the fact that they're going to hurt themselves. That's why I say: "Go on those eggshells." Avoiding those eggshells doesn't benefit you – it's a myth, it's the "normal" bit.'

'You're living at peace then,' said Denise.

'It's a false peace,' Sue shot back. She had been through rocky times with Joe as she had begun to reinforce boundaries, but her assertiveness had gradually seeded a new-found sense of mutual respect.

Dee did not seem convinced.

'They're dangerous men. They know how to use a weapon and it wouldn't make a sound,' she said. 'The most dangerous weapon's themselves.'

The meeting continued for a while longer before the women began to make their way home.

The first time I had visited Sue's house, Joe had been sitting slumped on the sofa, wearing a camouflage vest and taking slow drags on his e-cigarette. The lights were low and the tip glowed green in the semi-darkness. He spoke for an hour, almost without pause, as he recounted the six worst incidents seared into his memory from his thirteen tours of Northern Ireland. He later showed me the dates, documented in a service record he was given when he left the Army – known as a 'red book' for its crimson cover.

Joe's retelling left me profoundly unsettled. His tales were of blasts and gunshots, hate-filled streets and sudden death. The images returned to him with such vivid clarity that he could smell the burning petrol, hear the jeers of the crowds, and feel the texture of the brickwork he had crouched behind for cover.

Joe said:'I am still back in '92, '93, '94. I'm a young, fit soldier again. People are trying to tell me it's 2013 and I'm like: "You're fucking lying, you're playing with my head, you're messing about with me."

'The night terrors is the worst. You're lying in bed at night and you're having these nightmares. You wake up sweating and crying, then you start seeing people come out of the walls – terrorists. You're trying to move, you're trying to get away, but it's as if something's got a hold of you and you can't move.'

It was hard to reconcile the haunted figure on the sofa with the young man beaming from a photo snapped on his wedding day. Joe wore a glengarry and immaculate dress uniform, his arm draped around his smiling bride. He had been so affectionate in the early years of their marriage that soldiers had taunted him for being soft. Joe ignored them, insisting on giving Sue a peck as he left the house or walking with her hand in hand, proud to have forged the kind of enduring relationship that many others in his regiment had tried to build.

For the first part of their marriage, they lived in a two-bedroom house in a landscaped housing estate behind the wire of a large barracks. Sue soon discovered that Army homes were inevitably painted magnolia and that every time a soldier moved there was a 'march out' where unsmiling inspectors arrived at the door to assess your level of cleanliness to the last grain of soot. So zealous were they in their search for any evidence of slovenliness that they sometimes wiped a cotton bud around the rim of a keyhole in search of traces of grime.

Under the shadow of the 'march outs', Sue became an expert at dismantling a cooker and scrubbing it to a pristine shine, and acquired the improvisational skills of a West End set designer. When their Yorkshire terrier peed on the carpet, she used a cheese grater to crumble blue chalk to conceal the stain. A scratch on the anaglypta wallpaper vanished after an all-night session with paste made of flour and water. Parts of a fireplace were held together with Blu-Tack and a cereal packet was co-opted to serve as a corner of a door frame.

When their husbands deployed to Northern Ireland, Sue joined the other wives in adapting to life as a single parent, while living in constant fear that a pair of solemn-faced soldiers would knock at her door. Once the men did call – what Sue called her 'boots on the path moment' – to tell her Joe had been wounded during a patrol.

Adapting to the men's return was often harder than living with their absence. Young children would hide behind the sofa, barely recognising the hard-eyed men who barged back into their lives. Wives would have to relinquish their temporary roles as head of the household as their husbands reasserted their authority through obsessive micro-management. Neither had any inkling of what the other had experienced while they were apart.

Sue explained that the mutual silence was compounded by a tacit regimental understanding that the men would not talk about what they had done and the women would not ask, a culture that made it harder for many soldiers to seek help in later years. Officers' wives policed the unwritten contract.

'They'd have a coffee morning before the guys were due back,' Sue said, 'and you'd literally be told: "Meet them at the door with your best slap on, smile on your face, kinkiest underwear – make them forget about everything."

'Then usually, the night after they came home, they'd be

hauled back into camp for a compulsory bender – they used to call them a "smoker".'

Sue summed up the philosophy of this semi-official version of 'lager therapy': 'Have a pint, beat your mate senseless – all sorted in the morning. It's gone with the bruises.' Tempers ran so high that once Joe had his cheekbone broken by a friend.

Joe was medically discharged from the Army in 1997 due to back injuries and they moved into their home in Liverpool, revelling in the chance to paint each room a colour other than magnolia. But old habits died hard – it was a long time before Sue stopped dismantling and scrubbing the cooker every six weeks. Joe would trail after her while she was dusting – making sure surfaces were spotless. For years he suffered from nightmares, but said nothing. Sue put his compulsive streak down to the after-effects of Army life and did her best to shield their children from his low moods.

'For the fourteen years where we didn't know he had PTSD, he certainly showed a lot of the low-level symptoms,' Sue said. 'Other people are going to be tearing their hair out. We just got on with it. It all seemed normal to us.'

When Joe eventually went to the doctor he was given anti-depressants that made him irritable and he started to snap at Sue. She realised he was getting worse when they set up some IKEA furniture. To Sue's surprise, the assembly had gone smoothly – she knew the intricacies of do-it-yourself could be notoriously aggravating for get-it-done-yesterday infantrymen. Then Joe came back into the room a few days later, squinted at the table, and asked: 'Who set this up?' He wondered whether somebody had broken into the house.

Sue said he would go out to buy cigarettes and come back six hours later, with no idea where he had been. Or he would say he was going to give his dad a quick call and she would have to gently remind him his father had passed away years before. Once he looked at her over the dinner table and Sue had felt for a second that he was about to pay her a compliment. 'I'm sure I know you,' Joe had said. 'But just tell me who you are again?'

Joe began to behave increasingly erratically – making plans to leave home and declaring that he no longer loved her. Sue forbore as patiently as she could, telling herself that it was Joe's illness talking, but soon his outbursts took on more sinister forms. On one occasion, they were watching *Coronation Street* when Joe thought he could see figures flitting through the garden. He ran into the kitchen. Sue followed and saw him grab something from the dish rack. She fled with their son and the terrier. Joe stood at the front door brandishing a knife. Police arrived and he slumped to the ground – immobilised by a Taser.

Lost in his nightmares, Joe would confuse Sue for a terrorist and close his hands around her throat – only letting her go when he caught sight of himself in the bedroom mirror. Sue hit lows where she could no longer contain herself and would sit sobbing at her steering wheel in a car park at Tesco.

'Normal – I hate that word,' she said. '"Can't you wait for things to get back to normal?" What is "normal"?'

Joe had been awarded a war pension after being diagnosed with PTSD attributable to his service in Northern Ireland, but since he was no longer serving in the Army the NHS was responsible for his care. Joe said his trips to psychiatric wards made him feel like a character in *One Flew Over the Cuckoo's Nest*, the 1975 film set in a secure mental hospital in America. Once he became so frustrated after being admitted to a ward, within earshot of a grouse shoot, that he took a nurse hostage by grabbing him around the neck and only released him when staff promised to transfer him to a new unit. Another time, Sue asked for him to be moved because other patients were playing a combat simulation game on an Xbox.

The NHS referred Joe to Combat Stress for an assessment, but the charity's Audley Court facility wrote back to say that after careful consideration it had decided for various reasons that it was unable to admit Joe, describing him as a 'very complex case'. 'Moreover, we are a voluntary organisation and to contain a high-risk client on our unit is beyond our remit,' wrote a consultant psychiatrist working for the charity.

'Imagine going to hospital with pneumonia and being told to come back when you've got a cold,' Sue said.

Joe joined a waiting list to see an NHS psychotherapist and it was six months before his first appointment. The forty-minute sessions of CBT helped a little, but they were no more than what somebody with milder psychological problems might receive and there was scant evidence to suggest the approach would work for such a severe case of PTSD. Joe was still taking more than forty pills a day – for pain in his back as well as various drugs prescribed by his psychiatrist and for the after-effects of a recent minor stroke.

Joe's main source of solace outside his family was his outings with Blue Apple Heroes – and visits to a tattoo artist. Joe had acquired nineteen more tattoos in the five months before I met him. A cast of characters including Audrey Hepburn, Yoda, R2-D2 and Brian Bloodaxe crowded his arms and torso, and had begun to colonise his legs.

During one of my visits, I caught a first-hand glimpse of the pressures Sue faced. We were sitting chatting in the lounge when Joe suddenly froze – his eyes bulged and he seemed to be staring straight through me. His face was taut, his mouth fell open and he started muttering call signs as if he was talking on a military radio.

Sue, well drilled in de-escalating his flashbacks, was unfazed. She got up from the sofa, crouched down in front of him and spoke gently: 'Joe – you're at home, can you hear me? Blink your eyes if you can hear me. Joe – Sue. Blink for me. Can you hear me? Come on, blink for me, come on.'

Joe's face was taut but his eyelids flickered.

'That's it, you can hear me,' Sue said. 'You're at home. You're in Liverpool. You're safe. You're not in Ireland. You're just having a flashback.'

Perhaps half a minute passed – Joe's face remained blank and he seemed oblivious to our presence. Then he started awake and sucked in a sharp intake of breath. Had the flashback lasted a few seconds longer, Sue would have ordered me to leave the house.

A few months after our first meeting, Sue said Joe had finally started to receive more effective help through the NHS, and spoke highly of his consultant psychiatrist. Yet it had taken a long time, and a great deal of persistence on the family's part – resources which many ex-forces might struggle to muster.

'We have had to fight for three years to get the team in place that we now have,' she told me. 'I shudder to think how anyone goes on who has lost their family for whatever reason through PTSD. They are the guys that are left in the corner, rocking somewhere.'

Some months after my first visit to Liverpool Carers Centre, I attended another gathering of the Angels. The conversation turned to one of their greatest sources of heartache – the impact of their husbands' condition on their children. Many found themselves facing an impossible dilemma: was it better to stay in a marriage that might leave lasting emotional scars on their children or risk even greater pain through separation or divorce?

There was a consensus that the men's behaviour exacted a heavy toll. Sons might become withdrawn and anxious, while I had heard several stories of teenage daughters starting to cut themselves with razors. Some of the women said their children could not understand why their fathers were so angry, but Toni Collard, whose husband Keith had served in the Falklands and the Gulf War, explained that they had taught their daughter Grace about PTSD.

'For a child, they can't understand that, so we've always said "Mr Grumpy" – that's what we call PTSD in our house,' Toni told the group. 'So when he has his moments, where he needs to be left alone, when he is quite aggressive, when he is rude, I used to take Grace away and say: "Oh, it's Mr Grumpy, we need to give him some Daddy space."'

'Do you find double standards kick in a lot when they're unwell?' Sue asked. 'Something that they wouldn't put up with from the kids, they'll then do themselves, and vice versa?'

'He acts like a kid sometimes,' said Cheryl, whose husband Carl was tormented by his memories of serving as a peacekeeper in Bosnia.

Toni explained that when their daughter was younger her husband had been so protective that he insisted she carry a walkie-talkie when playing in the street: 'She didn't realise anything because it's just the way she's brought up.'

'See, my kids are still in that "I don't like Dad" stage,' said Denise. 'I then get it stuck in my head that I'm being a bad mum because I'm obviously not protecting my kids the way I should be. And then I'm thinking: "Well hold on, I shouldn't have to protect my kids like this," and then that's when all my emotions trigger off and then I turn to you for support and you help me because I find it hard.'

'We hold it together, don't we, when the kids are there?' said Cheryl.

'We've only had two times where we have had to "abandon ship", if you like,' said Toni. 'I think the children can sense something, but I will say to the children: "In the car, now." Thankfully, on both occasions, Keith has actually rung the police himself.

'I've come home to armed response in the street. When the police have finally let me in, my bath panel has been kicked in and my loft hatch has been ripped out because they're looking for the bodies of my children and me because they think that he's done something. How do you explain that to the children, it's awful isn't it?' she said, as other Angels nodded.

'The second time, he smashed up the house after we'd gone.

Everything, lovely wooden furniture – gone. When I got home, the police were at the house and he was already in the back of a police van. And a lovely policeman, who had actually served, came up to me and said: "He doesn't need to be in a cell. He needs a hospital, doesn't he?" And I said: "Yeah, he does."

'So they took him to the hospital. The police said to him: "Look, we can't wait around with you, we're going to have to leave you here. You'll be OK, won't you?"

'The hospital put him in a taxi and sent him home because there was no crisis team on to help him.

'We received a call the next day saying: "Did I want to be seen by the domestic violence unit?" and I said: "No, I just want some help for my husband."'

'It's very difficult to get people to understand that when the guys go into a flashback and violent episodes ensue that it's not domestic abuse,' Sue said. 'But I'm sure there's been a day when I said to him: "I don't know what's going on but if you're this angry, just punch me. Give me a slap and get it over with."'

Toni said: 'That reminds me of when people say: "Well, you have no injuries," and my husband says to me: "I wish I had a physical injury."'

'I said to Carl: "I'd rather your legs be blown off than this PTSD, I swear to God,"' said Cheryl.

'Screaming . . .' said Suzanna, whose husband Simon served in Northern Ireland. 'My husband wakes up screaming – that scares the life out of me. He doesn't lash out, he just screams.'

'Mine's woke up, jumped out and given the floor CPR before,' said Sue.

'We've all had that morning, haven't we, where they wake up in the bed, look over and say: "Why are you on the floor?"' she added. 'Or you wake up to a hand over your face going: "Shush, there's someone in the hatch."'

A universal problem was that it was often impossible to distinguish the symptoms of an illness from deliberate acts of vindictiveness or cruelty. Much as some women yearned to confront their men over the impact their moods were having on their families, they knew from experience that assertiveness could backfire. Several said they could not risk telling the unvarnished truth for fear of plunging their husbands into a fresh bout of self-loathing that would inevitably end in a new drinking binge, a shouting match or worse.

Cheryl was among those caught in the dilemma. She explained that Carl would be wracked with guilt for failing to be a better father after a period of heavy drinking to suppress his memories of Bosnia. At the same time, she was afraid that her husband might one day blame her for not having left him years earlier to protect the children from his anger.

'He's doing OK now, he's back on medication, off the alcohol, so fingers crossed,' Cheryl said. 'But that could all change in an hour.'

With the men frequently incapable of looking after themselves, a greater burden fell on the women. Suzanna said her husband Simon had loved cooking before he had joined the Army, but now he was so distracted that he tended to set things on fire. He had become a recluse and spent most of his time writing.

'He's avoiding things, which is working for him at the minute. But if he was to go out and meet people, then it could be anything and the anger would come back and the aggression,' Suzanna said. 'He's tried all the therapies and all the agencies and they've all let him down.'

'We are the best GP in the world for our husbands,' said Toni. 'Because we're the only one that's able to even slightly engage with them and we're the only ones that can get through.'

'Now and again, I see my real husband and I'm like: "Hiya!"' said Cheryl, with a bright smile. 'We make a joke of it because he's gone, he's totally different – he's a totally different man. One minute you can see the change in his eyes – he can be like the Devil.'

'I would love to turn back time and have my strong, working, healthy, fit, loving husband back,' Toni said. 'But PTSD has taken all that away.'

'Carl was lovely, everyone loved Carl,' said Cheryl. 'He was brilliant, he was hilarious, he was the best – he still is the best person I've ever met in my life. It's like it's ripped him away from me – he's just not the same any more. I feel robbed.'

'Those golden moments when you see your husband's personality coming out – that's what keeps us all going, isn't it?' said Sue. 'You'll have a golden moment every couple of months and you'll think: "That's what I'm fighting for and that's why I'm still here."'

The meeting ended, somebody put the kettle on and I spoke with Toni. She felt that PTSD had deprived her family of holidays, friends and a social life, yet at the same time, the struggle had brought out a softer side in her husband. Always a hard man, he seemed to have learned greater empathy after attending group therapy at Combat Stress, but Toni knew the memories of his service were buried in the shallowest of graves.

Once they had taken their daughter to the beach in Wales. She became stuck in the mud, and – though not in danger – called out to her father for help. Keith hesitated, saying he did not want to ruin his new shoes, but Toni could sense something was wrong. She later learned that the beach had evoked memories of dead Iraqi soldiers, half buried in the desert. The seaweed had reminded Keith of tufts of hair poking through the sand.

'If he goes on the sand he is convinced there are bodies under the sand,' said Toni. 'It's too much for him.'

Then she gave a rueful smile and added: 'Seychelles – never going to happen.'

The Combat PTSD Angels began to disperse and Toni headed into the car park, where Keith was waiting to drive her home.

13

'Fire in the Mist'

Trauma, body and brain

It was a bright summer's morning and the twin towers of the Dartford Crossing pierced a clear sky. Hugh Forsyth was at the wheel of his Citroën saloon, heading into the country from his home in South Ockendon in Essex. The prospect of crossing the gentle arc of concrete had once filled him with stomach-knotting dread, fuelled by visions of a suicide truck bomber demolishing the nearest stanchion and sending his vehicle cartwheeling into the Thames. Braving the busy underwater tunnel on the return trip was even worse: he had once been held up behind a car with Irish plates and had felt like he was about to combust. As soon as he reached home, he had run into the bathroom to vomit.

'This was an absolute nightmare for me one or two years ago,' Hugh said, as we merged with the four-lane stream of rush-hour traffic. 'I could hardly hold the steering wheel. I'd be shaking as I'd drive across it.'

This time, there were no more furrowed brows or compulsive mirror-ward glances. A white container truck rumbled along in front of us but Hugh barely gave it a second look. We reached the other side and left the scruffy warehouses and container parks of the estuary, cutting through a patchwork of fields and mature woodland as we drove towards West Sussex. The road dipped through tunnels wrought of ancient hedgerows until we reached an imposing red-brick farmhouse facing a meadow. A herd of half a dozen horses browsed among the dandelions, their tails swishing away flies.

Hugh parked by a barn, the sun-drenched timbers smelling of warm creosote, and approached Ko Li, a magnificent white gelding with an ivory-coloured mane. The horse had eyes like moist black marble and instantly recognised Hugh, who gave him an affectionate pat on the neck. Ko Li turned out to be an apt name for an animal that had served as a guiding light in Hugh's journey. It is drawn from the I Ching, the Chinese book of divination, and means Fire in the Mist.

From my travels across Britain, it was clear that there were thousands, perhaps many thousands of ex-forces who were stuck in limbo – not quite in crisis, yet not truly well. Some had been lucky – the treatments offered by the Army, the NHS, Combat Stress or others had afforded varying degrees of relief or recovery. Many others, though, had exhausted the officially sanctioned routes and remained caught between worlds, unable to leave the past behind and live fully in the present.

Hugh had spent years in this twilight. A gentle man in his mid-forties, he had been a corporal in the Royal Engineers, serving two tours in Northern Ireland, the first when he was eighteen, and a subsequent deployment in Bosnia. Much of his time had been spent working on teams searching for hidden bombs. The strains accumulated over more than a decade spilled over one afternoon in Bosnia in 1996 when a car overtook his truck then careered off the road. Hugh had run down to help and instead found himself surrounded by militiamen – he had left his rifle in the cab.

A few years later Hugh had – quite literally – dug his own grave. After a confrontation with his boss, and then his ex-wife, he had grabbed his old rucksack and stuffed it with an entrenching tool, a bottle of Southern Comfort and a statue of a mine-detector man he was awarded when he left the Army. As night fell, he had hacked a shell scrape in the garden of a nearby pub, scrawled a note, swallowed a handful of pills and lain down to die. He owed his life to a couple who had spotted him as they walked home.

Like many ex-forces who were given grace enough to survive their suicidal impulses, Hugh had done the rounds of psychiatric wards and eventually joined the old respite regime at Combat Stress in 2005. Though Hugh had attained a measure of stability, he had never felt more than half alive. There would still be times when he would be out walking his dog and he would see 'tilt rods' used to trigger Russian landmines standing in the long grass. Imagining the devices were strewn across the park, he would have to phone Tina, his new partner, to rescue him. Or he would creep downstairs while she was asleep and watch online videos of beheadings in Iraq, indulging an obsession with capture dating back to six months he spent as a twenty-year-old soldier roving Belfast in an unmarked car. He would feel so hopeless sometimes he would shout at Tina that she would be better off without him. When he had first arrived at the farm, his face had been a mask.

Hugh was among the first ex-forces I met and he taught me a great deal – though not in ways I would have at first imagined. In the two years I spent getting to know him, I became as convinced as he was that his recovery was due to a course of equine therapy he had undertaken at the farm – a form of psychotherapy that harnesses the healing power of horses. Advocates of the approach say it can foster the kind of rapid and enduring shifts in trauma survivors that even many years of conventional therapy might fail to yield. The programme, run outside the town of East Grinstead, had been developed by a therapist named Sun Tui. She had grown up with a more conventional British name but adopted her new identity to mark her progression as a healer. The name comes from the Chinese philosophy of Taoism and translates as 'Art of Living' or 'Inner Truth'. After growing up in a military family, and having briefly served as a reservist while married to an Army officer based in Germany, she had a particular affinity for helping ex-forces.

Sun Tui had developed an interest in the therapeutic gifts of horses after learning to ride had helped her conquer periods of debilitating depression following the loss of a child and subsequent divorce. She went on to study in the United States with Linda Kohanov and Kathleen Barry Ingram, pioneers of a school of natural horsemanship that hinges on cultivating trust with an animal rather than breaking its will. Sun Tui had since trained as a traumatologist and founded degree- and masters-level training qualifications in equine-facilitated learning, and had embarked on clinical research in cooperation with the King's Centre for Military Health Research.

Though Hugh had undergone a remarkable shift, it required a stretch of the imagination to see how horses might help resolve chronic symptoms of PTSD. It was easier to define what equine therapy was not: a day of riding ponies and feeding them apples, as Hugh had assumed when he first heard about Sun Tui's work from a member of staff at Combat Stress.

'You just feel something,' Sun Tui said during one of my visits to the farm. 'You get a glimpse of the universe that you're actually living in. You might not be able to hold that for any length of time, and I don't think you're supposed to. But what you do have is a sense of "Ah – there is something more, there is purpose."'

To help me understand, Sun Tui invited me for a consultation with her four-legged therapists, and a new vista opened in my understanding of trauma.

The farm sits on the lip of a shallow, wooded valley, and is surrounded by fields. On a hot August day the expanse had a dream-like feel. There were six horses grazing, including Ko Li, a beautiful chestnut Arabian mare named Isis, and a cantankerous thirty-year-old pony-sized bay called Jigsaw, who was the herd leader. Also known as Jig-Jog, Jigsaw was clad in an all-enveloping coat to protect him from midges, giving him a somewhat regal aspect. The farm is only a twenty-minute drive from East

Grinstead station, but when I half-closed my eyes I felt like I was surveying an expanse of East African bush. The feeling of isolation is an illusion, as Jigsaw proved one day when he broke free, wandered into a neighbouring garden and fell through the cover on a swimming pool.

I had come to attend a two-day introduction to equine therapy called Dare to Live developed by Sun Tui. Hugh, who had progressed so far that he was learning to teach equine therapy, wore a sticker on his polo shirt with his name written in felt tip. The three other participants were women, two of whom had served in the forces and who were considerably more at ease around horses than I was. We assembled in the barn – where a blackboard was emblazoned with the words DARE TO LIVE – IGNITE CHANGE, LIVE LIFE and chairs were arranged in a loose semicircle around an unlit wood-burning stove. A table bore various mystical accoutrements – amethyst crystals, candles, a packet of sea salt and a deck of cards – a kind of equine tarot. I picked number 27: 'Merlin's Spirit' – showing a black stallion nuzzling a foal. An accompanying book explained the symbolism: 'Redemption of the Masculine'; 'Mutual Transformation' and 'The New Hero's Journey'.

'It's an experience,' Sun Tui told the group. 'We can learn a lot of facts in our heads, but that doesn't always change the way we feel about ourselves.'

She began by explaining why horses are so suited to helping people work with difficult emotions: they seem to have an un-canny ability to sense feelings that humans may be hiding, even from themselves. The ancestors of Ko Li and Jigsaw evolved over millions of years spent trying to avoid being devoured by big cats. Their descendants have inherited a startle reflex more sensitive than that of a mouse and a razor-sharp sensitivity to the intentions of potential predators, including people. With those big, soulful eyes, they can see straight into you.

Sun Tui said horses could tolerate your anger, sadness or fear as long as you were not trying to hide them. The key to winning their trust was to achieve 'congruence' – ensuring that what you were feeling and how you were acting were in sync. You could only do this by first finding out what was really going on inside. That was where the crayons came in. Sun Tui handed out colouring boxes and told us to begin summoning messages from our unconscious by drawing a mandala on a page in our worksheets headed the 'Sacred Circle of Possibility'.

I glanced across at Hugh – a man who once made his living as a searcher in a bomb squad – but his face showed no trace of scepticism as he filled his Sacred Circle with an image of a path through forbidding mountains. I let my mind wander and produced a ship sailing on an ocean with a pair of stick figures on the upper deck. My brown crayon was too blunt to render the female of the pair as enticing as I would have imagined.

The next step was to turn our attention away from our thoughts and tune in to our bodies. Sun Tui directed us to sweep a lighthouse beam of attention through our heads, torsos, arms and legs to detect any sensation of discomfort, tingling, heat, cold or any other kind of feeling that we were generally too absorbed in our thought chatter to notice.

Testing his own role as trainee instructor, Hugh asked Sun Tui: 'Do you want me to say anything about the body scan?'

'We'll keep it to the clients for the moment,' Sun Tui said.

'OK,' said Hugh.

If any tension came up the response was to breathe out with an elongated 'Haaa' sound to stay grounded. Failing that, we learned to gaze into the distance and unfocus our eyes, which could have a similarly calming effect. The technique might sound a little esoteric, but the sometimes remarkable results of the now widely used therapy of EMDR were testament to the power of working with eye positions. As we began to relax, we were ushered into the field and Sun Tui issued each of us with a 'boundary tool' – a stick with a short rope attached – to allow us to set limits if horses came too close. It was time to meet the herd.

Naturally I was intrigued by Ko Li, the striking white gelding, but I feared others may think I was being somewhat grandiose if I tried to work with him so I sidled up to the shorter, chestnut-coloured Isis, who managed to bring a ballerina-like grace to the act of masticating grass. The mare, sensing my lack of authenticity, paid me zero heed and continued snuffling at the ground with agile black lips. I turned my back as instructed and performed the body scan. The goal was to override the instinct to suppress any difficult sensation you encountered and then 'expand' it by silently posing the question: *If this feeling could speak, what would it be trying to say?*

I felt a sadness welling up from nowhere and there were tears in my eyes. A sentence formed silently in my mind: *Time to let go.* I retreated from the paddock and Hugh asked gently: 'Do you want to talk about it?'

I shook my head, torn between a sense of shame at my own unexpected vulnerability and gratitude for his kindness. When Hugh conducted the same exercise he discovered anxiety roiling in his abdomen.

'Once I expanded it, it turned to pixellated yellow rays coming out my legs,' he said. 'I got a message that said: "*Stay rooted.*"'

After my encounter with Isis, I wrote down my insights on my worksheet:

- Horses are at one with themselves
- Not torturing themselves
- Can these horses help me to let go of the past?

I did not consider my musings any the less profound for having been written in capitals in blue crayon.

The cornerstone of equine therapy is a process known as 'join up' – also the hardest part to describe. Through some mysterious mind-meld, you learn to forge an almost telepathic bond with the horse. The entry-level version is to lead a horse around a paddock with no speaking or touching, and certainly without whacking it with a 'boundary tool'. When it works, the horse naturally falls into step behind your shoulder as if connected by an invisible halter. Sun Tui had advised me to visualise the horse doing what I wanted, then drop the image into my gut and project a beam of energy carrying my instructions. When this failed, I found myself miming something akin to slow-motion disco moves to attract Isis's attention. She responded by jettison-ing tightly packed clods of manure.

I might have failed to tune in to the collective equestrian frequency – but the exercise did have one very immediate result: I was forced to confront how I reacted to feelings of frustration. One part of my mind was saying it would be much easier if I was allowed to use the 'boundary tool' to show Isis who was boss. Another was telling me the effort was futile, and perhaps without the encouragement of Sharon Clifton, one of the instructors, I would have given up.

When Isis did eventually lift her head from her chlorophyll banquet and start to follow my lead I felt an unexpected thrill, even if my 'join up' only lasted for about ten seconds of the twenty minutes I spent trying. The energy beam I had projected was clearly too insipid. Hugh exuded greater confidence.

'It's like shooting laser beams out my stomach,' he said, miming cowboy-style shooting gestures with his forefingers. '*Peow* – *Peow* – *Peow*.'

The course closed with another mandala – 'Connecting the Sacred Circles'. I drew myself as a star-jumping stick man topped by a double helix of DNA. One of the women produced an intimidatingly professional-looking sketch of a horse. Months later, reflecting on my halting attempts to connect with Isis, Sun Tui suggested there could be hidden benefits to tears. 'If it rains one night in the desert, the next morning, within hours, there's plants growing,' she said. I could not deny that I had felt brighter after my two days on the farm, but I still had no real idea of how horses might have helped Hugh work through his symptoms of PTSD. That would require some reading.

For more than a century, psychotherapy has mostly proceeded on the assumption that the best way to help somebody is to sit in a room and talk. The approach was famously articulated in Vienna in 1893, when Sigmund Freud and Josef Breuer, his mentor, described how symptoms of trauma 'immediately and permanently disappeared' when a patient recounted a troubling event in the greatest possible detail. What became known as 'the talking cure' has since evolved into a bewildering array of branches, but almost all rest on the basic premise that clients will be able to resolve their difficulties primarily through a series of conversations with a (human) therapist.

A century later, this orthodoxy came under attack. In the mid-1990s, a number of therapists in the United States who had worked with Vietnam veterans and abuse survivors began to argue that the overarching faith in the power of words was misplaced. The mechanisms driving intrusive images, hyper-vigilance and explosive rage were buried in layers of the brain that were largely insulated from the influence of language. Psychotherapy needed to be retooled with a new emphasis on sensations in the body, rather than on thoughts in the mind.

Just as Myers had galvanised the debate on 'shell shock' with his 1915 contribution to the *Lancet*, so this new school of thought on trauma was spurred by an academic article. In 1994, Dr Bessel Van der Kolk, a Dutch-American psychiatrist, published 'The Body Keeps the Score' in the *Harvard Review of Psychiatry*. Van der Kolk drew on the latest theories of neuroscience to argue that traumatic experiences had a direct impact on the workings of the brain – disrupting the production of stress hormones, playing havoc with the brain's alarm system and preventing the normal processing and storage of memories. As I was talking to ex-forces about PTSD, Van der Kolk published a book with the same title, refining his ideas in the light of two more decades of clinical experience and advances in neurobiology. Trauma was not simply an event that had occurred in the past, he argued – it left an 'imprint' in the body and brain. The only way to resolve the symptoms of PTSD would be to restore a measure of balance to the delicate systems knocked out of equilibrium by the experience of overwhelming terror. Words alone might not suffice.

Van der Kolk has his fair share of critics in the psychiatric establishment, yet to me the book held an intuitive appeal. Here was a possible framework to account for the paranoia, surging anger, insomnia and numbing experienced by so many of the ex-forces I had met. Though Van der Kolk was by no means alone in emphasising the biology at work in PTSD, he had provided one of the clearest explanations of why the condition was not 'all in the mind' – as some sceptics in the Army still seemed to believe – and why telling somebody to 'man up' or 'snap out of it' was so futile. The condition was as much a physical injury as a broken leg.

'Feeling out of control, survivors of trauma often begin to fear that they are damaged to the core and beyond redemption,' Van der Kolk wrote. 'We now know that their behaviours are not the result of moral failings or signs of lack of willpower or bad character – they are caused by actual changes in the brain.'

The debate begun by Myers had resumed in a new form. Doctors in the First World War had begun by assuming that 'shell shock' was a result of brain damage caused by the pressure waves from exploding shells. The theory was quickly discredited and the origins of 'shell shock' were relocated from the brain to the psyche. Van der Kolk and like-minded psychiatrists had returned the emphasis back to the body, but in a very different way from their First World War predecessors, or even from contemporaries studying brain injuries caused by roadside bombs in Afghanistan or Iraq. Rather than scanning for evidence of tiny lesions caused by concussions, Van der Kolk wanted to understand how abuse in childhood or trauma in adult life could cause lasting disruptions to the physiological processes governing our response to threat.

To understand Van der Kolk's theory, it helps to make a fist. The wrist represents the oldest part of the brain, sometimes called the reptilian brain, which manages the basic functions that keep an organism alive – breathing, digesting, excreting and all the other things that newborn babies do. The fist represents the mammalian brain, present in humans and all other animals that nurture and care for their young. This layer is home to the limbic system – a halo-shaped component that governs our emotions, our flight-or-fight responses, and our ability to form lasting attachments with family and friends. Taken together, these two layers form what Van der Kolk calls the 'emotional brain' – the place where chronic trauma reactions reside.

Place your other hand over this fist, and you have a model of the outer layer of the brain, known as the neocortex – the crinkly dome familiar from science programmes. Though other mammals have a neocortex, the region is most developed in humans. Our frontal lobes give us the capacity for language and abstract reasoning used in the production of everything from flint arrowheads to atom bombs. They also contain mirror neurons, neural structures that underpin empathy – described by one neuroscientist as a kind of 'neural Wi-Fi' that allows us to feel connected to others and read emotional cues.

As we go about our daily lives, the 'emotional brain' is constantly scanning for any sign of danger. The process takes place in the amygdala – the brain's 'smoke alarm'. Formed of two almond-shaped structures, the amygdala monitors the stream of sense data from the eyes, ears, mouth, nose and skin for any evidence of a threat – helped by feedback from the hippocampus, a seahorse-shaped bundle of neurons that relates new input to past experiences. If the amygdala senses trouble, it can instantly trigger the release of powerful stress hormones, mobilising the body to fight or run. Once the threat is passed, the system gradually returns to normal, and the balance of decision-making power returns to the rational part of the brain in the dome-shaped neocortex.

But there are situations where the threat is so overwhelming, the terror so intense, that the flood of stress chemicals knocks the system permanently out of kilter. The risks are particularly high when the normal fight or flight response is blocked – perhaps because a soldier is pinned down by mortar fire, or trapped with his back to the wall as an assailant charges towards him with a bayonet. In such cases, the 'freeze' response may kick in: the victim is literally rooted to the spot with fear.

It helps to understand what can happen in humans by looking at the animal kingdom. When a gazelle is seized by a lion, it is programmed by nature to collapse unconscious – the 'flop' response. The move is sometimes called 'playing dead' but in fact the gazelle has no choice – it is an involuntary reflex hardwired by nature to make the predator lose interest. Military training aims to drum the 'freeze' and 'flop' responses out of raw recruits by conditioning them to fight or flee at all costs. But *in extremis*, even hardened combat veterans will nevertheless react similarly to the gazelle – sometimes experiencing an 'out of body' experience, as if watching themselves from above. According to one theory, this is the point where the sufferer literally 'blows a fuse': an onslaught of stress chemicals kills off neurons in the hippocampus and the brain loses its usual capacity to file memories of the unfolding horror in the past.

On the African plain, if the lion wanders away the lucky gazelle will hop unsteadily to its feet, then shake itself vigorously to discharge its pent-up energy and bring its stress hormones back into balance. It can then resume calmly eating grass as if nothing had happened. Humans, by contrast, are less adept at rapidly recalibrating their system. Van der Kolk believes that PTSD is caused by a fundamental reorganisation of the central nervous system that permanently changes a person's perception of danger.

In this altered state, the brain's survival mechanisms react instantly to the slightest reminder of the original threat. I had heard many accounts of this process in action: a dive for cover in response to a low-flying jet; an abusive outburst triggered by a bumped trolley at the supermarket; treating a smudged plate on the dish rack as a matter of life or death. In such cases, the amygdala – the 'smoke alarm' – had hijacked the system. Trauma survivors might often have no conscious awareness of the connection between their devastating overreactions and a life-threatening situation many years before.

Such overwhelming experiences not only threw the body's stress response out of balance, they also skewed memory. As Van der Kolk explained, parts of the brain that provide a sense of time and perspective, a certainty that 'that was then, and this is now', go blank. It is as if a secretary who normally sorts the contents of an in-tray into the correct files is swamped by an avalanche of papers and they start spilling all over the floor. Flashbacks occur as the brain tries in vain to process these images into some sort of coherent order but succeeds only in adding to the chaos.

These action replays are not like everyday recollections, akin to pictures in an album. During a flashback, the brain bombards the sufferer with sights, sounds and smells so real they feel like they are actually back in combat. One veteran compared the experience to being trapped in a space helmet with a video of the traumatic incident cued up to play in the visor at any moment – just as Hilary Horton had been forced to keep watching the film of the white-tiled kitchen at her medical outpost in Al Amarah. Sufferers begin to organise their lives around keeping such flashbacks at bay, perhaps through alcohol, or seemingly harmless activities such as extreme exercise. Some seek to avoid triggers altogether by retreating into the narrow world of the recluse.

When I reached Van der Kolk by phone at his office at the Boston University School of Medicine, he explained that talking therapies such as CBT (cognitive behavioural therapy) can play an important role in helping people reconnect with others and understand what is happening to them as they start to confront their condition. But to really heal their symptoms, the balance between the 'emotional brain' and the rational brain must be restored. Words alone cannot accomplish this task because the rational part of the brain is impotent to talk the 'emotional brain' out of its own reality. When the 'smoke alarm' is triggered, no amount of insight will switch it off.

'Talking, the understanding part of the brain, is basically an interpersonal part of the brain – it has to do with you and me getting along with each other,' Van der Kolk said. 'The imprint of trauma is not in the social system primarily. It's primarily in the self-preservation part of the brain.'

For real change to take place, the body needs to appreciate that the danger has passed and learn to live in the here and now. Van der Kolk advocated various kinds of approaches based on working with the breath or the body, or mindfulness exercises in which somebody learns to hover as an observer over their thoughts and feelings. The goal was to learn to safely approach their traumatic material as a first step to releasing the blocked energy from the time of the incident – a little like the way a gazelle shakes itself down after a brush with a lion. Van der Kolk has also pioneered group therapy work, where clients can re-enact and resolve traumatic scenes as other group members play roles from their past.

Not everyone shared Van der Kolk's convictions. His critics feared it might be risky to unleash his methods more widely without first validating them with much more research, and some suspected that the neuroscience he cited remained much cruder than he implied. Even some experts who were sympathetic to Van der Kolk's thesis were concerned that his accounts of the mechanisms involved in PTSD neglected to mention important parts of the 'emotional brain' that would need to be engaged for trauma treatment to be successful.

For his part, Van der Kolk believed that the fiercest resistance to his approach stemmed from the vested interests of professionals who might have built their careers on promoting the virtues of talk. He told me: 'For reasons that I don't quite understand these notions are considered controversial. Some people consider me as the main spokesperson in the field – others say that I am a nut who overstates his case. Only time will tell whether our substantial knowledge about the way the brain is changed by life experience will be taken seriously and guide the development of effective treatments.'

While I could lay no claim to any scientific expertise, Van der Kolk's model provided one potential explanation for how equine therapy had enabled Hugh to live life in a higher octave. The exercises I had tried at Dare to Live – tuning in to sensations, and working with the 'haaa' breath – were precisely the kind of body-awareness techniques Van der Kolk advocated. The horse acted as a kind of force-multiplier – its sheer size and power anchoring a trauma survivor as they explored feelings they may never have otherwise felt safe enough to confront. The 'join up' exercise aimed to restore a sense of connection to others by activating the same pathways in the 'emotional brain' that govern human relationships.

'That person gets all "connected up" – it's as though the light gets switched on,' Sun Tui explained. 'The horse wants to connect with it.'

Perhaps more remarkably, Ko Li, Isis and the other horses seemed to know intuitively how to help. Take Jigsaw, for example, the grumpiest and scruffiest horse in the herd. He had arrived at the farm full of aggression and tormented by a skin condition known as sweet itch. Sun Tui said he knew what it meant to be an outcast and often bonded with ex-forces.

'He comes into his own when working with people who have pain and suffering,' Sun Tui said. 'He's kind of the horse that you might call "a master of sadness". He can really help people to connect to that in a graceful way that allows tears to flow. Nobody likes him because he's scraggy looking. He chooses them – and they start to see something. He hits them in their heart.'

Sun Tui described how one ex-serviceman came to the farm struggling with confusion and sadness after being separated from his family. He felt drawn to Isis, but the chestnut mare treated him with the same Zen-like indifference I had encountered.

'Meanwhile, right at the fence-line is Jigsaw in his dirty, smelly blanket – staring, completely fixated,' Sun Tui said.

She had suggested the former soldier approach Jigsaw instead.

'What?' he replied. 'That dirty, smelly old thing?'

Sun Tui removed the blanket to reveal Jigsaw's radiant brown and white coat. She told the man how Jigsaw had started life at the farm not knowing how to communicate except through lashing out.

'He just burst into tears,' Sun Tui said. 'The two of them just connected, inseparable, for that afternoon and the next day.'

Hugh had described a similar breakthrough with Ko Li. He had been working with Sun Tui for two weeks, when a BBC crew arrived to shoot an item about her work. She asked Hugh to demonstrate the 'join up' technique, but Ko Li refused to budge. Hugh felt like a child trying to move a marble along a table using willpower alone. As the crew waited, Sun Tui took Hugh aside.

'This isn't just a trick,' she said. 'Really do that "Haaa" breath, really drop your energy down to your stomach, then visualise Ko Li. Really believe that he will do it.'

Hugh repeated silently: *I really need you to do this Ko Li because I really need this to go right.*

When he tried again, Hugh felt a sensation like a lightning

bolt shooting from the crown of his head to the soles of his feet. The knot in his stomach loosened and he felt a profound sense of peace suffusing his body. It was as if he had been catapulted back into his eighteen-year-old self, before he had set foot in Belfast. This time, Ko Li strolled right behind his shoulder.

Hugh told me: 'It was literally like a magnet. He grabbed hold of you and – pfff – "there you go, you're safe, sorted and nothing's going to damage you".

'I was like a young kid again. That spark I had of "I can do anything" – that's the feeling I got back. It was like: "This works, it really works." It took from my head all the grief, all the PTSD, all the worry and it just went phhhh . . .

'What you get with the horse is real. They don't see the soldier, they don't see anything else – they are seeing the real you.'

One afternoon, as I was chatting with Sun Tui outside the barn, Hugh wandered over to join us with his parents, Emma and Hughie senior, who were paying their first visit to the farm. Hugh's father, who had served twenty-two years in the Army and left as a sergeant major, could hardly believe the progress his son had made since his darkest days.

Hughie, who wore a wide-brimmed hat against the sun, said: 'We didn't realise he was suffering from PTSD. It was hard for us to figure out why he had changed.'

'I'd had my big breakdown,' Hugh said. 'I thought the answer was retrain, get another job, get another career, move out of the area, get a fresh start.'

'We thought everything was fine,' Emma said. 'And then it's just as bad as ever.'

'That is very much the nature of trauma, though,' said Sun Tui. 'When you're in the thick of depression you might not know it, but other people can see it, and the people who love you will keep on fighting for you.'

'I remember one time we sat for two weeks solid,' said Hugh's father. 'All we did was talk and eat dinners. Talk, drink tea and drink coffee, twenty-four hours a day. Just talk, talk, talk.'

'I didn't think that a young lad, with a half a career under his belt, had seen enough and done enough to warrant having PTSD,' said Hugh.

'I phoned off work so I could be there twenty-four hours a day,' said Emma. 'Talking wasn't helping: we were too close.'

'From a clinical point of view, you were in a helpless position and doing everything you could do with what you knew,' Sun Tui said. 'I can only imagine it must have been living hell watching your lovely son struggling like this, intuitively knowing as parents he wasn't safe on his own.'

'We went away one weekend to see some friends – bank holiday,' Emma said. 'While we were away he slit his wrists. I said: "I'm going to get to the bottom of this. I'm going to find out exactly why he's doing it."'

Emma said her son's response was that he had tried to kill himself because they had gone away for the weekend and not left him any milk.

Emma recalled: 'I saw red and said: "Right, you're on your own." That's when we said: "enough's enough".'

'Can't remember that,' said Hugh. 'I didn't even remember doing that to my wrists. I lost four days completely. I remember lying in bed and you were really angry. I remember looking down and seeing all the bandages. I was so confused, I was like: "No, I never did this. I've already survived an overdose." There was no way.'

'Now we know the PTSD trauma part is an injury to the brain,' Sun Tui said. 'It is treatable. That's where Hugh's an inspiration to so many.'

Later Hugh led his father on a 'join up' exercise with Isis. To Sun Tui's astonishment, it was only a few minutes before the stubborn Arabian was walking calmly behind the older man's shoulder.

'That's stunning,' she called across to them. 'That's "join up" with heartfeltness and connection.'

Father and son exchanged glances as Isis went back to her grass.

14

'Machine-gun Mind'

Discovering inner peace

In November 2007, a 250-strong group of veterans of the Falklands War returned to the islands on a week-long pilgrimage organised by the South Atlantic Medal Association, a group named after the medal awarded to the 26,000 people who took part in the campaign. Among them was a former soldier named Gus Hales, who had grown up in the pit town of Nuneaton in the West Midlands, where his father had worked as a coal miner. At the end of the visit, former soldiers, islanders and officials filed into Christchurch Cathedral in Port Stanley for a Remembrance Sunday service. The church was filled to capacity and some pilgrims were diverted into a nearby hall where proceedings were relayed on a screen.

Gus is a tall, compact man whose rugged complexion bears testament to his love of the outdoors. Like many of the others attending the service, he had worn a navy blazer and pinned on his South Atlantic Medal. As the congregation filed into the church, Gus worked his way towards a pew behind the front rows reserved for dignitaries. A naval officer tried to redirect him but Gus told him he needed an aisle seat because of a bad leg. The VIPs seated in front of him included the veterans minister flown in from London, the governor of the islands, who cradled a cocked bicorn hat decorated with ostrich feathers, and a fierce-looking brigadier. A vicar supervised proceedings from the pulpit.

Airborne raids rely on speed and daring and Gus, who had served in 9 Parachute Squadron, a unit of the Royal Engineers, had taken the philosophy to heart. He had realised while running through his mission in his mind that timing would be critical. Make it too short, and there was a risk his intervention might fall flat. If he tarried too long, however, the vicar might recover quickly enough to shout him down. Gus calculated the optimal duration: precisely two minutes.

As the service wore on, Gus sat with his head bowed. The only outward sign of his nervousness was his tendency to absently wipe his hand across his upper lip. Somebody handed the veterans minister a piece of paper and he began to recite a passage from St Paul's Epistle to the Romans. Gus thought the words sounded lazy and formulaic and a surge of anger dissolved his remaining self-doubt. The minister sat down and there was a pause as the vicar put on his glasses. Gus strode up the aisle and took position behind the lectern. Fixing the minister with his gaze from a few paces away, he began to speak.

'I'd just like to say, on occasions like this, humble soldiers are very rarely ever asked to say anything,' Gus said. 'I'm not on the programme, but I'd just like to say this.'

Gus reminded the gathering of the veterans who had committed suicide since the end of the war, then paused, closed his eyes, and took a deep and deliberate breath. Despite a lump that had formed in his throat, Gus's voice was even and clear as he recited his poem from memory:

'Every year on Remembrance Sunday
I sit in the corner of a British Legion Bar
Dressed in blazer, shirt, regimental tie
And polished shoes, with my head held high.
But deep in my mind, where nobody goes,
I see a wooden cross where the wind of victory blows.
"Three Cheers for Victory," I heard the politicians say

But they never asked me about my victory.
And, if they did, I would have explained it this way:
It isn't your flags or your emblems of war,
Or your marching of troops past the Palace's door.
It isn't Mrs. Thatcher on the balcony high,
Reaffirming her pledge to serve or die.
But it's the look and the pain on a teenager's face
As he dies for his country, in a far off place.
It's the guns and the shells and the phosphorous grenades
The dead and the wounded, the freshly cut graves
Or a grieving wife or the fatherless child
Whose young, tender life will be forever defiled.
Or the alcoholic soldier with a shattered mind
Who takes the suicide option for some peace to find.
Well, that's my victory but no one knows
For it's deep in my mind where nobody goes.'

On the words 'deep in my mind' Gus pointed to his forehead. The applause erupted before he had returned to his pew. A woman in a striped jacket seated midway down the nave rose clapping and others joined in a standing ovation – though not the officials and military officers seated at the front, who remained frozen in their seats.

After the service, former soldiers and Marines arrayed in their medals and blazers poured into the churchyard and took turns to congratulate Gus, who had put on the maroon beret of the Parachute Regiment. They offered handshakes and hugs as a videographer recorded their words.

'That has been the most moving part of the week,' one said. 'It was absolutely fantastic.'

'People like it,' another added. 'It's important, to all of us, mate.'

Gus told them that all he had wanted was for the voices of the soldiers and their families to be heard: 'It gets lost, doesn't it?'

The pilgrims then made their way to a memorial grove where

a tree had been planted for each of the 255 members of the Task Force and three islanders who had been killed in the war. The custodians had chosen hardy species of cypress, ash and mountain pine to ensure these 'living graves' would survive the bitter gales that whipped Port Stanley each winter. In an annexe, several younger saplings had taken root, planted to honour men who had taken their own lives long after the fighting ended.

I had first heard of Gus through Danny White, the former Royal Marine whom I had visited in East Sussex. Danny knew Gus and had shown me a clip of his recital on his phone. Even through the tiny screen, Gus projected a mesmerising intensity. I wondered what must have happened to have transformed him from a saluting recruit into a renegade soldier-poet.

Danny seemed reluctant to put me in touch with Gus directly, explaining that despite his foray in the cathedral, he was an intensely private man. His name came up a few weeks later when I went to see Dr Dafydd Alun Jones, the psychiatrist who had worked at Ty Gwyn. Gus had once been among his charges and he gave me a number for his home in the Welsh borders. Gus's wife Angela answered and told me she would pass on my request. I rang every few weeks, until eventually, six months after my first call, Gus invited me to visit his old family home in a quiet street in Nuneaton. As we drove from the station, he pointed out Mount Judd, a towering, grass-covered slag heap left from his home town's mining heyday.

Gus led me into the living room, which served as a sometime pit stop for his racing bikes. At the age of fifty-seven, the legacy of pent-up emotion from the war still propelled him like a dynamo and Angela estimated he must have covered almost 8,000 miles – enough to reach the Falklands. I guessed the decor was little changed since Gus's parents' day, but one feature appeared to be a newer addition – a wall alcove housing a collection of wood and stone Buddhas. A card for a funeral he had recently attended of a fellow Falklands veteran lay on the sofa. Gus said the man had driven onto a hillside, fixed a pipe to his exhaust, and gassed himself in his car.

'To think that thirty years on, this can still trouble to the point where they just don't want to live,' Gus said. 'So the Falklands is a distant memory to a lot of people – to us it's something we live with every day.'

Like many of the ex-forces I had met, Gus had joined the Army in large part due to a lack of other options. After leaving school, he had worked for a time as a fitter maintaining mining machinery, but he had no desire to follow his father underground. He toyed briefly with the idea of becoming a vicar but at the age of nineteen he joined the military, hoping to discover his own version of the fierce camaraderie his father's generation had found in the pits.

When Argentine forces seized the Falklands, Gus and his colleagues in 9 Squadron were part of the hastily assembled Task Force. Gus recalled that as they had neared the archipelago, one of the padres had given the men on his ship a rousing speech, warning them that some would kill and some would be killed, but that every man would be expected to do his duty. To Gus, then in his mid-twenties, the words had sounded like an echo from the days of Nelson.

Gus's first mission was to secure unexploded ammunition in the aftermath of the Battle of Goose Green on the eastern side of the island. He then joined a reconnaissance team sent ahead of the bulk of the British force to survey minefields. They returned to a small settlement at Fitzroy to report, and Gus found himself overlooking the cove where the Welsh Guards were moored on the *Sir Galahad*. To Gus, the transport looked as vulnerable as a beached whale.

An air-raid warning sounded and Skyhawk jets streaked low over a hill. There was a tremendous series of thumps and flames blossomed on the craft. Soldiers began to fire and Gus loosed off some rounds at the passing jets with a machine gun before it jammed. As helicopters began to ferry casualties ashore, Gus joined one of the chaplains in a four-man stretcher party.

'A chopper came off the boat, and they'd got a casualty on it,' Gus said. 'There was a fella stood in the door. His waterproofs had melted in the heat flash. What it must have done is shrink and gone black and gone into his skin. He was still smouldering, his hair was on fire. His face had blackened and scorched – but contracted.'

Gus tensed as he recalled the scene.

'He was stood in the helicopter like this . . .' Gus stretched his arms out in a crucifixion pose. 'When I looked down, his leg was hanging off, but he was stood on it. So it's like almost totally severed, and kind of hanging off by the tendons, bits of trouser, bits of plastic – he was somehow standing on it.

'We all stopped like that,' Gus said, his face registering the open-mouthed shock he had felt. 'For some reason the padre was just able to lean forward and pull him onto this stretcher. And I remember thinking: "fucking hell".

'We turned away and we started running with this bloke – his leg was gone off at a right angle, he was smouldering, and the smell of it . . . As we were running, somebody said: "Where the fuck are we going?" We were just running with this bloke, and we didn't realise where to go with him.

'The padre said: "There's a community centre." We just ran there.'

Gus remembered running as fast as he could, yet dreading what he would encounter when the next batch of wounded landed: 'It was like we were running forever, running at top speed – but feeling as though I was dragging my heels because we didn't want to go back for the next chopper.

'We dropped him off on this floor, went back and there was

another chopper coming in and we must have gone back ten, twelve times. At this community centre was something like a couple of medics – that was all that was there. Well, these medics must have said: "We need to get drips in them."

'There was no stands for the drips – I was standing there like a Christmas tree with a drip in my pocket going down to this fella, a drip over my shoulder going down to this fella, another drip over this shoulder going down to that fella, to curling my hands like that . . .' Gus gestured as if he was holding a bottle. '. . . And a drip going down to this fella. And all of these blokes are groaning, the stink of the burning flesh . . .

'I remember just thinking: "I don't know what to do." It's like: "Just stand here." But you're just surrounded by this. And that was a nightmare for years: "I've got to get out of here, I can't take this." But on the other hand, the compassionate side: "I need to be here for these blokes, they're in a shit state."

'Blokes just kept coming and coming, and I think eventually something turned up – a table or something – I was able to put these things on it. Then we went outside. Then all the guys that walked off the *Galahad* were coming up the hill.'

Gus could clearly remember the way skin dangled down like translucent sets of washing-up gloves from the burned men's hands. One of them asked Gus for a cigarette and he retrieved a pack from the soldier's webbing. He lit a cigarette then placed it in the man's mouth – a kindness he repeated for several of the others who could not use their fingers. Soldiers tried to cool the casualties down by sluicing them with a hose.

'So one bombing incident takes a couple of minutes and the debris just goes on and on,' Gus said. 'It's something I remember quite well, but tend not to dwell on.'

He paused, lost in such a deep well of thought it seemed for a moment he had vanished from the room.

'And then we were off clearing mines,' he said. 'Two o'clock in the morning being shelled in the minefield. Yeah – perhaps parts of that I'd rather not revisit.'

'I realise it's a very difficult thing,' I offered, weakly.

'Getting through what I saw at Goose Green, the mines, the *Galahad*, there's still more to cover,' Gus said, then paused, as if considering whether to continue. 'Maybe just leave that for a bit,' he said. 'If that's OK?'

The loss of the *Sir Galahad* was a major blow, but the advance continued. Some days later Gus found himself waiting in the freezing darkness in the lee of a ridge standing between the Task Force and Port Stanley. Flares floated on parachutes, casting a flickering pall over files of British troops snaking across the lower slopes under the shriek of incoming shells. To Gus, the panorama looked like a scene from the First World War. As he waited for the order to advance, he felt an inexplicable sense of euphoria, as if past and future had dissolved, and his personal fate was no longer of the slightest consequence. He was witnessing history, yet touching the realm of the timeless. Then the order came to cross the 'start line' and Gus dropped to his knees to begin clearing mines. There was an explosion followed by screams. *Does somebody need help?* A runner appeared and told him he needed to move faster. *Tell the Boss I'm moving – it's a minefield.* Another shell landed closer and Gus felt a burning sensation as the blast sucked air from his lungs. *I survived that one – OK, keep going.*

The Falklands campaign might have ended badly for Britain, but the lines of poorly trained Argentine conscripts gradually crumbled, and soon white flags were flying over Port Stanley. After the ceasefire, Gus took a helicopter to Ajax Bay, where the Army had converted a refrigeration plant into a morgue. He wanted to attend the burial of a friend, a twenty-two-year-old lance corporal who had been shot on Mount Tumbledown in the final hours of the war.

Gus and other young members of 9 Squadron took turns to carry the stretcher bearing the grey body bag towards a trench that had been dug in preparation for a mass burial service. Soldiers had discovered at the start of the war that the shell scrapes they dug in the peaty soil quickly waterlogged. The same held true for graves. As the carrying party drew nearer, the floor of the pit began to pool with brackish water.

Gus recalled the hymn they sang: 'Dear Lord and Father of Mankind'. As they reached the line 'Forgive our foolish ways!' Gus thought of the Nelsonian speech the soldiers had been given as they approached the islands. He felt he was being ordered to seek forgiveness by the same religious authorities that had sanctified the killing. More than thirty years later, he could not revisit that moment without his voice filling with anger.

'In other words: "Go and do your duty – now you've done it, ask the Big Man upstairs to forgive us,"' Gus said, his voice rising. 'And I just thought: "You bastard." It was like: "I'm finished with this bullshit."'

As he stared into the grave, any faith Gus had once had in the Church evaporated and the shock and grief of his friend's death surfaced anew.

'He was full of life, like all the lads. And we were very close. Couple of nights before he went up Tumbledown, we sat on this mountain together, freezing our bollocks off. Hadn't eaten for about four days. No food had got to us,' Gus said.

He recalled how they had talked: '"What are you going to do when you get back?" "First thing, I'm going to have a pint and shag." All that stuff. And here he was – dead. Now we've got to appeal to some greater authority? We've been very foolish, have we?'

Gus's jaw was tight and his gaze cut across the living room.

'That was like a seminal moment – the confusion set in,' he said. 'I couldn't square the circle. I couldn't round it off. I couldn't understand. Here was something in me saying: "For Chrissake, we're human beings, we shouldn't be engaged in this. This is awful."'

At the end of the service, Gus took a last look into the sodden burial pit, and noticed the body bag that contained his friend had begun to float. His remains were later repatriated to Britain to be cremated and Gus attended his funeral to say goodbye a second time.

'When you come away you think: "Why didn't I die?"' Gus said. 'All this is emotional stuff – you're locking this away, not thinking about it. Unless that feeling is somehow expunged, it's always going to be there gripping at you. That's how I can still feel today, thirty-two years on.'

Before Gus had deployed to the Falkands, he had been a model soldier who almost never missed a day of work. When he returned, he started to question orders and was constantly in the sick bay with some ill-defined ailment. He was tormented by nightmares, but could not find the words to speak even to his wife Angela, who had served as an Army nurse and had worked in the Falklands after the war.

Gus left the Army and they moved to a cottage in Yorkshire, where he spent eighteen-hour days working on renovations, venting his anger by laying into the brickwork with a hammer. He bought a model kit and would spend sleepless nights painstakingly building a replica galleon. Soon his mind was dominated by half-buried memories of the Falklands and he developed a compulsive antagonism towards authority.

'The police was my thing for ten years after the Falklands,' Gus said. 'I'd fight any policeman – just the mere look of them. There was this kind of "anti-authority" as well: "Nobody tells me what to do. I've been in a war." Madness. Because guess what: you might be able to get away with one policeman, but they've got radios and ten turn up. You're never going to win.'

Angela, who had worked with survivors of prisoner-of-war camps in the Far East earlier in her nursing career, knew Gus was suffering from the legacy of his combat exposure, but did not know where to turn. Their GP told them he did not believe in PTSD and that Gus was suffering from temper tantrums. Police registered his rages as 'domestic troubles'. One day, he went out walking with Angela. His face filled with vulnerability as he whispered: 'Please help me. I think I'm going mad.' When Gus ended up in a psychiatric ward the staff were at a loss so they locked them into a room together so Angela could do her best to soothe him. Gus spent the night under the bed, searching for mines.

'It was becoming part of me bit by bit,' Gus told me. 'If you cut off your little toe, you're all right. If you cut your next toe off, you're all right. Cut eight toes off, you fall over. You're coping until you can't stay upright any more. Probably took ten years.'

Gus sought solace in treks along the Pennine Way or through Pembrokeshire in south-west Wales, sometimes bedding down in the porches of country churches. One time he sheltered from a downpour at a church in the village of Cold Ashton in South Gloucestershire and was mesmerised by light pouring through a stained-glass window depicting Christ on the cross.

'All my mind said was: "More suffering." It didn't seem a helpful image to me,' Gus said. 'When your mind's full of agony, the last thing you want to do is see somebody else going through all that – that's how it felt.'

Eventually, Gus found his way to Ty Gwyn, where he met another former soldier named Billy Fitzgerald, who lent him a book on Buddhism called *Seeing the Way*. Gus was particularly struck by the story of a Vietnam veteran who said that it was impossible to forget a war, but there were techniques you could use to transform your thoughts and feelings. Gus wanted to know more so Fitzgerald took him to Amaravati, a Buddhist monastery at the eastern end of the Chiltern Hills in Hertfordshire, where they joined monks and nuns for lunch. Afterwards, Gus requested an audience with one of the monks, who had also served in the Royal Engineers, and began to pour out his tale.

'I can't get the Falklands out of my mind,' Gus told the monk. 'It's obsessive, it's all I ever think about.'

Not a glimmer of curiosity crossed the monk's face.

'Oh,' he replied. 'They're just thoughts.'

Then he got up and walked out.

Gus could not believe that he had driven all the way from Wales to be treated so rudely. He fumed silently but agreed to stay for afternoon tea, where he met the monk again. He told Gus that if he could start to see his memories of the Falklands for what they really were – mental phantoms – they would lose their power. On the drive back, Gus pondered his words.

'Everybody else until then had made me feel special for feeling that way. It's like: "Oh, come here and sit down. You were in the Falklands? I read about that, I was at school when that was going on. Must have been terrible." As humans, we love that attention, don't we?' Gus said. 'This guy wasn't the slightest bit interested – that was the Awakening.'

Fitzgerald took him to a meditation group in the Welsh town of Colwyn Bay. Gus was told he could quieten his churning thoughts by directing the focus of his attention onto his breath. At first the simple-sounding task seemed impossible as his mind see-sawed between projections into the future and a futile compulsion to rescript the past. Gus persisted, doing his best to concentrate on the sensation of exhaling through his nostrils.

And then it happened: for a few seconds, the fog of thoughts about the Falklands cleared. It was like a milder version of the epiphany he had experienced on the 'start line' on the night of the advance. Gus realised his mind had been functioning like a machine gun – thoughts firing in an automatic stream like the belt-fed rounds he aimed at the warplanes that bombed the *Sir Galahad*.

'Once you let the first shot off, the rest just come, so there's never any space between thoughts,' Gus said. 'When I went to this meditation session, I remember noticing some space between a couple of thoughts. It felt like forever – it was probably ten seconds.

'I remember coming out of that and thinking: "I had ten seconds of peace." I wasn't thinking about the Falklands for ten seconds. For fifteen years, never had no peace in my mind. To get ten seconds of peace is just amazing.'

'Then the realisation came: "If I can get ten seconds, what about a couple of minutes? What about ten minutes? A ten-minute break from myself?"'

Gus decided to deepen his practice by enrolling on a retreat in Herefordshire to learn a 2,500-year-old meditation technique known as Vipassana, which means 'to see things as they really are'. Vipassana is taught at ten-day boot camps in centres around the world where students rise before dawn and spend ten hours a day on their cushions. There is no talking for the duration, apart from in brief interviews with supervisors, and participants are banned from making eye contact, and from using mobile phones or even pens. Something about the discipline appealed to the soldier in Gus and as the days passed he honed his ability to turn his attention within. Half-forgotten memories bobbed to the surface and he discovered nuggets of long-dormant sadness. As Gus neared the final day, his mind returned to the funeral at Ajax Bay and he convulsed with tears he had never allowed himself to shed.

Gus was by no means alone in seeking relief by sitting still. A growing body of clinical research and neuro-imaging studies suggests that meditation can slowly change the way the body responds to stress, helping practitioners to overcome depression or anxiety. In PTSD, the inhibitory functions of the brain that allow a degree of control over powerful impulses or emotions often fail, leaving sufferers liable to overreact to minor frustrations or freeze at an innocent touch. Meditation seems to strengthen neural circuits in the prefrontal cortex that help restore a degree of self-control.

Though Gus believed his years of Vipassana practice had saved his life, he emphasised that he was far from cured. Nevertheless, he had discovered a way to ride the waves of his turmoil instead of being capsized and his example had inspired others. He invited me to Liverpool to meet a couple of other ex-forces who sometimes joined the short retreats he led in a cottage in Derbyshire.

We met at Maggie Mays on Bold Street in the city centre, a cafe decked out in 1950s style with a menu offering 'scouse' – a traditional Liverpudlian lamb stew. Also present were Jon, a former Royal Marine who had fought in the Falklands, and George, a former Army Commando who had served in Northern Ireland. George was later joined by his wife Susan, whom I recognised from the first Combat PTSD Angels meeting I had attended at Liverpool Carers Centre.

George had met Gus while they were staying at Audley Court, the Combat Stress facility in Shropshire. Intimately acquainted with the Spiral, George would wake from nightmares and rush to the bathroom to vomit, nostrils filled with the smell of burning flesh. Unable to control his anger, he would lash out at his wife Susan, then disappear for a few days before attempting a reconciliation. Gus taught George the basics of meditation and at the end of their stay he marched him to the computer room to enrol him onto a ten-day Vipassana retreat.

'He said: "You can do it. Just remember: don't go with your Commando green beret on,"' George said.

Inevitably, George's Commando training did kick in, and he

sat on his cushion determined to ride out the ordeal through sheer willpower. In the evening he could not understand why his jaw hurt so much – until he realised he had spent the day clenching it. At night, monsters seemed to loom out of the walls, but he stuck out the ten days and called Gus.

'I felt like I was losing my mind,' George said, recalling their conversation.

'You were,' Gus said. 'There's all this shite you've got in your mind that was just going out.'

George enrolled in another ten-day course and went deeper still. He felt as if his body was dissolving and healing hands were pushing through his chest.

'It's amazing – I suffer with sciatica, slipped disc. I was getting up and walking as if I had no pain,' George said. 'I felt loose. I felt free.'

One night, George was walking through the compound and was transfixed by the luminous intensity of the light bulbs.

'Everything was dead bright – crystal clear and shiny and sparkly – so much so that I stopped and went "bloody hell".'

'It's called samadhi,' Gus said. 'Your awareness is so sharp, you start noticing each and every thing. Listen, it's a bit like in Buddhist texts there's a famous phrase, it's called . . .'

Gus broke into a recitation in Pali, a language used in early Buddhist texts. Jon and George did not blink – it was not unusual for Gus to pronounce such stanzas, or underscore a point with snatches of his own verse or a quotation from Shakespeare.

'What it means is: "We live life with dust in our eyes,"' Gus said. 'When that dust starts to clear, you see things clearly and properly for the first time. That's the Awakening, isn't it?'

'It's constantly revealing itself to you,' Jon said. 'Something can happen in your life – you can think: "I'm looking at it entirely differently than I would have done if I hadn't found meditation and mindfulness." At the end of the day, it's only a thought, and thoughts arise and pass away. And once you get your head round that . . .'

'. . . that's massive,' Gus said.

'Then you start looking into the mind and how it creates things,' Jon said. 'You can get to a point where there's a sense of calm. It's like dry-cleaning your brain I guess – the ultimate cerebral enema.'

The trio knew that there is a raw physicality to the emotional residue of combat, linked to changes in the body and brain that cannot be controlled by willpower alone. And yet their diligent work on the meditation cushion showed them how ingrained habits of negative thought had made their suffering worse. Gus had used the image of a machine gun spraying bullets to describe the way his compulsive rumination about the Falklands had run wild. Through meditation, the men had learned they could choose whether to pull the trigger.

'Take a war, say the Falklands,' Gus said. 'It's a thoroughly negative experience. It sets up patterns of negative thinking. The more you're rehearsing it, the more you're thinking it, the more negative you're becoming – until you're totally in a negative zone. You can't see no good from it, you can't see no good in humanity. The negative thinking reinforces negative thinking, and that's what's called the Wheel of Samsara. And how do you get out of that? If somebody comes along and says something to you, you'll tell them to fuck off.'

Jon agreed: 'That brings you right back to the Bullshit Bingo again: "Jon's not very well, poor old Jon." You can play all those bullshit games, or you can say: "I'm not playing it any more."'

'I think there's a lot of soldiers, squaddies, who truly want to get out of the mess they're in,' said George. 'And if they found Vipassana, their lives would change.'

'Some people don't want to get out of it,' Jon replied. 'It's no good saying to someone whose sitting in Wetherspoon's every day getting bollocksed: "Listen, mate, there's a way out of this."'

'That's the illusion of PTSD,' Gus said. 'People stick with it because they think it's getting them somewhere. It's just creating misery, but they think there's some kind of reward – attention, appreciation, applause. "Without this I'm nobody." But when I've got this at least I get a welfare officer visit me, I go to Combat Stress, I go to see the psychologist and talk about "me" for hours.'

Jon nodded. 'But nobody told me I can sit at home by myself and see all this bullshit and stand back from it and go: "They're just thoughts."'

Jon and Gus did not wish to sound callous – they knew as well as anybody that the anguish that had followed them home from the Falklands was real. Yet they had also learned how the feelings of guilt or hopelessness could acquire a curiously addictive quality – luring their sufferer back like a drug. Meditation had not erased their memories. Their diligent practice had gradually altered the very structure of their brains – giving them a new-found capacity to move *through* their pain to inhabit a new world beyond.

'It's amazing. So many people it could help – meditation,' Jon said. 'But people think you're all trippy hippy. They think us four went away in a cottage for four days and were all drinking each other's urine and playing bongos. The western mind is screwed, mate. The Buddha – talk about being ahead of the game.'

Later, I spoke to Susan about the changes she had seen in George.

'To me, the best thing he ever did was the meditation,' she told me. 'I'm just so glad he found Gus when he did. He doesn't go off his rocker like he used to. He's found that little space between thinking and saying.'

Susan would later speak at a Combat PTSD Angels meeting

about George's experience, hoping other husbands might discover some peace of their own.

Towards the end of the pilgrimage to the Falklands, Gus and the videographer had broken away from the main group to climb Mount Longdon, where the third battalion of the Parachute Regiment had engaged in some of the fiercest fighting of the war. The pair trudged over olive-drab tussocks, passing black tarns and the forlorn detritus of battle: empty boxes of mortar rounds; countless spent cartridges and a pair of rusted stretcher poles. Gus had not fought on Mount Longdon, but had lost a friend on its slopes: Corporal Scott 'Scottie' Wilson, one of the twenty-three British soldiers killed in the twelve-hour assault to take Longdon and subsequent two days of shelling from Argentine forces stationed on Mount Tumbledown.

The summit of Mount Longdon was a natural fortress: a jagged heap of frost-shattered granite mottled by splashes of lichen. Port Stanley was visible as a distant smudge against the blue of the South Atlantic. A six-foot metal cross dominated the peak, set in a plinth engraved with the names of the dead. Gus reached a spot among the stones where previous pilgrims had planted miniature wooden crosses, some bearing weathered photographs of men in red berets. One had cracked a can of Boddingtons and left it as an offering. A plaque commemorated three of the teenage paratroopers who died – two of them had been seventeen and a third had been killed on his eighteenth birthday.

'Today I have a sixteen-to-seventeen-year-old daughter myself,' Gus said. 'All those years ago I saw these guys – if you like – as comrades. But now, as I've got older, I kind of look on these seventeen-year-olds as my children.'

He put on his maroon beret, then knelt down and opened his pack to retrieve a foot-high brass statue of the Buddha, presented to him by monks and nuns at Amaravati. He gave the figure a final polish and knelt down to place it in a niche where it stood with an outstretched open palm and a serene smile.

'Having found Buddhism, and how much it's changed my life, this is the zenith of that moment – to leave a Buddha here as a symbol of enduring peace, and that's a really joyful moment,' Gus said, as the videographer captured his words.

'Yes, we get caught up in wars, yes, we get caught up in unwholesome and unskilful behaviour, but there's always hope. To anybody who visits this spot: stop worrying, stop suffering, be at peace with yourself. And be at peace with everything around you.

'With that act, the war's over,' he said. 'It's truly come to an end – and I can now move on.'

As the mist thickened, Gus began the journey back to Port Stanley, the town he had helped to liberate twenty-five years before.

15

'Like a Phoenix'

New horizons in therapy

In the early nineteenth century, a wealthy Scottish trader sank his fortune into building Manor Hall, an elegant country pile at Doune, outside the town of Stirling. The granite-and-sandstone mansion boasts more than fifty rooms, a dumb waiter and a film-set stairwell, but the most striking feature is the tower, an ornate structure commanding panoramic views. Above the front door, a Latin inscription reads: *Duris non frangor* – 'I am not disheartened by difficulties'. Manor Hall was in the midst of a major renovation when I visited, but the slogan had been left untouched. It was a fitting motto for the home's new role as a clinic dedicated to resolving the toughest cases of trauma.

Across Britain, I had been struck by the skill and commitment of many clinicians working in the military, the NHS and charities. And yet, despite their dedication, there seemed to be an endless procession of ex-forces who were still searching for meaningful help for PTSD, addictions, depression or other life-sapping burdens. Some had learned to cope with their symptoms, at least on better days, but fewer had returned to a true state of wellness. It was perhaps unrealistic to hope that everyone could make a full recovery. But those who had made the most striking shifts often seemed to have followed unconventional paths – equine therapy, for example, or Vipassana meditation. Their symptoms might not have vanished completely, and they might still need support in the future, but the peace these men had tasted suggested that fundamental change was possible. It also posed a challenge to the medical establishment: how to go beyond coping with trauma and deliver true healing?

I had heard about Manor Hall from Dr Alastair Hull, the consultant psychiatrist and psychotherapist who, during his decade of running an NHS traumatic stress clinic in Perth, had seen many ex-forces who had all but given up hope of getting better. I had asked him if he knew of anywhere offering promising new treatments in Britain, and he had arranged for me to meet two of his fellow trauma psychotherapists, psychologists named Dawn Harris and Colin Howard, the co-founders of the new Centre for Trauma at Manor Hall.

Harris and Howard had spent much of their careers working in the Scottish prison system and latterly in private practice, often despairing at the lack of in-patient facilities for those suffering from the most severe and complex cases of PTSD. For years, they had dreamed of opening an independent clinic where trauma survivors – civilian or military – could be given tailor-made care for as many weeks or months as they needed, rather than being funnelled through a standardised programme. The turning point came when the owner of a large construction company agreed to back their vision in return for a share of their revenue from private clients, insurance companies and NHS referrals.

I arrived six months before Manor Hall was due to open, and the house was still a building site. The imposing edifice was swaddled in a scaffolding cocoon and the corridors reverberated with the sound of saws and drills. The two psychologists gave me a hard hat, hi-vis vest and protective gloves and led me between the stone columns flanking the front door.

Even in its gutted state, the house felt like a special kind of haven. Harris and Howard planned to create a nurturing ambience in the twenty-six-bed sanctuary – more boutique hotel than psychiatric unit. Safety features put in place to minimise the risk of self-harm would be discreet: several rooms were equipped with shatter-proof windows and stripped of any fixtures that might be used to string up a noose. Similarly, workmen had installed panelling around the stairwell to make it impossible to jump from the balcony. Though the waiting list was so far comprised of civilians, Manor Hall also hoped to treat ex-forces, and several senior staff had served in the military. Like Ty Gwyn, the house had a distinct echo of Craiglockhart near Edinburgh, where W. H. R. Rivers had treated Siegfried Sassoon.

As we climbed the tower, Harris and Howard explained that there would be more to the therapy than tranquil views. They were determined to put into practice the insight that seemed to lie behind the most remarkable transformations I had encountered: the key to lasting change lies in recognising that trauma is stored in the body as much as in the mind.

'All the trauma that anybody experiences, from big trauma to small trauma, is held by the body,' Harris said. 'So the brain can lie to you lots of times, but the body can't.'

'The body always remembers. The body always keeps the score,' said Howard, echoing the words of Bessel Van der Kolk.

Treatments in Britain have come a long way since the First World War, when dazed conscripts might be subjected to bursts of electricity or left to languish in county asylums. And yet, for all the advances, the results of the standard approaches to treating trauma have been mixed, with many of the ex-forces I met feeling they had yet to achieve a breakthrough. Harris and Howard would offer a new way to treat PTSD, one they saw as something akin to psychotherapy's holy grail.

The protocol had been devised by an American psychologist named Lisa Schwarz. Her work was not yet widely known in Britain, but it had been embraced by a scattered community of practitioners in the United States and Europe. Given the enthusiasm at Manor Hall, I was keen to find out more. They had arranged for my visit to coincide with Schwarz's latest trip to Glasgow and she invited me to try her approach for myself.

With her mop of shoulder-length curls, gritty sense of humour and ready, mirthful laugh, Schwarz is not an average denizen of the often staid world of mental health. While some practitioners derive their authority from their status in the clinical hierarchy or the number of letters after their name, Schwarz radiates the confidence of a bare-knuckle boxer. Having treated thousands of people during more than twenty-five years as a psychologist in the United States, she has no shortage of clinical experience. Yet I soon learned that there was a deeper dimension to her credentials: Schwarz had not flinched from facing the depths of her own pain. In the parlance of psychotherapy, she had 'done her work'. She was in Glasgow to train about sixty therapists in her treatment method, which she had named the 'Comprehensive Resource Model'. The technocratic-sounding title did not quite do her approach justice.

Schwarz gave me a pair of headphones and led me through an exercise to visualise a grid of energy flowing through my body. Music panned left to right as I practised 'earth breathing' – a technique designed to keep me anchored firmly in my body as difficult feelings began to surface. I was told to imagine inhaling air from the molten core of the earth – drawing it up through caves, slabs of stone and soil and into my leg, then holding it at the base of my spine before exhaling it through my other leg. Once I got the hang of it, the exercise had a distinctly calming effect.

Next came 'heart' breathing – inhaling into my solar plexus from the earth and sky – then sending the exhale from my heart to whatever part of me needed healing. As the session progressed, and waves of sadness and anger began to surface, we dispelled them using 'fire breathing' – I was told to picture myself as a dragon blasting flames and smoke, and breathe out, as if fogging up a mirror. From time to time, Schwarz posed questions about what I was experiencing by repeating her 'magical question': 'Ask your body, not your brain – take the first answer that comes to you, and don't think.'

I found the session surprisingly powerful: by the end I had shed tears, shouted out and unearthed pockets of emotion I had never realised I carried. As the soundtrack in the headphones switched to the guttural chanting of Tibetan Gyuto monks, I felt a curious sensation in my chest, as if hands were rummaging around in my heart area. A pins-and-needles feeling tingled across my face and I was left feeling exhausted but lighter.

After our session we joined Ron Schwenkler, an American therapist who had contributed to the development of the model, and who was helping Schwarz at the training workshop. During our conversation and in subsequent email exchanges, Schwarz explained how she had developed her technique partly by drawing on ancient healing traditions she had encountered during her own long quest.

'To be able to do this work, it helps to have gone through something yourself that tore you down to skeletal proportions, and come back out of that, like a phoenix that rises out of the ashes,' she said. 'I had my own trauma history that challenged me to "get busy living or get busy dying".

'I tried both and for years lived in a way that made me feel like I wanted to die almost every day. My go-to coping skills almost killed me, and had devastating effects on my family. Staying "asleep", slumbering through my pain instead of facing it, took me so far down I couldn't bear to look at myself. So how to get out of that? It strips you of your humanity to live in that lifestyle.'

Schwarz said the true stripping down began when she eventually faced up to what she had done to her son and her parents. But it was just this kind of painful personal work that had helped her discover and refine the tools she used to treat trauma.

To understand Schwarz's method, it helps to employ a metaphor for the way traumatic events can leave an imprint on the
body and brain. She visualises the residue as 'capsules' containing
memories, raw emotion and self-defeating beliefs that have become lodged in the central nervous system – picture if you will
a kind of psychic sludge. People might avoid such feelings for a
lifetime, blotting them out with alcohol or converting them into
psychological symptoms such as panic attacks or depression and
in some cases physical illness, especially migraines, skin conditions or stomach problems. An inner deadening descends that
makes it impossible to feel a spark of connection with others,
or even with oneself. Schwarz knew from experience that there
were no short cuts to reversing this process: the 'capsules' had to
be unearthed so the fear, grief, rage and shame that seeped out of
them every day could be faced fully and dissolved.

'The work we do is to allow a person to love themselves again
through a healing process based in love, safety and connection,'
Schwarz said. 'Not to sound corny, but love heals – it really does.'

This was not the first time I had heard talk of a game-
changing new approach to PTSD. Just as doctors had adopted
a bewildering range of treatments for 'shell shock' in the First
World War, barely a week seemed to pass without a new study
or news story on revolutionary remedies for PTSD – the vast
majority originating in the United States. They ranged from the
ultra-sophisticated to the disarmingly simple. Some rested on
delicate physical interventions – such as a technique known as
stellate ganglion block, which involves injecting an anaesthetic
into a bundle of nerves (the stellate ganglion) that sits near the
base of the neck. Others were costly but less invasive, such as
hyperbaric oxygen therapy, administered through ninety-minute
periods in an oxygen chamber, or video game-style 'virtual
reality' simulations designed to help veterans come to terms with
incidents in Afghanistan or Iraq. Nature offered simpler remedies
– some extolled the therapeutic benefits of medical marijuana

and one study pointed to the healing properties of blueberries.

There was nothing like the same scale of research taking place in Britain, though there was some notable work under way. In Oxford, the Scars of War Foundation, established in 2011, said it had launched a five-year brain-scanning project to better understand PTSD. At Cardiff University, psychiatrist Dr Ben Sessa was leading a team of researchers exploring how MDMA – the main ingredient in the recreational drug Ecstasy – might be used to enhance conventional trauma therapy by enabling a patient to engage more deeply with disturbing memories without being overwhelmed. They aimed to see MDMA licensed for use in treating PTSD in Britain by 2021.

I also encountered a growing number of therapists and life coaches, often ex-forces themselves, who espoused new psychological techniques that they believed could resolve trauma symptoms, often in only a few sessions. Some paraded beneficiaries who spoke with almost evangelical enthusiasm about how they had been rapidly 'cured' of PTSD. Such claims presented a dilemma. Given the scale of unmet need, and the limitations of existing talk therapies, new thinking was required. Yet if there was one thing I had learned on my travels, it was that treating trauma is no job for amateurs.

Schwarz's approach struck me as different. Unlike some techniques I had encountered, her method had been embraced by highly trained trauma specialists in Scotland who could draw on a wealth of clinical experience. Dr Alastair Hull had spent years practising and teaching both CBT and EMDR, but believed that Schwarz's model provided a far more effective toolbox for tackling the most difficult cases of PTSD. Several other consultant psychiatrists, including Dr Frank Corrigan, who had co-edited a textbook on the neurobiology of trauma and dissociation, were equally convinced and the Glasgow workshop was being attended by more than sixty therapists in search of alternatives to the existing approaches, including ten doctors.

Though Schwarz's model had not been validated by formal clinical trials, Hull, Corrigan and their colleagues believed it chimed with an evolving understanding of the neurological underpinnings of trauma reactions that surpassed even the theories advanced by Bessel Van der Kolk in his book *The Body Keeps the Score*. Schwarz's ideas seemed to them to build on the best work being done in the field but take it a stage further by providing a more versatile range of techniques to heal wounds at the very deepest layers of the brain – parts that widely used therapies such as CBT might not reach.

Schwarz's core goal is to help a client confront their most traumatic experiences without the risk of being damaged by the process – a perennial danger in treating PTSD. She does this by equipping them with various techniques – called 'resources' – that enable them to remain comfortable even as they work through extremes of emotion attached to their worst memories, always the most harrowing stage of existing therapies.

In one resource-building exercise, trauma survivors are led back in time to reconnect with their 'core self' – the pristine essence that existed long before they began to experience the harsh realities of life. It might not be a stretch to suggest that this was the place A.J. had discovered in his 'meeting God' experience; the serenity Gus Hales had tasted through meditation; and the 'lightning bolt' feeling of reconnecting with his teenage self that Hugh Forysth had encountered in equine therapy. Other 'resources' included the various breathing exercises I had tried and a special technique for working with fixed eye positions.

Once the client had learned to trust their new tools, the work of healing old wounds could begin. A session would typically involve visualising an encounter with a younger, struggling version of yourself to provide the comfort – the feeling of 'not-aloneness' – that was missing at the time of the trauma. You could offer words of encouragement, looking into 'your' eyes, or breathe together. If at any time a client's feelings began to boil over, they could use one of the 'resources' to rapidly regain their poise. The priority was always to avoid any risk that opening people's trauma 'capsules' could make them worse – as described by a number of ex-forces who had had unhappy experiences of CBT or EMDR.

When clients felt so damaged that the task seemed impossible, there was an even more potent option available: enlisting the help of a 'power animal'. Schwarz taught therapists to lead their clients through an exercise to visualise an invisible ally: it could be an animal, something else from the natural world – an oak tree, or a rock, for example – or a 'spiritual being', typically an angel, though in my session I was surprised to encounter a regal elven woman leading a magnificent black horse. Known in therapy-speak as an 'internal attachment figure', this new companion would serve as a guide, sage and guardian when confronting the worst events of the past.

While talk of imaginary creatures might prove jarring for more conventionally minded therapists, the exercise was designed to fulfil a very specific neurological purpose. Just as a horse serves as a human proxy in equine therapy, so working with a 'power animal' aims to energise dormant neural pathways in the 'emotional brain' that govern our ability to form healthy connections – known in psychology as 'attachment' or 'attunement'. It was thought that trauma in early life or adulthood could cause these circuits to atrophy, which accounted for the cut-off feeling I encountered in so many ex-forces with PTSD. Schwarz and Hull believed that working with a 'power animal' provided a means to fire up these circuits again and bring healthy human relationships back within reach.

The beauty of 'power animals' was that clients were not limited to one – some conjured up a whole menagerie to assist them in daily life. Schwarz, for example, had a wolf-dog hybrid who advised her while she was teaching. Hull's collection included a honey badger, whose dogged capacity for excavating hives despite the stings of angry bees proved an asset in difficult meetings. One former soldier had an eagle, which circled over-head looking for signs of danger, and a grizzly bear who had taught him he could be tender as well as tough. It took several weeks for my own guide to materialise, and in a form I would not have anticipated – an Amazonian butterfly fluttering on brilliant vermilion wings.

In some respects, Schwarz's approach was not quite as avant-garde as it might sound. Plenty of therapists had explored ways to reverse changes to the brain and nervous system associated with PTSD, whether it be through yoga, various types of bodywork or techniques to unblock trapped emotion through 'tapping' on the meridian lines used in acupuncture – each backed to varying degrees by a growing evidence base. Schwarz's supporters saw her method as a versatile way to promote rapid and lasting heal-ing without the need of stables, an ashram or a studio, and in a way that experienced therapists could use alongside their existing techniques.

There would be sceptics. Many psychiatrists had poured scorn on the finger-wagging and flashing lights of EMDR until years of research showed the technique worked. Schwarz was acutely aware that many might be wary of the more mystical-sounding elements of her model and proposals had been drawn up for a large-scale study in Britain and the United States, where another practitioner had gathered extensive data over two years of using her methods with military veterans. Schwarz was also working with Hull, Corrigan and others on an academic book to explain the breathing exercises, 'power animals' and other techniques in the light of the latest neuroscience.

The two psychiatrists were not afraid to stake their reputations on Schwarz's approach. In April 2015, Hull and Corrigan threw down the gauntlet to the psychiatric establishment by pub-lishing an academic article questioning the value of CBT for the most serious cases of PTSD – an unusual public challenge to much of the trauma work done by the MoD, the NHS and Combat Stress, which had placed CBT at the core of its flagship six-week programme.

In two articles in the *BJPsych Bulletin*, the peer-reviewed journal of the Royal College of Psychiatrists, Corrigan and Hull questioned the evidence base used to justify the widespread use of CBT for the most severe cases of PTSD. They pointed out that many studies used to justify the approach were based on people who had few problems apart from a one-off traumatic experience – making them easier to treat. There was very little research, by contrast, to prove that CBT was effective for 'complex' cases of PTSD in which a sufferer has experienced multiple traumas over many years, like many of their patients who had served in the forces. Corrigan and Hull argued that CBT often made little headway in such cases for precisely the reasons identified by Van der Kolk: words alone could not help shift traumatic reactions lodged deep in the 'emotional brain'. They wrote:

> The over-optimistic claims for the effectiveness of cognitive-behavioural therapy (CBT) . . . do not best serve a group of patients greatly in need of help. Given the limitations . . . it is essential to investigate other approaches consistent with the evolving understanding of the neurobiological underpinnings of traumatic experiences.

In other words: it was time to give 'power animals', earth-, fire- and heart-breathing and the other techniques in Schwarz's model a fair hearing. While many would take some convincing, there was at least one former soldier who was certain that Schwarz's blend of neuroscience and shamanism had saved his life.

On the day I visited Manor Hall, Hull had arranged for me to meet one of his clients, the former Special Forces soldier who

I knew as Steve Townsend, and who had served for more than twenty years in the military. We spoke in one of the consulting rooms in a modern annexe to the main house, flanked by trees dappled with autumn hues.

A well-built man in his late forties who had once been a champion Army distance runner, Steve had a shaved head and a hint of shadow on his chin. Even at rest, something about his expression communicated that there was no time whatsoever for any bullshit. He was inclined to be suspicious of journalists and the only reason he had agreed to speak to me was that he wanted me to write about Hull's work.

'Because of Alastair, I don't have to look over my shoulder every step of the way,' he said. 'I don't need to walk into a room and the first thing I do is look for a weapon.'

Steve explained that the trigger for his breakdown had been the loss of two of his closest friends from the Army, who had died in quick succession some years earlier. His wife eventually persuaded him to see his GP, but Steve found him less than helpful. He was eventually referred to a therapist who tried CBT and taught him some relaxation techniques, but they made scant headway.

'When the demons come at night – and they often do come at night – controlled breathing does fuck all to control your state of mind,' Steve told me. 'You need something else – you need something deeper.'

Steve began to drink to dull his anguish, but he could not stop the thoughts bouncing around his mind – he compared them to a rubber ball ricocheting off the walls of a prison cell. He barely slept, but when he did the worst images from his tours returned in nightmares. During the day, even the most innocent of sights would spark a volley of dark imaginings.

'I remember sitting in a greasy spoon cafe in a fairly large town. There was a young mother, toddler on her knee – the kid had a slice of toast and was gumming on it,' Steve said.

A thought had come to him: *What would she do if she knew I was a killer?*

'That mother would be running away if she knew she was sitting with a murderer,' Steve said. 'When you take somebody's life, that's ultimately what you become.'

He paused.

'When you look somebody in the eye and you know they're dying and you know that it's you that made that happen, you become very aware that that person, that individual, is looking at death – which makes you death. And that's a very dark thing to live with.'

Steve gave a rather hollow chuckle, briefly closing his eyes.

'People have said to me in conversation – not knowing me or knowing about me – that taking the life of a human being is never acceptable. I say, if you think that, you've never been in a war zone.'

He drew breath.

'I was part of a group of people who called an airstrike on a fuel convoy where twenty-seven people lost their lives in less than sixty seconds. I was directly responsible for that.

'There's not an operator in life who still doesn't walk down a street and look in shop windows to see if somebody is behind him, because these are the instincts that keep you alive. Having these thoughts is part and parcel of who I am and what I've done, but you can't live your life like that in normal society. Because it keeps on eating you up and gnawing away at you and destroying you.'

Losing hope of ever getting better, Steve had begun to make plans to end his life. He had practically given up on the NHS, but had persisted for his wife's sake. Eventually he found himself in Hull's consulting room. During their first session, which lasted ninety minutes, Steve barely uttered a word.

Hull knew he had to offer him something that would at least pique his curiosity enough for him to return, so he began explaining how PTSD can affect different layers of the brain: 'I just got the chart out and started taking him through the neurobiology of trauma. After about an hour and a half he said: "OK I'll come back." The first thing for me was not letting the guy out the room without giving him something that would get him back in.'

As their sessions progressed, Hull began to use some of the techniques from Schwarz's model and eventually suggested they try something different in the next session – an exercise to find his 'power animal'.

The idea set Steve thinking. A dog lover, he naturally considered some form of canine, but the image triggered associations with the black dog – Winston Churchill's symbol for his depressions. Steve dismissed the idea of a dolphin as impractical – though he gave more serious thought to raptors and eagles. He briefly auditioned a giant viper but realised it might not be suitable.

'It just would have been too aggressive all the time,' Steve told me. 'I don't need that. If there's any type of aggression needed then I'm more than capable myself.'

At their next session, Hull led Steve through an exercise they had done before – visualising a 'sacred place' that evoked feelings of safety and calm. Steve imagined himself sitting in his interior sanctuary, waiting for his power animal to reveal itself. At first nothing happened. And then a creature appeared and there were no more doubts. Steve's 'power animal' was a sleek and muscular jaguar – a creature imbued with stealth and guile that could stay close without ever being seen. The big cat felt so real that the possibility that it might inadvertently materialise was a half-serious consideration.

Steve put his jaguar's protective powers to the test when Hull asked him to close his eyes and led him back to one of his most disturbing memories: being beaten as a small boy by his alcoholic father. Hull told Steve that although the animal might not be able to stop what was happening, he could kindle a feeling that he would not have to face his fears alone.

'I'm standing there as a small child, standing underneath this cat, with huge paws on either side of me, almost my head against its chest,' Steve said. 'I'm feeling the vibration of this thing breathing – it was incredibly powerful.'

Hull told Steve he could call on the jaguar outside of therapy sessions, and he soon sensed it padding beside him wherever he went. His 'power animal' proved its worth one evening when Steve stopped at a service station for a coffee and encountered a group of drunken young men spoiling for a fight.

'For me, with my history, I'm worried that I'm going to hurt someone and this is not going to end well,' he told me. 'I don't care – if I'm provoked in that way, I'm going to react, and I'm not going to stop until they stay down.

'Now I can have a conversation with my "power animal": "Listen, it will all be fine, walk away. Even if someone does provoke you, what's the worst thing that can happen? You're a couple of minutes late for your coffee." A "power animal" gives you options.'

During one session, Hull helped Steve work on his insomnia. He invited Steve to imagine he was at home asleep and to 'look through closed eyelids' to notice who was standing guard. Steve realised his jaguar was protecting him. As he began to drift off at home, he could again hear the big cat breathing – and woke after the first proper sleep he could remember in years. If troubling memories surfaced, they talked them through together.

'There are many things that I have participated in, I would go as far as saying "performed", that I would never share with anyone else,' Steve told me. 'If I need to talk about a traumatic event that's occurred, I process it with my jaguar. I don't need to talk to another human being about it. He will give a measured response and talk about why it's happened.'

I knew even before asking that Steve would not reveal its

name. I wondered if he felt the jaguar was a projection of his own mind, perhaps an image summoned from his unconscious, but he shook his head.

'Do I see this as part of my "higher self"? No. It's very different – it's a being in its own right. We share ideas, but he's not me. He looks at things from a completely different perspective.'

Steve tried to help me understand.

'When you have been – I hate to use this phrase – indoctrinated, brainwashed, however you want to call it – into viewing issues in a set way, which is what happens in the military, it's very difficult. When you come out of the forces, you're not allowed to look at life that way any more.

'It's like being introduced into society like a little child again. Just like holding on to a teddy bear, I feel like my power animal is holding my hand.'

Since he had started working with Hull, Steve had found a new lease of life working with young people as an adventure sports instructor and assessor. Hull had encouraged him to start running again and he had shed the excess weight he had gained while trapped in the Spiral.

'Not that long ago, I didn't care much about how other people were feeling,' he said. 'I was only concerned about myself. I didn't think society gave a fuck about how I felt. It's gone full circle. Now I understand how young people feel. The fact I can give something back is amazing.

'It's a game-changer for me and I'm sure it will end up being a game-changer for others. There are options.'

Somewhere in the room, just out of sight, the jaguar flicked its tail.

Conclusion

Learning to sit still

One February day, I took a final trip on the Number 57 bus from Perth to the Wellmeadow in Blairgowrie. As usual, June Black met me outside the Angus Hotel and we drove across the bridge over the river Ericht. It was a crisp afternoon and sunlight played on the crests of the Sidlaw Hills as we reached June's estate. Aaron's medals were still on display by her mantelpiece, but his shrine was gone from the living room. The Black Watch soldier figurine, 'Black Swan' pendant and lucky horseshoe had been moved to a permanent display in an alcove under the stairs. Though June would still walk past them many times each day, the mementos would no longer dominate her home in quite the same way.

Ever since June had learned of her son's journey through the military mental health system, she had nursed the hope that the Army might offer an apology. Not long after he died, she had attended suicide prevention training in Perth, participating in role-play exercises to learn how to help the vulnerable escape the 'river of suicide' before they reached the waterfall. In the years she had since spent trying to come to terms with the loss of Aaron, June believed she had faced up to what she perceived as her mistakes as a mother – mistakes made without the benefit of the insights hidden in his medical notes. She wanted the military to hold up a similar mirror.

'I thought he was a man, a soldier, he could handle anything life could throw at him,' June said as we took a last look through the plastic crate containing Aaron's documents. 'I was wrong. He was a strong-minded laddie – I never knew how fragile he was.'

After almost three years of deliberations, the Crown Office, Scotland's prosecution service, decided not to launch a Fatal Accident Inquiry into the events leading up to Aaron's suicide. Having exchanged lengthy correspondence with the MoD, officials had established that Aaron's request for follow-up support after he left the Army had gone unanswered because of a 'systems failure' in the way computerised information was shared between mental health staff and social workers within the military. The MoD had since rectified the problem. The Crown Office had concluded that the lack of follow-up could not be said to have caused or contributed to Aaron's death, and therefore it would not be in the public interest to investigate the case any further.

The decision came as another blow to June, who had hoped an inquiry would have highlighted the importance of providing troubled young service-leavers with potentially life-saving support. Even in death, it seemed to June that Aaron had been overlooked. Though his name would not appear on any war memorial, June had seen to it that his headstone bore the inscription 'HERRICK 10' – the computer-generated code name for Britain's operations in Afghanistan in 2009. James Forrester thought the inscription apt – he considered his friend to be a casualty of war.

'You'll get some old sergeant major that will argue he was just weak and things like that,' James told me. 'They never knew him.'

It is of course impossible to know for sure what killed Aaron, someone returned from Afghanistan thinking the high would last for ever. The trauma symptoms noted by a psychiatrist may have played a part, especially in combination with alcohol. Yet Aaron may equally have been a casualty of peace – unable to withstand the sense of futureless isolation that engulfed him when he left behind friendships forged under fire. His problems were emblematic of the difficulties faced by thousands of young men from inner cities or small-town estates who looked to the Army to provide them with a way out but left after only a few years of service. Well-trained and tightly cohered to their group, many found going into combat easier than returning home. Entitled to less support than those who had completed longer careers, they often struggled the hardest.

Drinking heavily, suffering symptoms of post-traumatic stress and besieged by self-destructive impulses, Aaron had not been an easy twenty-two-year-old to help. That was precisely why he needed help the most. Had he been bleeding from a bullet wound, he would not have been discharged until he had been bandaged. But men and women like Aaron had been allowed to walk away, bleeding from wounds that could not be seen. If personnel were not grabbing lifelines thrown by the military, then the military needed to start throwing new lifelines.

Since October 1914, when 'Case One' arrived in Myers's care, the system for tending to the mental well-being of soldiers has grown up in a piecemeal and ad hoc fashion, overshadowed by the Army's stubborn ambivalence towards psychological injury. The paradox is that many of the men and women I met had proved that remarkable recoveries were possible – even for those who had spent many years trudging the darkest stretches of the Spiral. For some, the suffering they endured on leaving the forces cracked the shell of their military persona and allowed a deeper, more authentic self to shine through – provided wise enough help was on hand to support a prolonged and often painful rebirth. By the time my jouney ended, I had become convinced that it is time to replicate that transformation on a collective level, by re-imagining trauma services – military and civilian – so that everyone has the best achievable chance of learning not merely to cope, but to heal. Even at a time of austerity, the goal might not be as utopian as it sounds. Relatively small investments now could save vast sums in terms of future care and avert untold suffering, but summoning the courage to make them will require some new thinking.

Researching this book was like visiting two parallel worlds. In the first, mental health issues in the military were deemed to be broadly under control. The authorities in this world often criticised the media for feeding harmful and misleading stereotypes through sensationalist coverage of PTSD and it was received wisdom that there was no evidence of a 'ticking time bomb' of psychological wounds sustained in Afghanistan and Iraq. The general attitude seemed to be that a small proportion of soldiers had always found it difficult to adjust after war – a problem for which there was, regrettably, no solution. All things considered, the system for their care was not bad, and gradually improving.

The second world resembled the aftermath of an earthquake. Disparate teams of rescuers were digging with varying degrees of urgency, tenacity and skill to reach unknown numbers trapped beneath the rubble. Some were using obsolete or even potentially dangerous tools and many of the would-be helpers were competing rather than cooperating. The tales of shaken survivors who were lucky enough to be unearthed suggested that there might be many more in urgent need of help. Nobody in authority seemed to be taking the rescue effort in hand.

Our system of military mental health care is just like this rescue effort – haphazard, beset by rivalries and based largely on approaches that lag behind the latest theories of how trauma affects the brain. Despite the research done in the past decade, nobody can say with any certainty what the impact of thirteen years of intense operations in Iraq and Afghanistan involving the deployment of more than 200,000 people will be on future demand for psychological support. Given the suffering endured by many hundreds of members of the 26,000-strong Task Force that Britain sent to the Falklands, where the ground campaign lasted seventy-four days, it is not surprising that some foresee trouble ahead.

'The fact that so many have already come forward from Afghanistan with problems leads me to believe that in the next eight, ten, twelve years there's going to be massive numbers,' said Leigh Skelton, the former clinical director at Combat Stress. 'I don't think we're anywhere near the peak.'

Sue, the founder of Combat PTSD Angels, just one of a growing number of support groups for military carers across Britain, said many members sensed their partners were struggling but feared they might have to hit rock bottom before acknowledging the true scale of their distress: 'There's lots of guys probably that are borderline PTSD,' she said. 'But they say: "the lid's on my box" and they don't want to look at themselves too closely.'

It would be wrong to subject services to arbitrary criticism – not least because of the risk of discouraging people from seeking help. Nevertheless, I met many in the military mental health sector who were all too aware of the limitations but were constrained by professional considerations from speaking out. It would be more dangerous to continue pretending that the current system is fit for purpose. As Gillian Taylor, the occupational therapist working in Yorkshire, put it: 'Until we all sit round a table and say: "The infrastructure here has got great big gaps in it", we're going to stay where we're at. We have to provide sustainable support at a local level – and that means working together.'

Within the military, the biggest problem is still stigma, an echo of the Victorian values that ruled in the days of Myers. Serving generals in the United States have spoken publicly about their private struggles. Examples of similarly courageous senior-level leadership on the issue in Britain are much harder to find. Soldiers need to be convinced that seeking help will not damage their careers, or too many others will concur with James Forrester: 'They've got a duty of care on paper, and that's about as far as it goes.' This was a little harsh – I had got to know uniformed psychiatric professionals who cared deeply. But it was well past time to make a decisive break with the fear and prejudice evident since the days of 'shell shock' and adopt a visionary new strategy.

It is unfortunate that Britain's military reflexively adopts a defensive tone when discussing PTSD and other disorders, concerned over its media image and the threat of compensation claims. Instead, it could turn its problems into a virtue by seizing a new mantle as a mental health champion – sharing its vast experience of managing stress with the civilian world and invigorating campaigns to erode stigma in society as a whole. This may not be as counterintuitive as it sounds. The MoD has already made strides in combatting racism and homophobia in the forces, and has set an example by creating the TRiM system to spot and help people in difficulty. It could share what it knows to help companies and other large organisations do the same. There could be few people better placed to demonstrate that even the strongest men and women can sometimes struggle than people like A.J., Hilary Horton, Steve Townsend, Hugh Forsyth and the many others I met. A braver military could turn its experience of dealing with depression, anxiety, trauma and alcoholism into a national asset, and join forces with researchers in Britain and the United States in an expanded effort to assess the scope of the damage done by brain injuries caused by blasts in Iraq and Afghanistan.

Without even realising it, the Army is already a past master at influencing the parts of the brain targeted by the latest trauma treatments. Sergeant majors have not traditionally taken much of an interest in the neurobiology of 'attachment' and 'attunement' or the fight–or–flight response, but military training has evolved over centuries to harness these very mechanisms to rewire the circuitry of the 'emotional brain' to mould raw recruits into cohesive fighting units. Infantrymen are conditioned to react to threats quicker than the rest of us – and with fight rather than flight. One therapist working at Combat Stress used the analogy of a television – most people are able to switch off when they relax, whereas his clients felt like they were on permanent stand-by mode. Furthermore, the bonds forged by soldiers in war can resemble the profound familial ties of early life, which is why grief and guilt over lost colleagues can be so shattering. As A.J. has pointed out, the difficulties faced by many ex-forces are not necessarily due to the 'horrors of war' – they might equally be connected with the unacknowledged bereavement they experience on leaving the group. You do not have to be suffering from PTSD for such feelings to push you into the Spiral.

One possible response would be to envision a new approach to military training – one that lays as much emphasis on learning to resolve difficult feelings as it does on skill at arms. The Army has already begun to evolve away from the disciplinarian regimes of the last century towards a model that places more value on coaching skills. To its credit, the MoD has established the Joint Stress and Resilience Centre at the Defence Academy in Shrivenham to develop stress-management courses. The effort needs to be exponentially bigger, more ambitious and embedded in the heart of military life.

Where commanders once prescribed 'lager therapy' to regulate their men's emotions, recruits could be taught mind–body techniques throughout their first year, not as an add-on, but as a core part of what it means to be a soldier. These could exploit the latest theories of neurobiology in the same way as the breathing exercises and 'power animals' of the Comprehensive Resource Model (CRM) I had experienced in Glasgow. While mindfulness should not be seen as a panacea, the US Marines and Army, not noted for their lack of war-fighting prowess, have developed significant programmes to employ the technique, validated by a growing body of research.

Some will recoil at the idea of harnessing meditation and mindfulness to serve the military – nobody wants to see ancient techniques for opening the heart co-opted to build a more efficient killing machine. It would be a dangerous delusion to imagine that the psychic cost of participating in war – and committing the act of killing – can somehow be magically erased. Healing inevitably demands a confrontation with deep reservoirs of personal pain. Nevertheless, after many conversations with ex-forces, I was more inclined to see the military as a reflection of society, not a separate entity – its members no more or less deserving of compassion than anybody else. In a perfect world, there would be no need for soldiers. But if there is to be conflict, then let's give those we send to fight the tools to cultivate compassion, empathy and restraint – qualities that are arguably even more vital in war than in peace.

It is also time for a new vision of transition from military service to civilian life. In the current system, there is a notable disparity between the training recruits receive when they join the Army and the preparations for leaving. The core purpose of basic training is to reorganise a young person's mind and body for combat. Yet the current 'resettlement' process largely consists of talks on CV writing, advice on housing and benefits, and perhaps some vocational classes. We might teach former combatants a bit of tiling or plumbing. What we do not do is teach them how to sit still. In the United States, many Iraq and Afghanistan veterans who enrol in college under the GI Bill do not complete their degrees – some estimates say more than 80 per cent drop out – often because they are simply unable to focus. In Britain, the King's Centre for Military Health Research has pointed to a clear correlation between serving in combat and the risk of committing a violent offence. One former Royal Marine spoke for many ex-forces when he said: 'They let me out with the safety catch off.'

Nobody should leave the military without being equipped with a new 'safety catch' – a way to connect with their calm centre, the basic goodness that lies within us all. Hugh Forsyth discovered this through Ko Li, Gus Hales found it through meditation, A.J. found it through his Gibson Les Paul, and Steve Townsend found it through his jaguar. It seems perverse to wait until former servicemen and women reach crisis point before helping them to discover what A.J. calls their 'Rock'. There is a wealth of techniques, some of which I had sampled on my travels, that could be used to help ex-forces recalibrate themselves to face the potentially deadly pressures of civilian life.

Such 'transition training' could also erode stigma by providing an explicit acknowledgement that serving in the military can produce profound changes. I have yet to meet a former soldier who says they were unaffected by the experience of deployment or combat. Good or bad, these changes need to be embraced, explored and managed. For those suffering from PTSD or other serious conditions, the programme would provide an extra safety net to maximise their chances of receiving meaningful help. The model of individually tailored, open-ended, holistic treatment offered at Manor Hall could be replicated around Britain to ensure even the least well ex-forces can have the best possible chance of recovery – using a wide range of existing and novel treatments, for however long it takes. Such centres could provide integrated care for those ex-forces self-medicating trauma symptoms with drugs or alcohol – filling a big gap in the current system.

Lastly, 'transition training' would enable the military to do something it is not very good at – saying 'Thank You'. There is no universal ceremony to mark the end of a military career, no equivalent of the passing-out parade performed by newly trained soldiers. Some units are better than others, but it is not uncommon for the last contact ex-forces have with the military to be a letter warning them they are liable to be prosecuted if they fail to return all their kit. Establishing a formal farewell would be a simple yet powerful symbolic gesture towards forestalling the collapse in self-esteem that has pushed so many onto a downward path.

Just as the military has an opportunity to re-imagine its relationship to mental health, so could the NHS and charities re-imagine their approach to veterans. Throughout my travels, I discovered a wealth of services on offer for ex-forces – but was struck by how many struggled to find help. The problem is not one of resources, but one of political will. A dynamic retired senior officer could be appointed to a new post in the Cabinet Office with the power to liaise between ministries to streamline services for veterans and cut through the confusion. The first task would be to create what clinicians call a 'care pathway' to clearly allocate responsibilities and ensure ex-forces can access the right services at the right time. The proposed accreditation scheme for military charities offering mental health support should be rapidly implemented to minimise the risk that vulnerable people might be harmed by amateurish or inappropriate treatment. Veterans might not necessarily require much in the way of separate services – but they do need to feel acknowledged and understood. Early intervention can prevent manageable problems spinning out of control, but after years of immersion in the military, many will walk away if their first encounter with a GP or mental health professional seems to confirm their suspicions that civilians will never appreciate what they have been through. The NHS is making a sincere effort to handle ex-forces more sensitively and its success stories could help encourage the many who are shy of seeking help to come forward.

On a more fundamental level, the British medical establishment needs to bring its trauma services, patchy at best, into the twenty-first century – as much for the sake of civilians as for the sake of service personnel. As the consultant psychiatrists Frank Corrigan and Alastair Hull have argued, it is time to acknowledge the limitations of CBT and validate a new wave of body-based approaches that could help ensure that people suffering from the most severe cases of PTSD are not branded 'treatment-resistant' when they do not respond to talking therapy but are given a genuine shot at healing. In this way, the years of tribulations that spurred some former service personnel to eventually open their minds to novel techniques, often out of sheer desperation, might not have been time wasted after all. By demonstrating the power of working with the parts of the brain that words cannot reach, they have unearthed a profound gift for all survivors of trauma.

The unexpected friendships that developed during the course of my journey persuaded me that there is a great danger in treating ex-forces as a tribe apart. The men and women I met who had survived the Spiral had much in common, but they were above all individuals – the term 'veteran' has as many meanings as it does people entitled to wear the badge. For some, their experiences still cast such a long shadow that it seems premature, even disrespectful, to speak of a search for meaning. But there were those for whom the quest to relieve their suffering gradually brought them into harmony with deeper dimensions of themselves. War is inherently dysfunctional – to resolve conflict through killing is a form of collective madness. The aftershocks might just reveal new ways of being human and whole.

Acknowledgements

From the outset, this book has been a team effort: the hardest work was performed by the many people who were courageous enough to revisit some of their most troubling memories. In some cases, their inner voyages set ripples of difficult feelings in train and led to more than a few sleepless nights. I would like to thank all of them for the generosity of spirit they showed in welcoming a notebook-bearing stranger into their homes – I hope they feel the result was worthwhile. There are also many people who have been quoted only briefly in the preceding pages but who have played a critical off-stage role. I would like to thank them all, and many others for providing invaluable encouragement and advice, including:

Former members of the Armed Forces: Stephen James Smith, Jonathon Le Galloudec, Andy Grant, Anthony Beattie, David Brown, Stuart Tootal, Hugo Farmer, David True, Giles Price, Thomas Martienssen, Byron Kirk, Howard Leedham, Nick Leason, James Saunders, Andrew Lord, Adrian Leitch, Trevor Philpott, Adam Randle, Leigh Groombridge and Brian Brown. At SAMA, I received invaluable pointers from Mike Bowles, Rick Jolly and David Cooper. For information on Ty Gwyn, I am indebted to Robin Short and Sylvia Quayle. A special thanks also goes to those still serving in the forces: Captain Robert Campbell and Major Cormac Doyle.

Many family members who have been touched by some of the issues broached in this book have also been extremely helpful. They include Elizabeth Synge and Andrea Burns and also Julia Molony and Sue Hawkins, who run the Ripple Pond support group for forces wives.

A number of academics, researchers and other experts have extended an uncommon welcome to a trespasser on their territory and provided important comments, corrections and insights: Edgar Jones, Peter Leese, Jamie Hacker Hughes, Helen Parr, Eva Cyhlarova, Davide Ghilotti, Aly Renwick, Susan Klein, Michael Burgess, Ben Sessa and Neil Greenberg.

Journalist colleagues have also very kindly shared contacts without whom this book would not have been possible: Ben Farmer, Tom Coghlan, Adrian Massie-Blomfield, Toby Harnden, Stephen Paul Stewart, Chris Terrill, Richard Burdge, Rob Crilly, Rich Oppel, Emma Graham-Harrison and Kate Devlin. At Studio9 films: Fiona Lloyd-Davies, Selin Thomas and Lucile Smith.

Many friends offered words of encouragement that served as a more invigorating boost than they may have realised: Farah Haq, Michael Georgy, Orla Guerlin, Katie Nguyen, Barney Jopson, Ayesha Babar, Jasper Thornton, Declan Walsh, Carolyne Faulkner, Izzy McRae, Andrew England, Mark Turner, Fiona O'Brien, Andrew Rice, Anna Gát, Maurice Xiberras, William Wallis, Eliza Griswold, Daniel Wallis, Val and Paul Lynch and Susan Mayberry.

The medals for heroic patience in listening to my endless talk about veterans or for volunteering as first readers go to: Justin Quirk, Tulip Mazumdar, Daniel Simpson, Beth McLoughlin, Finbarr O'Reilly, Yara Bayoumy, Sadia Bundgaard, Kate Holt and Genevieve von Lob.

My approach to this project has been shaped by the influence of many of my previous editors, but at Reuters I would particularly like to thank Michael Williams and Alix Freedman (for instilling much-needed discipline), as well as John Chalmers, who kindly supported my unexpected decision to tackle this subject. At the *Financial Times* special thanks go to Demetri Sevastopulo, Tom O'Sullivan, Joanna Rollo, James Lamont and Jane Crust.

Acknowledgement is also due at the MoD to Jan Kemal and Jennifer Maxfield; at the MoJ to Emily Poyser; at the Royal Society of Medicine to Rosalind Dewar; and to Nicola Hudson of Combat Stress.

Much of this book was written in libraries and cafes. Thanks are due to the staff at the Wellcome Library and Wellcome Café. I am also particularly grateful for the hospitality shown by Tanya Kebo and Dana Velagic at Café Plenty in Hampton, and by Haitham Gabril at Café Du Panache in Hampton Hill, as well as by the staff at Hampton Library.

Remaining in Hampton, I would like to thank my father John, my mother Susan and my sister Katie for all their love and support over the past two years – it has been good to be home.

Lastly, thanks to my agent Sophie Lambert of Conville & Walsh and the team at Portobello Books, including Seren Adams, Pru Rowlandson, Sara D'Arcy and Iain Chapple, as well as copy editor Martin Bryant. Above all, I am indebted to my editor Laura Barber, whose idea it was to tackle this subject, and whose vision, skill and patience were the catalysts that transformed my heap of half-formed ideas, odd notions and story fragments into *Aftershock*. I feel deeply privileged to have been asked to make such a journey, and to have forged so many new friendships along the way.

Notes and Further Reading

Below are listed some of the key books and articles which informed *Aftershock*, though this is by no means an exhaustive or comprehensive list of sources consulted. There are also various additional notes on the material in several chapters and some suggestions for further reading.

A wealth of additional reports and publications on military mental health and many of the issues discussed in this book can be found at the website of the King's Centre for Military Health Research: https://www.kcl.ac.uk/kcmhr/publications/Index.aspx

The Veterans and Families Institute at Anglia Ruskin University is also exploring research and academic activity in relation to the British military, veterans and their families.

Introduction: The Spiral

On common mental disorders in the forces:

Goodwin, L. et al., 'Are common mental disorders more prevalent in the UK serving military compared to the general working population?', *Psychological Medicine*, advance online publication 2015.

On rates of PTSD and other disorders in the forces:

MacManus, D. et al., 'The mental health of the UK Armed Forces in the 21st century: resilience in the face of adversity', *Journal of the Royal Army Medical Corps*, 2014; 160(2): 125–30.

Hunt, E. J. F. et al., 'The mental health of the UK Armed Forces: where facts meet fiction', *European Journal of Psychotraumatology*, 2014; 5.23617.

On suicide after leaving the forces:

Kapur, N. et al., 'Suicide after leaving the UK Armed Forces – a cohort study', *PLoS*, 2009; Med 6(3): e1000026.

1. 'Welcome Home, Soldier Boy': The hard return from war

For more detail on the Black Watch tour in 2009, see:

Aviation Assault Battlegroup: The 2009 Afghanistan Tour of the Black Watch, 3rd Battalion the Royal Regiment of Scotland, Barnsley: Pen & Sword Aviation, 2011.

On Aaron Black's arrest:

Lowson, A., 'Handcuffed soldier legged it from police', *Daily Record*, 18 February 2011.

2. 'Case One': 'Shell shock' and the origins of military psychiatry

Myers's article on 'shell shock' in the Lancet:

Myers, C. S., 'A contribution to the study of shell shock', *Lancet*, 1915; 185: 316–20.

On the history of trauma reactions:

Abdul-Hamid, A. K. and Hughes, J. H., 'Nothing new under the sun: post-traumatic stress disorders in the ancient world', *Early Science and Medicine*, 2014: 19(6); 549–57.

Ghilotti, D., 'The burden of the invisible scars: a study of the psychological damage suffered by British war veterans after active service in the war zone', MA Dissertation, Cardiff University, 2010.

Shay, J., *Achilles in Vietnam: combat trauma and the undoing of character*, New York: Simon & Schuster, 1994.

Sources on First World War military psychiatry:

Corns, C. and Hughes-Wilson, J., *Blindfold and alone: British military executions in the Great War*, London: Cassell, 2001.

Jones, E. and Wessely, S., 'Battle for the mind: World War I and the birth of military psychiatry', *Lancet*, 2014; 384: 1708–14.

Leese, P., *Shell shock: traumatic neurosis and the British soldiers of the First World War*, Basingstoke: Palgrave Macmillan, 2002.

Moran, Lord, *Anatomy of courage: the classic WWI study of the psychological effects of war*, London: Constable & Company, 1945.

Myers, S., *Shell shock in France 1914–1918: based on a war diary*, Cambridge: Cambridge University Press, 1940.

Shephard, B., *A war of nerves: soldiers and psychiatrists in the twentieth century*, London: Jonathan Cape, 2000.

Watson, A., *Enduring the Great War: combat, morale and collapse in the German and British armies 1914–1918*, Cambridge: Cambridge University Press, 2008.

Hopkins, J. *Problems, politics and personalities in the treatment of mental and nervous casualties in the British Army 1914–1918*. PhD thesis, University of Leicester, 2002.

Details of Albert Troughton's letter:

'How can we judge him?', *Coventry Telegraph*, 17 August 2006.

3. 'The Trigger': Outwardly untouched, wounded within

For more details on the Royal Marines' 2006–2007 tour of Afghanistan:

Southby-Tailyour, E., *3 Commando Brigade: sometimes the best form of defence is attack*, London: Ebury Press, 2008.

For more on snipers in Afghanistan:

Cartwright, J., *Sniper in Helmand: six months on the front line*, Barnsley: Pen & Sword Military, 2011.

4. 'Delayed Massive Trauma': Soldiers, therapists and the 'invention' of PTSD

Sources on Second World War psychiatry:

Jones, E. and Wessely, S., *Shell shock to PTSD: military psychiatry from 1900 to the Gulf War*, Hove: Psychology Press, 2005.

Thalassis, N., *Treating and preventing trauma: British military psychiatry during the Second World War*, PhD thesis, University of Salford, 2004.

Jake Wood's account of suffering PTSD after Afghanistan:

Wood, J., *Among you: the extraordinary true story of a soldier broken by war*, Edinburgh: Mainstream Publishing Company, 2013.

On the 'rap groups' held by Vietnam veterans:

Lifton, J., *Home from the war: Vietnam veterans, neither victims nor executioners*, New York: Simon & Schuster, 1973.

On the controversies around PTSD:

Young, A., *The harmony of illusions: inventing post-traumatic stress disorder*, New Jersey: Princeton University Press, 1995.

Hunt, N., *Memory, war and trauma*, Cambridge: Cambridge University Press, 2010.

Brewin, C., *Post-traumatic stress disorder: malady or myth?*, New Haven: Yale University Press, 2003.

5. 'Lager Therapy': Pouring petrol on the fire

On the history of alcohol and the military:

Jones, E. and Fear, N. T., 'Alcohol use and misuse within the military: a review', *International Review of Psychiatry*, April 2011; 23: 166–72.

On the death of Mark Connolly:

Dailyrecord.co.uk, 'Black Watch soldier who killed friend with one punch is cleared', *Daily Record*, 7 July 2012.

On current levels of drinking:

Fear, N. T. et al., 'Patterns of drinking in the UK Armed Forces', *Addiction*, 2007; 102(11): 1749–59.

Interviews with Dave Salt and Professor Gordon Turnbull were conducted in parallel with the filming of a story about ex-forces, PTSD and alcohol abuse called Dead Man Walking, *broadcast on BBC2* Newsnight *on 4 September 2013.*

On access to treatment:

Alcohol Needs Assessment Research Project (ANARP), *The 2004 national alcohol needs assessment for England*, Department of Health.

6. 'No Safety Catch': Ex-forces and criminal justice

On the history of Armed Forces and crime:

Emsley, C., *Soldier, sailor, beggarman, thief: crime and the British Armed Services since 1914*, Oxford: Oxford University Press, 2013.

Some recent reports on veterans in prison:

Napo: *Armed Forces and the Criminal Justice System: A briefing from Napo, trade union, professional association and campaigning organisation for probation and family court staff*, September 2009.

DASA: *Estimating the proportion of prisoners in England and Wales who are ex-Armed Forces*, MoD, 2010.

Howard League for Penal Reform, *Report of the Inquiry into Former Armed Service Personnel in Prison*, 2011.

HM Inspectorate of Prisons: *Ex-service personnel supplementary paper: veteran data from HM Inspectorate of Prisons' inspection surveys*, 2014.

The results of the government's 2014 review:

Phillips, S., *Former members of the Armed Forces and the criminal justice system: a review on behalf of the Secretary of State for Justice*, November 2014.

On the case of Jimmy Johnson:

Renwick, A., *Hidden wounds: the problems of Northern Ireland veterans on Civvy Street*, London: Barbed Wire, 1999.

Morgan O'Connell's comments on Johnson were quoted in an article by Sean Rayment in the Daily Mail, *9 April 1996.*

On ex-forces and violence:

MacManus, D. et al., 'Violent offending by UK military personnel deployed to Iraq and Afghanistan: a data linkage cohort study', *Lancet*, 2013: 381: 907–17.

On the attack at Nad-e-Ali:

This account is based on personal correspondence with Liam Culverhouse and newspaper reports, including:

Rayment, S., 'Murder at Blue 25: British soldier speaks of betrayal in Afghanistan', *Telegraph*, 4 April 2010.

Rush, J. 'Former soldier who lost his eye in Afghanistan attack that killed five colleagues faces jail after admitting killing his toddler daughter when he got home', *Mail Online*, 8 November 2013.

Kenber, B., 'British soldiers were "unlawfully" killed by rogue Afghan policeman', *The Times*, 21 May 2011.

Press Association: 'Child death review finds "failures"', *Press Association Regional Newswire – East Midlands*, 26 February 2014.

Dolan, A., 'Soldier Liam Culverhouse jailed for killing his 20-month-old daughter after surviving a rogue attack in Afghanistan as it emerges he feared being alone with child', *Mail Online*, 18 January 2014.

7. 'Life's Easier with your Eyes Closed': Searching for a way out

The MoD's study on suicides among Falklands veterans:

Defence Statistics (Health): *A study of deaths among UK Armed Forces personnel deployed to the 1982 Falklands Campaign: 1982 to 2013.* MoD, 2013.

A response to the study from Combat Stress:

http://www.combatstress.org.uk/news/2013/05/dasa-report-falklands-veteran-suicides/

For more on the Welsh Guards in Afghanistan:

Harnden, T., *Dead men risen: the Welsh Guards and the defining story of Britain's war in Afghanistan*, London: Quercus, 2011.

The BBC film featuring Dan Collins:

Broken by Battle, BBC1 *Panorama*, 15 July 2013.

For more analysis of suicide data see:

Gee, D., *The last ambush: aspects of mental health in the British Armed Forces*, London: Forces Watch, 2013.

On suicide after leaving the forces:

Kapur, N. et al., 'Suicide after leaving the UK Armed Forces – a cohort study', *PLoS*, 2009; Med 6(3): e1000026.

8. 'Maintaining the Assets': How the military tends its psychological wounds

For more on the prevalence of stigma in the Armed Forces:

Murphy, D. and Busuttil, W., 'PTSD, stigma and barriers to help-seeking within the UK Armed Forces', *Journal of the Royal Army Medical Corps*, jramc-2014-000344. Published online first: 18 December 2014.

On rise in PTSD cases:

Farmer, B., 'PTSD rises by a fifth in British military', *Telegraph*, 1 August 2014.

'The Last Ambush' report:

Gee, D., *The last ambush: aspects of mental health in the British Armed Forces*, London: Forces Watch, 2013.

The stigma study:

Fear N. T. et al., 'Does anonymity increase the reporting of mental health symptoms?', *BMC Public Health*, 2012; 12: 797.

9. 'Failing Your Soldiers': Left to fight alone

Newspaper stories on veterans:

Armstrong, J., 'Iraq war veteran who survived suicide bomb returns veterans badge over treatment by Cameron's government', *Mirror Online*, 1 October 2014.

Hind, S. 'Former soldier claims army sent him on firing range despite knowing he was suicidal', *Daily Record*, 16 September 2014.

Taylor, J., 'Anfield pitch protestor revealed as war hero sniper protesting against mental healthcare from Ministry of Defence', *Liverpool Echo*, 23 February 2015.

10. 'Veterans Champions': The NHS on a war footing

The 'Fighting Fit' report:

Murrison, A., 'Fighting Fit: a mental health plan for servicemen and veterans', MoD, 2010.

Hilary Horton's story is also recounted in this newspaper story:

Goldwin, C., 'Lights signal end of Iraq trauma', *Telegraph*, 20 February 2012.

11. The Pinball Machine: Into the maze of military charities

On the history of combat stress:

Reid, F., *Broken men: shell shock, treatment and recovery in Britain, 1914–1930*, London: Hambeldon Continuum, 2010.

On Johnson Beharry:

Judd, T., 'Iraq hero goes on warpath', *Independent*, 28 February 2009.

The Combat Stress study on the six-week programme:

Murphy, D. et al., 'Mental health and functional impairment outcomes following a 6-week intensive treatment programme for UK military veterans with post-traumatic stress disorder (PTSD): a naturalistic study to explore dropout and health outcomes at follow-up', *BMJ Open*, 2015; 5: e007051.

On military charities:

Gribble, R. et al., 'Public awareness of UK veterans' charities', *RUSI Journal*, 2014; 159(1): 50–7.

Edwards, A. 'Fraudster tricked injured war heroes including Simon Weston to support his veterans' trust but spent cash on speedboats and women', *Mail Online*, 5 March 2013.

'Sir Richard Dannatt calls for military charities to work together', *Telegraph*, 15 January 2011.

The Lord Ashcroft transition review:

Ashcroft, Lord, *The Veterans' Transition Review*, 2014.

12. 'Living with Mr Grumpy': When your partner has PTSD

One of the Combat PTSD Angels meetings I attended was filmed for the BBC Newsnight story Dead Man Walking broadcast on 4 September 2013.

13. 'Fire in the Mist': Trauma, body and brain

On trauma and the body:

Van der Kolk, B., *The body keeps the score: brain, mind and body in the transformation of trauma*, New York: Penguin, 2014.

Levine, P. A. with Frederick, A., *Waking the tiger: healing trauma*, Berkeley: North Atlantic Books, 1997.

Rothschild, B., *The body remembers: the psychophysiology of trauma and trauma treatment*, New York: W. W. Norton & Company, 2000.

Turnbull, G., *Trauma: from Lockerbie to 7/7: how trauma affects our minds and how we fight back*, London: Bantam Press, 2011.

On equine therapy:

Kohanov, L., *The Tao of Equus: a woman's journey of healing and transformation through the Way of the Horse*, Novato: New World Library, 2001.

Shambo, L. with Young, D. and Madera, C., *The listening heart: the limbic path beyond office therapy*, Chehalis, WA: Human-Equine Alliances for Learning (HEAL), 2013.

14. 'Machine-gun Mind': Discovering inner peace

The film documenting the 2007 pilgrimage:

Falklands 25: the 2007 Pilgrimage, British Forces Broadcasting Service.

For more on the treatment of casualties from the Sir Galahad:

Jolly, R., *The red and green life machine: a diary of the Falklands field hospital*, London: Corgi Books, 1983.

Note: David Cooper, the Padre of 2 Para who organised the treatment of casualties from the Sir Galahad *at Fitzroy, had the following recollection of retrieving the wounded from helicopters which he sent me in an email:*

> In most cases when the heli landed I ran to it, established the number of casualties on it and then signalled to those sappers [engineers] from 9 Squadron how many I needed and whether they needed any stretchers. Once they reached the heli, I then unloaded the casualties – if on a stretcher with their help; if not with the help of the aircraft loadmaster, generally by lifting them onto a stretcher in the aircraft and

then out and away to the village hall. In one case the loadmaster stood back and refused to help. [This appears to be the incident described by Gus Hales.] It was a particularly serious case and very messy. I knelt over the casualty [who was lying supine in the helicopter], grasped him to my chest and lifted him out of the heli and onto the stretcher where he was then taken to the hall. He did not stand, but it is conceivable that he appeared to stand since I was holding him upright to get him from the heli and onto the stretcher, though he was facing outwards and I was holding him facing me. He was in a bad way and would have shocked anyone seeing this level of injury for the first time and at close quarters. There were a large number of casualties and helicopters and it was a physically and mentally demanding time.

— Personal correspondence, 28 May 2015.

On the battle of Mount Longdon:

O'Connell, J., *Three days in June: a unique insight into the last three days of the Falklands War*, Kindle: 2013.

15. 'Like a Phoenix': New horizons in therapy

Hull and Corrigan's articles on limits of CBT for complex PTSD:

Corrigan, F. M. and Hull, A. M., 'Neglect of the complex: why psychotherapy for post-traumatic clinical presentations is often ineffective', *BJPsych Bulletin*, 2015; 39(2): 86–9.

Corrigan, F. M. and Hull, A. M., 'Recognition of the neurobiological insults imposed by complex trauma and the implications for psychotherapeutic interventions', *BJPsych Bulletin*, 2015; 39(2): 79–86.

The book Corrigan co-edited on trauma and dissociation:

Lanius, U., Paulsen, S. and Corrigan, F. M., *Neurobiology and treatment of traumatic dissociation: toward an embodied self*, New York: Springer Publishing Company, 2014.

Glossary

Afghan	Afghanistan
Bergen	military rucksack
Casevac	emergency evacuation of wounded
CBT	cognitive behavioural therapy
Chinook	twin-rotor military helicopter
contact	engagement with enemy, firefight
CRM	Comprehensive Resource Model
DCMH	Department of Community Mental Health
EMDR	eye movement desensitisation and reprocessing
FOB	forward operating base
GPMG	general-purpose machine gun
Gulf War syndrome	a phrase coined to describe a disparate range of unexplained symptoms affecting some veterans of the 1991 Gulf War
HESCO	defensive barrier formed of earth-filled cages
IED	improvised explosive device
ink	tattoo
KAF	Kandahar Airfield
KIA	killed in action
Landie	Land Rover
MoD	Ministry of Defence
MTBI	mild traumatic brain injury
OC	Officer Commanding
op	operation, mission
PTSD	post-traumatic stress disorder
R & R	rest and recuperation
Regiment, the	Special Air Service (SAS)
RPG	rocket-propelled grenade

Index